INDIA

INDIA

Labyrinths in the Lotus Land

Sasthi Brata

William Morrow and Company, Inc., New York

Tenderly, for Barbara,
to whom I owe *almost* everything

Library of Congress Cataloging in Publication Data

Brata, Sasthi.
    India, labyrinths in the lotus land.

    Bibliography: p.
    Includes index.
    1. India—Civilization—1947–   . I. Title.
DS428.2.B73 1985   954.04   85-11509
ISBN 0-688-04780-7

Printed in the United States of America

First Edition

1 2 3 4 5 6 7 8 9 10

BOOK DESIGN BY JAMES UDELL

Acknowledgments

Conventional politesse requires an author to acknowledge indebtedness to at least a handful of people who "read the book and made helpful suggestions." In my case, however, only Pat Golbitz, my editor at Morrow, read the typescript during its incubation, and successfully deflected me from obvious pitfalls, mostly by persuasion, but sometimes by harsher methods when urgency demanded. My gratitude to Pat transcends the barriers of ritual politeness.

Mostly, I have been encouraged and stimulated by conversations with friends in India. Within the journalistic fraternity, there was Rahul Singh, Vinod Mehta, Rajinder Puri, Saeed Naqvi, and Nihal Singh, Raj and Romesh Thapar. Elsewhere, there was Momeen Latif, Salman Khurshid, Leena and Arup Chauduri, Mukul Sharma, and Aparna Sen.

For material help, Indian Airlines tried to smooth my internal passage through India to the best of its ability. The chairman emeritus of Welcomgroup Hotels, A. N. Haksar, laid on lavish hospitality, especially at the Lord Wellesley Suite in the Windsor Manor (Bangalore). Ratna Sahai cosseted me on behalf of the Oberoi organization. Chota Chudasma of Air India facilitated my transatlantic travel. Niranjan Desai, the minister of culture at the Indian embassy in Washington, ensured a close liaison with the Festival of India in the United States.

My old school chum Santanu Chaudhuri, patiently aided by his lovely wife, Swasti, put me up at his palatial abode in Calcutta, and listened to my midnight ruminations for days on end, with an altruism that went far beyond the call of friendship. Hari Dang feted me at St. Paul's School in Darjeeling with a warmth that I could not have possibly deserved.

Kevin, Ken, and Bob, of the tribe of Borgers in New York, heroically came to my rescue when I landed in Gotham City totally computerless and jammed in crisis.

Back home in London, Susannah helped to sort out my myriad files and Sirkka befriended me with loving tenderness. Judy

Williams typed the original proposal in one of those marathon sessions, each day after a full eight-hour stint as a ship broker at the Baltic Exchange in the City of London. I owe Judy a greater debt than mere words can convey.

Finally, I must not forget to thank my agent, the redoubtable Miss Lowenstein, who conceived the idea of this book, and nursed the project through its period of frequently troublesome labor.

Author's Note

I left India for Europe in 1961. Since then I have lived as a voluntary exile from the land of my birth in various different cities of the world. During this odd quarter of a century, I have revisited India over a dozen times, mostly on journalistic missions on behalf of British newspapers and television.

I covered the insurrectionary movements in West Bengal in the late sixties, reported on the war of liberation in Bangladesh (1971), visited most of the neighboring countries, attempted to expose the inequities of the Emergency in 1975 and thus fell out of favor with Mrs. Gandhi's government. In 1977, when the Janata (People's) party came to power, I was back in grace. When Indira Gandhi was sent to prison, I was there in Parliament to witness the drama.

Of the six prime ministers that India has had since independence, I have interviewed the last four. As a result of my journalistic assignments, I have had the opportunity to meet some remarkable people, including the internationally renowned filmmaker Satyajit Ray. Vijaya Lakshmi Pandit, Nehru's sister, and a former Indian ambassador to Washington, Moscow, and the Court of St. James's in London, became a personal friend.

Though I have lived principally in London over the past twenty years, I have always kept in touch with events in my motherland. My access to British and Indian media has enabled me to portray each country to the other, and I have been very lucky in the informative response I have had from both sides of the old Imperial Divide.

My perspective is therefore different either from that of a foreign newspaper correspondent stationed in Delhi for a limited period or from the way in which a domiciled Indian perceives native affairs. In this book I have tried to eschew both the extremes of rabid chauvinism and the disapproving disdain of a superior Occidental encountering the grotesque miseries of the mystic Orient for the first time. I have attempted to observe and describe India as if I were, in the immortal phrase about Cavafy, "standing at a slight angle to the universe."

The absence of one single source to which the Westerner can turn for a bird's-eye view of the whole of India, in all its myriad aspects, led me to contemplate writing the book in the first place and my publishers to respond with such heartening enthusiasm. This is not a guidebook, nor does it aspire to lead the scholar into the maze of the latest facts and figures about the country. Statistics in India are both unreliable and notoriously in flux. Thus I have been content to accept secondary sources when a mere glimpse of the dimensions was all that I intended. If *The Times* (London) correspondent informs me that the population of India is rising by a million a month, I have accepted his word, even though he might be out by 5 percent either way.

Since there are a multitude of specialists on each of the topics I have covered, it is entirely possible that the word of one authority whom I may have quoted is vehemently contradicted by the assertions of another. Once again, it has been my intention to paint a general picture in broad brushstrokes rather than delve into minutiae.

In conclusion, I shall allow myself to quote a snippet from the letter I wrote to my editor in New York from Bombay, the first stop in my journey, through the length and breadth of the land, specifically for this book:

> From out of my window in this hotel, there are ships to be seen, and steamers, and little dinghies bobbing up and down on the Arabian Sea. Spearing the horizon there are giant oil rigs that would make J.R. in *Dallas* gaup with envy. Right in front of me, there is the *Gateway of India,* a monument to King George V, the first British monarch to visit the country. A day's tariff in this hotel (one hundred dollars) is more than what a junior reporter earns in a whole month on a national daily. Inside, you would not believe that it was India, but for the pictures on the walls and the sights from the window. I look out at black croaking crows (kites) defecating from the air and when I am on the street, they splatter my dark gabardine suit with the casual impunity of urchins. Pigeons copulate on rooftops and leave behind their barnacled offerings as mementoes to transient lust. As dusk falls and the orbing sun rolls down the sea like a

red round billiard ball on green baize, the promenade thickens with strolling humanity "taking their ease" in the cool evening breeze.

Earlier in the day at Nariman Point, the hub of Bombay's commercial center, with sweat sucking silk shirt to skin like glued cellophane, an eclectic tout sidles up to me and whispers: "Change dollars, sir, pounds, no problem. Want pretty girls, young boys? All on hand. Very good rates!" The accents and locution are not from Manhattan's Forty-second Street, but the sentiments are sadly similar. I retire from labor and prepare for the grueling marathon ahead; thirty-two cities, five villages, and some six industrial centers, and all the miracle, magic, and maddening devastation that is India.

In this book, both as a native son and as an exile in a foreign land, I have tried to show why India, in all its myriad aspects of despair and splendor, of destitution and opulence, of majestic modernity and primitive superstition, may yet be an Oriental sphinx whose secrets can and should be unlocked.

—S.B.
MANHATTAN
FEBRUARY 1985

Contents

Acknowledgments
5
Author's note
7

PART ONE
Prologue

1. *Laying Out the Canvas*
15

PART TWO
Inception

2. *Black Hole and Bubbling Brilliance*
91
3. *Rituals at Wounded Knee*
120
4. *Desserts in the Barren Kingdom*
146
5. *Land of the Magic Carpet*
169

•

PART THREE
Ethos

6. *Deities and Devotees*
197
7. *Caste Typing*
218

CONTENTS

PART FOUR
Systems

8. Clockwork Lemon
235

9. Slaves and Masters
247

10. The Robot and the Plowshare
258

11. Debates and Dialecticians
268

12. Oyster World with Thorns in the Thigh
276

PART FIVE
Currents

13. Avenues of Ink
289

14. The Celluloid Mirage
297

15. Ascent to the Apiary
307

PART SIX
Epilogue

16. Quo Vadis, India?
321

Selected Bibliography
326

Index
331

PART ONE

Prologue

1

Laying Out the Canvas

*E*very time I return from India, there is a sense of loss—imprecise, suspended, like a hole without a ring. Yet there is also a feeling of release, as if one had just escaped death by drowning. There is instant shock, even now, after twenty years of exile, in that first collision between West and East, in climbing down from a British Airways jumbo onto the sweating, indolent tarmac of Bombay airport. The fly-infested stalls, open sewers, reckless defiance of elementary hygiene, implode within my consciousness just as violently as they did exactly two decades ago, when I first revisited the country of my birth after two years in Britain.

But subtly, through a process of natural and unperceived mutation, the picture changes. Details become blurred, the landscape grows around one like a well-worn cloak. Beggars continue to exist, their mutilated limbs and oozing sores persist in objective reality, but with time, even within days, they no longer assault the eyes. Unmentionable phenomena register visually, but they get shunted to the side, till finally they are bleached out of conscious cognition.

One boards a taxi in Calcutta, and learns to ignore, even vehemently whoosh away, the eleven-year-old mother carrying a cretinous and skeletal baby in her arms, knocking on the window, tearfully begging for a penny. One puts on a Savile Row suit, and dines at the Bengal Club (the oldest in India) where eight-foot-tall oil portraits of Philip Mountbatten and Elizabeth Windsor adorn the main marble hall. Disease, squalor, and the unrelenting sun, even in winter, become familiar companions. One learns, perforce, to forget that there is another world, alternative visions, other ways for the human animal to survive.

For not far from the surface of one's turbulently stirred and stirring mind, there is guilt, and the gnawing angst of having to accept personal incapacity. Intractable problems of poverty and indescribable human misery induce the very fatalism that one so comfortably condemns on the ~~electric Olivetti~~ *Internet computer* back home in the West.

Ovid was wrong when he wrote "There is nothing permanent in the world except change." In rural India, in the villages of Bengal, change is an alien concept: that rickety bullock cart, the same iron plow, the changeless bony skeletons wrapped tight in dark shiny skin, endure immutably. Mud huts and dung cakes still provide shelter and fuel as they did centuries ago. Everywhere one turns, there is fathomless pain, in unblinking eyes, the deep expressionless stares of those who have plumbed the depths and transcended despair.

It is possible that traffic is worse somewhere in the world other than in Calcutta. If it is so, I have not seen it. I used to think that Rome was horrendous—all those hooting horns, no indications, an arbitrary free-for-all. But Calcutta beats the lot. On a stretch of main road, you have clearly marked signs for left and right moving vehicles. Yet all of a sudden you find yourself on one narrow lane, being forced onto the curb because five closely packed lines of motioned motors are assaulting you from the other direction. Forget about laws; don't think about complaining. Take shelter and run! Climb up on the pavement and hope that you won't have a collision.

Yet again, when you get into a taxi or a private car and shut your eyes to an imminent calamity, accidents seldom happen. Miraculously, everyone seems to have an intuitive sense of what can and cannot be done. Monoxide fumes may choke your lungs, mendicants and pedestrians may be run over, chaos may seem to prevail, but if your chauffeur is driving, and you are reclining on the backseat, the soporific splendor of timeless India will engulf you. Of course, you will be perusing *The Statesman* or *The Times of India* under the reading lamp, and if some journalist friend on a short sojourn from the West informs you that just a minute or so ago a child was about to be knocked down under the wheels of your own car, you will snort with superior disdain and wonder why these "bloody exiles" don't get rid of their supercilious feelings of concern before they come back to visit the place where they were born.

But if there is destitution, there is also opulence and grandeur on a scale unimaginable in the West. And the contrast is shattering. In the palatial establishments of Calcutta's old rich, more money may be spent on a single evening than what the butlers and *chaprasis,* who serve the drink and dish out the food, may earn in a whole lifetime. Gracious living and lavish hospitality are assumed norms, not the exceptions. In one house where I stayed, the hostess wore a gold-brocaded sari that cost more than five times the annual wage of her cook. My host related a story about a hand-cut glass vase that his grandfather had bought in Czechoslovakia in the mid-1800s. The golden retriever had knocked it down with a wagging tail, and the only comment that was made, as the precious glass shattered on the marble floor, was "Wasn't that a beautiful sound? You could tell it was the authentic stuff." This was long before insurance money could be claimed for broken furniture, at least in India.

An image that sticks in my mind, symbolically defying the taboos on cliché, is of a New Year's Eve party. A large roomful of gorgeous ladies, clad in gold, silk, and diamonds, shimmering and twinkling in the dim light, with acres of winter lawn sloping off into the distance. Gingerly approaching middle age, with massive posteriors encased in all-embracing saris, the women presented faces of serene lust and insurgent civility, rolls of grotesque fat undulating like waves on six-inch-wide exposed midriffs. And the music? Postpubescent disco barbarisms of the latest crazes from New York and London. This was among the top crust of Bengali society, where married couples had been wedded by parental selection.

While Scotch whisky and Martinis flowed (a bottle of Scotch

is forty-five dollars from the bootlegger, ten dollars a shot at an ordinary bar), and the men stood around talking about their latest jaunts in Tokyo, Chicago, or Paris, the women sat in long rows on the other side of the room, nursing their fruit juices and colas, occasionally getting up to wobble their flabby behinds on the dance floor. One hundred yards down the drive, a burning *choola* (portable coal cooker) belched out thick noxious fumes into the still cold air while the gatekeeper and his family of six prepared themselves for their only daily meal of *chapatis* (flat unleavened bread) and *dal* (lentil soup).

At another time, in another place, we have just had dinner, some six of us, at the Grand Hotel in Calcutta. My American friend comes out of the restaurant and strides down the long marble corridor, leaving the rest of the company behind. She is attired in a silk jumpsuit from an *haute couture* house in Paris, and she doesn't mean to be rude. The Indian lady in the company walks with slow, stately steps, allowing time to weave around her gait, rather than the other way about. Though I understand them both, I am stranded in the middle. I can no more explain to the American woman that, according to local custom, walking at that imperious speed after a good meal is a sign of bad manners, than tell my Indian friends that this impetuous foreign creature thinks that once we have done one thing, we should promptly get on to the next item on the agenda. Time to her is precious, but oh, in such a different way. One needs a translator for social mores. And I, Tiresias, strung astride two worlds, able to see the same incident from two sharply opposed perspectives, can tell neither party what is right and what is wrong. Not because I do not know, but because right and wrong—morality—does not enter the arena: You cannot compare apples with elephants.

But if time has a different accent and manners wear sharply contrasting costumes, then erotic temple architecture and ascetic holy men sitting naked in the foothills of the Himalayas totally defy Western comprehension. How does a nation where sensuality and sex are so widely paraded accept the rigid norms of Victorian morality in daily life? How does ancient sexual licentiousness live side by side with taboos that even a teenager would refuse to accept in London or New York?

Try walking down a Delhi street hand in hand with a girl, and catcalls and boos will fall on you like showers of confetti on a newly wedded couple. Try kissing her on the lips in public and a near riot is sure to break out. Yet postpubertal virgins in orthodox Hindu homes are taught to worship the phallus in order to get a "good husband" *(shiv puja)*. There is a famous temple called *Lingaraj* (the exact transliteration would be "Kingprick"), while figurative representations of the female pudenda are littered around thousands of holy shrines, with the penis stuck in the middle.

The vast Indo-Gangetic plains of Hindostan, bounded by the sturdy Himalayas in the north, and the oceans in the south, were known to the West from well before the Christian era. Alexander of Macedonia attempted to march in from the Northwest with a massive army, conquered a tiny tract of land within India, and was forced to retreat under pressure from his own exhausted soldiers, a while before Caesar landed on the British Isles. Then there was a whole array of plunderers, from Ghenghis Khan and Tamerlane to the Great Moguls.

Over the past two millennia, India has been repeatedly invaded and vanquished by nomadic tribes from the arid, inhospitable deserts of central Asia because the land offered the prospect of stability and luxury. In ancient times, there was certainly overland trade between Greece, Egypt, and the northwestern kingdoms of Hindostan. In the Southeast, there was maritime trade with China and the nations of the Malay Peninsula. Each marauding invader came in the hope of more permanent booty with less onerous exertions. And every time, the conqueror was absorbed by "Mother India" till they assumed the new identity that their colony had conferred upon them.

The newer nations of the West, such as Portugal, the Netherlands, and later, France, were after the same sort of thing, except that they tried it by the sea route. And they were mostly unsuccessful because they landed in unpropitious times and places.

By contrast, the British were far less troublesome. Initially, they did not bring an army with them. Queen Elizabeth's Charter of Assent to the East India Company in 1599 specifically set out the objectives of trade as being paramount. Of course the legitimate interests of the traders were to be protected wherever necessary by the use of arms, but territorial conquest was not the declared goal.

Due to several curious coincidences, the last foreign intruders into India successfully ingratiated themselves in the courts of two successive Mogul emperors by providing surgeons to administer to the medical needs of members of the emperor's family.

Indeed, the British were the least irksome of all the Western incursors. All they wanted was trade, in exchange for which they would provide handsomely for the imperial coffers. It was not the kind of offer that Indian emperors, with huge hungry armies, were likely to refuse in those days. Especially as the Anglo-Saxons projected an impeccably civil and nonbelligerent mien. While the Portuguese, the Dutch, and the French fought and squabbled for laughably small patches of land, the British went straight to the top, asked the emperor for a license to trade, and established themselves as friends rather than as rapacious conquerors, with the inciting odor of military hegemony in their nostrils.

The ploy worked in India, just as it would beat their European competitors on the continent of North America less than a hundred years later. Duplicity has always been a characteristic of the British at their most grasping, diplomatic best.

From Marco Polo, the Venetian traveler who visited the country in the thirteenth century, to the Portuguese sailor Vasco da Gama, who landed on its west coast two hundred years later, the Europeans had long been intrigued by the sprawling civilizations of the Indo-Gangetic plains.

That intrepid voyager of the stormy seas, who set out from Genoa and discovered a whole New World, was after the emeralds and spices of the mystic East. Of course, Christopher Columbus chanced upon infinite new vistas unknown to the Old World, and accidentally spawned the dynamic new civilization that we now call the United States of America. But we must not forget that he named the natives he saw on first landing "the Indians."

Both curiosity and old-fashioned avarice drove the explorers toward the land where there was gold and silk and diamonds and spices, of which the West had heard but never seen. Some six hundred years ago, the nations that made up the country we now know as India were the richest in the world, just as Britain was the wealthiest imperial power two hundred years ago.

Since then much has changed. The British have come and gone,

India has exploded an atom bomb, minor and major wars have been fought with neighboring China and Pakistan. Both population and poverty have escalated beyond human comprehension. Urban India has sprinted after and caught up with the consumer craze of Western civilization. Television sets and transistor radios have begun to sprout alongside the bullock cart and the iron plow.

The visiting Westerner is awed, intrigued, and baffled by stupendous contrasts. India is as diverse as the continent of Europe—climatically, architecturally, linguistically, and in many other ways. There is such a riot of flamboyant colors that the American or European must often shelter behind dark glasses. There is squalor and filth that no number of TV documentaries can so indelibly imprint on the mind's eye as real life may.

Snowcapped mountains in the North give way to the most flat and luscious green in the South. You can have a Sahara or a safari, according to where you happen to be. One thousand-year-old temples may be sitting next door to modern satellite communications complexes (in Thumba, South India), while nuclear scientists may start the day by offering *puja* (devotional offerings) to a clay god.

To any outsider, there may seem to be not one but several Indias, each unique and sharply different from the other. The South Indian looks, talks, and dresses differently from the anglicized Punjabi in the North, who may wear a suit, relish European cuisine, and sprinkle his conversation with the argot of the West.

Just as the climate changes from chilling frost to torrid heat, as one travels down the meridian from the northern idyll in Kashmir to the southernmost tip at Kanniyakumari, jutting out into the Indian Ocean and hovering over the equator, so does the architecture, the language, the facial features, and even the color of the inhabitants. Fair Caucasian profiles give way, gently, imperceptibly, but unmistakably, to shiny black Dravidian skin, pouting lips, and blazing white teeth.

Each area has its own customs and language, and views the past at an angle ever so slightly tilted away from its neighbor. Regional loyalties are fierce. Sporadically, communal and religious dissension (as in the recent explosion at the Golden Temple of the Sikhs in Amritsar, resulting in Mrs. Gandhi's assassination and the consequent carnage), explodes into riots and mass desecration.

21

With fifteen major languages, each with its own rich literature, and over two hundred principal dialects, India is a diverse nation. Foreigners often see this diversity as potential for Balkanization. Centrifugal forces are perceived as powerful antidotes to the notion that India shall ever remain an undivided entity.

It has been argued, not least by the protagonists themselves, that India as a nation never did exist till the British arrived on the scene. They crept in stealthily as traders, secretly imported an army, sowed seeds of war among local rival princes, and established a military hegemony over the entire landmass bounded by the Himalayas in the North and the oceans in the South. They called it "India" for want of a better name, and created a single nation, ruled by a foreign power, for the first time in five thousand years.

There is much truth in this thesis. But as usual with imperial conquerors who pillaged and plundered (the Kohinoor diamond is still in safekeeping at the Tower of London), there is a great deal of travesty as well. It is true that there was no nation called "India" before the British swooped in. But there was "Bharat," and the word is enshrined in one of the greatest epics of world literature—the *Mahabharata*.

Since Indians are notoriously devoid of historicity, we do not have a clear notion about the boundaries of this great epical land, but we may be fairly certain that it stretched from the North in the area now called Delhi down to the very South.

Way back in pre-Christian times (324 B.C.), there was the Maurya empire, which extended from Herat in Afghanistan to Madurai in the South. A couple of millennia later, during which time the same territory had been split up into a multitude of separate principalities and kingdoms, the last great Mogul emperor, Aurangzeb, deployed his military might to bring the whole country together under one national umbrella, and that was only as late as the seventeenth century.

The British, however, are right in claiming that they were the only *modern* power that exercised direct control over the length and breadth of the vast subcontinent. In their own self-interest, they established an excellent system of railway and postal communications which, however long it took in the days of the steam engine, was nevertheless more efficient than horses and elephants.

Insurgents, however far from the center in Delhi, were aware that news would reach the viceroy within days, and that troops would be sent out with swift dispatch. Apart from the Indian mutiny in 1857, there were remarkably few gestures of defiance against the governing agency in all of the two-hundred-odd years the British ruled India.

Native princes preferred a "white" skin to be in charge, rather than one of their own kind, who could never be trusted not to be harboring expansionist ambitions.

By a superbly efficient policy of "divide and rule," by appearing to remain above the fray, and yet squeezing every ounce of self-interested juices from regional and religious rivalries, the British managed to exercise power and bring political cohesion to an exceedingly disparate group of people.

But at some stage or another the bluff was bound to be called. And it happened in the form of Mohandas Karamchand Gandhi, an impoverished itinerant barrister, who had been called to the bar in London, had attempted to practice in South Africa, and finally returned to his homeland in disgust, failure, and frustration.

It is possible that, had he been allowed to go on practicing in Durban at the turn of the century, Gandhi might never have set foot in India again. There may never have been the bloody calamities of the Hindu-Muslim riots in 1946, which eventually led to the partition of the country and the birth of the two independent nations of India and Pakistan in 1947, when the British handed over power.

Gandhi, who acquired the title of Mahatma ("Great Soul") for propagating the nonviolent mode of political action, injected a sense of nationhood against which the British were powerless. Opinion, however, is divided about the efficacy of his tactics. Some commentators argue that, without Gandhi, the foreign yoke would have been thrown off much earlier. Repeatedly, at the crucial point, when victory seemed in sight, Gandhi would go on a fast, urging the hotheads to cool it so that violence was not provoked. To many it appeared that he was more concerned with stamping his own image on a brand of political action than with liberating his own people.

No one denies, however, that the man brought the whole of the Indian peoples together for the first time in many a century, and thus earned the right to be called the "Father of the Nation."

Gandhi forged a national ethos that developed its own momentum and would sooner or later win against the military might of an imperial power based some five thousand miles away.

Paradoxically, it was the shared experience of foreign domination that brought Indians together as they had not been for eons in the past. The British also left a unifying legacy of a lingua franca which could be understood and spoken by the entire country.

In their homeland, Indians may call themselves Bengalis or Punjabis or Gujaratis, and speak in their own tongues among members of their own community, but immediately as they encounter a foreigner or come abroad, they become Indians first and foremost, and converse mostly in English even among themselves.

Although the literacy rate is still very low (less than 30 percent in most parts of the country, though somewhat higher in others), the educated Indian speaks and writes in English. Of course there are local non-English dailies with enormous circulations, but the opinion-forming forums are English-language newspapers and journals. All India Radio (AIR) still broadcasts its networked news to the whole country in English, and parliamentary debates, even today, take place mostly in the imported language.

The diversity of India's linguistic and regional differences is overlaid by a pervasive subconscious awareness of a people with a unique and shared cultural heritage that is different, and perhaps even superior, to that of its neighbors or of any other nation in the world.

It is this labyrinth of contrasts, contradictions, and paradoxes that perplexes the Western mind: how opulence and poverty can so easily coexist; how Harvard-returned economists can sit in mud huts and advise illiterate villagers to become self-sufficient, and not hanker after material goods; how the most populous *democracy* in the world can have a political system where one family has ruled (with two small interruptions) for over three decades, and has installed a forty-year-old political novice in the driving seat, with the largest ever popular vote, mainly because he is the grandson of Jawaharlal Nehru and the eldest male heir to the viciously slain Indira Gandhi.

For half my life, I have written and talked about India, addressing a Western audience. To my countrymen, I have tried to act as interpreter and guide to the mores of the Occident. Sometimes these two roles have come into sharp conflict, as they did during the Emergency in 1975, when Indira Gandhi's government abruptly and crudely withdrew all human rights from the entire population, instantly throwing over five hundred political opponents into jail.

As all foreign journalists had been expelled from the country, I was given a commission from *The Guardian* newspaper (London) to cover the Indian Emergency. People in Britain, more perhaps than in America, were stunned by what had happened. India, the darling progeny of Western democracy, had suddenly and uncharacteristically succumbed to totalitarian rule. Indira Gandhi, Harrow-educated Jawaharlal Nehru's daughter, had begun to behave as if she were any other tin-pot dictator.

Disbelief and sorrow, rather than anger, characterized the responses of the liberals in England in the summer of 1975. So, both to satisfy my own curiosity and to inform the Western world as to what was happening in the country, I traveled around India incognito for ten days, and returned to write a full-page "extra" for *The Guardian*.

I described the conditions, tried to explain what had brought all this about. Why Mrs. Gandhi, with her back to the wall, was passing retroactive legislation (she had a rubber-stamping majority in Parliament at the time), which would make her immune from the law courts. People in Delhi were going about in fear lest they be arrested for anything they said. Politicians (those who were lucky enough to be out of jail) and journalists did not talk in whispers; they simply did not say anything at all. Stories were floating around about prominent Opposition leaders (among them Morarji Desai, who was eighty at the time, and would go on to become prime minister) who had been incarcerated, and how some of them had been beaten black and blue, with electric shocks to their testicles at crucial moments of the interrogation.

The piece, which was published under the title "Rape of the Lok" (people), created a sensation. Not only because it reported events and reactions that were quite literally unthinkable to the liberal mind, but because it threatened to destroy an illusion: that Britain had spawned India in its own image, that whatever else happened in the rest of the world, India, enmeshed in gargantuan chaos and grotesque inefficiency, would continue to behave like a proper little democratic child and go on paying its dues to the concept of liberal democracy that England had bequeathed to the world.

It was inconceivable to the British intellectual and political mind that there might be people in this world who actually preferred the dictatorial *dunda* (rod) to adult franchise. It was overlooked that dictatorship *does* bring some instant benefits. Mussolini did make those famous trains run on time; Hitler brought hyper-inflation under firm control in Germany. The masses often respond more warmly to the short-term rewards of totalitarian rule than to the abstruse ideals of democracy.

When prices go down in shops, trains run on time, the palms of clerks in government offices do not have to be greased for the smallest jobs, when street crime abates, then men with empty bellies may choose to opt for one meal a day rather than be glamorously seduced by the power of the "vote."

I had to report that the average person on the streets and in the bazaars vigorously applauded the new regime (it was the middle-class intelligentsia who complained most vociferously). There were large billboards on top of tall buildings in New Delhi that carried the slogan INDIA IS INDIRA, INDIRA IS INDIA. Huge floats carrying her statue called her a goddess, in flaming neon letters.

Of course, this was not a new debate. But as it *was* a debate, it implied that there were points to be made on both sides. In developing countries, the concept of democracy may appear to be an unaffordable luxury—especially if you happen to be staring up from the bottom end of the ladder.

On my return to London, I was sought out by the BBC and the independent television networks. In one interview, I said at the end, as an off-the-cuff remark, that I shouldn't be surprised if she (Indira Gandhi) was the target of a potshot attack by someone. If you drive people into a corner where they feel they have nothing to lose, anything can happen. These few sentences created an international diplomatic scene of which I was wholly unaware at the time.

Next morning, three burly detectives from Scotland Yard came to arrest me in my house in Hampstead. Under instructions from the British Foreign Office, they wanted to confiscate my private papers, and demanded to know the addresses of all the people I had visited in India. When I verbally responded with the equivalent of the one-finger sign, they said they were under pressure from the (Indian) Ministry for External Affairs to apprehend me, so that I could be extradited back to the country of my origin. Modestly, I might claim to have been the only writer about whom there was a full-scale debate in the Indian Parliament, where a resolution was eventually passed: I was called a "traitor to India." The government was instructed by the legislative body to seek my extradition from the United Kingdom so that I could be tried for treason in India.

In India, the *Guardian* article was circulated secretly (in *samizdat* fashion), and years later there were those who were kind enough to tell me how much it meant to them at a time when all hope seemed wholly lost.

Fortunately, I managed to remain at large as the holder of a British passport, of which the Indian authorities seemed blissfully unaware. And the storm blew over!

It was a dark two years for India. Much to the eternal shame of politicians like James Callaghan (British prime minister between 1976 and 1979) and Henry Kissinger, the dictatorial stance adopted by Mrs. Gandhi was mutely and implicitly applauded by the Western world.

Although the actual imposition of the Emergency was always piously condemned, editorials in papers such as *The New York Times* and *The Times* (London) talked of "a hard smack in the bottom" (or its metaphorical and linguistic equivalent), to bring that hideously corrupt and inefficient country back to its senses. Expressed between the lines, there was a sneaking admiration of the firm action taken by a woman who was faced with the impossible task of trying to govern what, to many journalists and commentators, was an ungovernable country. Dictatorship was never openly condoned, but allowances were made. Both within and outside India, arguments that have been rehearsed a thousand times over began to be reiterated to justify the barbaric brutality of coercing human minds to obey the whims and dictates of one single person.

As an Indian, I felt disgust and hatred when intellectuals and novelists such as Michael Foot (the man who was to become the next leader of the Labour party in Britain) and Iris Murdoch returned from a freebee junket sponsored by the Indian government, and waxed eloquent about how marvelously "efficient" the country had become under the new dispensation.

Personally, I felt deeply ashamed and bitter. I did not like having to live in England, with every kind of freedom I wanted, while friends of mine were in jail, or muffled, back in India. But glorious news was to follow. Two years later, in 1977, Indira Gandhi did call an election, even if it was only to try to establish her legitimacy in the eyes of her peers and mentors in Europe and America. She was defeated by an overwhelming majority, even losing her own seat in Parliament. Democracy was restored! And India proved to the rest of the world that governments can change without a gory coup.

As the only country among developing nations that has functioned continuously under a Western system of democratic adult franchise for nearly four decades, India can boast that since independence in 1947, there have been no political executions, no gory battles around the palaces of power, no worse feuding in the political arena than that with which the West is all too familiar.

In India, politics is inexorably connected with the minutest details of everyday living, for the richest industrialist to the lowliest villager. Whether it is caste or child marriage, bonded labor or women's rights, the power of politics is pervasive. In the West, many institutions that are taken for granted today owe their origins to political action. In India, these institutions are not yet in place.

When the Westerner finds politics distant or boring, he is assuming that his streets will be swept, that his eighteen-year-old daughter will be entitled to vote, that glaring injustices will be righted in the courts, that his wife would be able to divorce him if she finds the marriage intolerable, that he is guaranteed freedom of expression, that he will be able to worship whichever god he wishes, and so on. But none of these institutions took shape overnight, nor were they part of the natural dispensation of things from time immemorial (in Switzerland women got the vote only in 1971).

The frequent and facile assumption that politics and "the real India" can be observed and experienced in isolation is a jaundiced and romantic view. If he so wishes, the Westerner *can* treat politics as being peripheral to the central business of his life, because the parameters that ensure his civilized and democratic existence were wrung out of political battles that were fought long ago. This is not the case in India.

The moral imperative to eradicate untouchability required the political acumen of a Mahatma Gandhi to install into the consciousness of the nation. It was a crucial political move by Lord William Bentinck, the then governor general of India, that banned *suttee* (widow burning) in the country. A woman's right to divorce was not originally enshrined in the republic's constitution, and it required parliamentary legislation, which met with widespread opposition from Hindu die-hards. Caste discrimination was another issue over which long and bitter political campaigns were conducted.

Of course social progress is not instantly attained simply by writing a few paragraphs into the statute book. But the value of a democratic constitution and reforming legislation lies in the declaration of an ideal to which a nation tries to aspire in theory, though it might take a long time to achieve in practice. Caste discrimination still exists in India, but even the poorest peasant from the lowest caste knows today that when he is being victimized, his exploiter is violating the law. And every so often, a case comes up in the courts in which the concept of equality before the law is triumphantly upheld, and the wrongdoer is punished.

During World War II, Vijaya Lakshmi Pandit's husband died in the hospital, leaving no will. And though Mr. Pandit was a fairly rich man, Mrs. Pandit was left penniless because her husband's entire estate was claimed by her in-laws. British-Indian law at that time did not recognize the rights of a widow over her late husband's property. As the Nehrus had given away most of their wealth to the nation during the independence struggle, Mrs. Pandit had to support herself and bring up her daughters on the charity of her brother, Jawaharlal, and the largesse of friends. The little that she had inherited from her father had been either spent or pooled into the joint family resources, which were also claimed by her late husband's brothers. As there were no obvious jobs that a woman could do at the time to earn a living, Mrs. Pandit was in the pitiful condition of being thrown into a pool of penury after having enjoyed a life of affluence both in her father's house and in her husband's. After independence, Nehru, the new prime minister, set about trying to introduce legislation that would put a stop to such obvious injustice. But it took him nearly six years to get the Hindu Code Bill (which enabled a widow to claim her late husband's property as a right, even if he had not left specific instructions in his will to that effect) passed by Parliament. There was much political gossip in Delhi, which accused the prime minister of riding a personal hobbyhorse because of the experience his sister had suffered, while attempting to project the impression that the bill was motivated by principle and impartial ideological conviction. Whatever the truth, it was the only occasion in which Nehru blackmailed his parliamentary colleagues (most of whom opposed the measure) by threatening resignation.

In the mid-1950s, when I was still in school, a second cousin of mine some ten years older than myself was being fixed up for marriage. He was a handsome young man of twenty-five who had graduated with creditable grades from the university. Employed in a reasonably lucrative job, my cousin was a desirable catch in the eyes of parents with marriageable daughters.

His father hoped for several things from the potential bride and her family. Being Brahmins themselves, she would of course have to belong to the same high caste. In addition, she would have to be attractive, pleasant mannered, good at housework, and most crucially, her family would need to be sufficiently well provided to pay for a handsome dowry. As it was a joint family in which all the sons and their wives, as well as the daughters, lived in the same house, the money would not go to the groom, but had to become part of the common fund—in other words, his father, being the head of the household, would have total control over it.

With the inciting prospect of this large injection of cash, my uncle had become fairly agitated to get the ball rolling, select a bride, and set a date for the wedding. But the groom himself did not appear to be very keen. And contrary to norm, the mother also did not seem very anxious to see her son married off at that time.

My cousin stalled for a long while, with excuses including his career prospects being unsettled, his desire to take a master's degree by attending evening classes, his attempts to go abroad, and other incidentals like persistent headaches, and so forth. When none of this worked anymore, my uncle's patience was exhausted. He set about consulting middlemen and organizing "inspection cere-monies" of the potential brides (elsewhere, I shall describe in de-tail what these customs are).

But once again, the groom-to-be raised objection after objec-tion (usually conveyed to the father through the mother, since respectful sons *never* discuss such delicate subjects with the pater-familias) about each candidate. One was not sufficiently educated, another did not have a fair enough complexion, yet another was too short, and so on. Mind you, he had not yet actually *seen* a sin-gle woman who was likely to become his wife. All his objections were based on verbal data provided by his mother, who, in turn, had got it from the middleman, buttressed by a passport-size pho-tograph.

Finally, my uncle exploded in a violent temper. He told his wife to inform the son that all this dillydallying would have to stop. A candidate with all the appropriate credentials was selected, and a date was set when a team, including the prospective groom, would visit the girl's house. The time for this auspicious inspection was set for seven in the evening, so that my cousin would have plenty of time to come back from work and change into his best clothes.

The appointed day duly arrived, and the clock struck six, but there was no sign of the would-be groom. My uncle was getting distinctly fretful, ruminating out aloud about how irresponsible and unpunctual the younger generation had become.

Came seven o'clock. Still no trace of the errant young man. My uncle was now in a fury, which he vented on his wife, who was more than usually subdued, and did not seem to share either her husband's impatience or his apprehension that something might have happened to my cousin.

The clock marched steadily on, inflaming my uncle's already explosive temper by the minute. He was angry with his son for having flagrantly disobeyed a parental order—this was a much more insubordinate form of the verbal excuses he had been making. But more than that, my uncle was worried about the repercussions from the girl's family. If word got around that the prospective groom was unreliable or that he was being press-ganged into marriage against his own wishes, then the price (dowry) in the market would fall drastically.

When the mother could not stand the rantings and ravings

anymore, she broke down and confessed to her husband that she had known all along that her son would not turn up that evening. He had been seeing a girl for the past three years, and was waiting for her to graduate from college before getting married.

As the girl came from a poor family, there would be no question of a dowry. She was also from a lower caste.

When my cousin came home at ten that night, my uncle stripped his son's shirt off his back, took hold of a pair of leather sandals, and beat the young man for over twenty minutes, till the welts burst and blood streamed down, while the rest of the family, including the mother, watched the spectacle in silent despair.

At the end of that session, my cousin, who had put up no resistance all through, bent down and touched his father's feet, asking forgiveness. When he was asked to renounce this "low-caste, penurious girl" and he refused, with a silent shake of the head, he was ordered out of the house, and the rest of the family were severely instructed never to see or speak to him again.

I heard about this incident through family gossip, and months later I asked my cousin why he had tolerated such violent indignity so meekly. The reply was: "He *is* my father and had my best interests at heart. I should not have deceived him, and made him lose face with the girl's family."

But the young man did marry the woman of his choice.

Thirty years on, the changed political and social climate in the country would almost certainly prevent such a scene occurring again. Young people are far more conscious of their rights, and the taboos on intercaste marriages have been challenged frequently enough in the courts to inhibit such tyrannical behavior.

In my own case, I fell in love with a girl who was in the same class in college with me. We had been seeing each other for three years, and though we had kissed and fondled a little, it did not occur to either of us to go any further. Proper sex was strictly for the married.

Since she belonged to the same caste (Brahmin) as I did, there were no barriers in that sphere. But her parents did not like me. Between us, however, we had firmly agreed that we would get married after I came down from the university.

As we were of the same age, it was much more urgent for her

to be married (she was twenty at the time, and girls even in their late teens were then considered to be on the shelf). So she, too, had stalled, but finally without success.

Her mother threatened suicide and her father proposed to disinherit her (she was an only child), if she did not do their bidding. Under constant and coercive pressure, she had agreed to go through with the usual inspection ceremonies. But she had kept the news of all these developments from me because she did not wish to upset me while I was preparing for my finals.

On the last day of my exams, she came to see me at college. We drove out into the country, petting and kissing more daringly than we had ever done before. For over two hours, I talked about my hopes and dreams, what we would do after we got married, all the wonderful places in the world we would visit together.

We drove back to town, and then, just as she was getting out of the car, two streets away from her house (in case her parents spotted us), she said, "I am getting married next week," and sprinted away in the dark.

Four days later I left Calcutta, not wishing to be in the vicinity of such vicious cruelty.

She had met the man whom her parents had chosen only once. He was twelve years older than she and had a degree in mechanical engineering from Glasgow (Scotland) University. He worked at a good job, and had bright prospects.

Years later she told me about her wedding night—how, when she had screamed out in pain, he had slapped her face and shouted, "Keep shut, woman, and try to help me!" At thirty-one, and educated in Britain, he, too, was a virgin.

That was twenty-five years ago. Once again, the political and social mores in contemporary India would not allow such coercion. Nor would a woman put up with it so meekly, if it was attempted.

After Mrs. Gandhi was ousted from her throne in 1977, I went back to India to have a look at the old country. *The Statesman,* the oldest (founded nearly two hundred years ago) and most prestigious English-language daily in India, asked me to write for them. I started filing vigorously, ventilating my erstwhile frustrations and angers.

In one of my articles I pointed out that the minister of information (a veritable Goebbels in disguise) under Mrs. Gandhi's Emergency regime had commented on record, about press censorship in India, "When we asked them to bend, they crawled. Obediently!"

My columns from London tried to analyze that something in the Indian temperament which is malignantly addicted to the dispositions of a dictator. The articles did not make the writer very popular, but the paper received a large number of letters every week, and sold more copies on the newsstands. It must have been obvious to any anglicized reader in the country that I did not much care for Indira Gandhi and her authoritarian propensities.

During that visit in 1977, I asked for an interview with Morarji Desai—octogenarian, urine-drinking (yes, he actually drank a cup of his own urine every morning for health reasons), nonsmoking, teetotal, vegetarian who wants to become prime minister of India. I was flatly refused. Largely because I was thought to be a sexual libertine, and a beef-eating wine-bibber to boot. (Brahmins, by birth, are not supposed to drink alcohol, and eating beef is as much an anathema to Hindus as pork is to an Orthodox Jew). On assuming power after Mrs. Gandhi, the new prime minister announced at an international press conference that he had not had "carnal congress" for the previous fifty years, and in Paris, at a banquet hosted by Giscard d'Estaing, then president of France, Morarji Desai refused a toast because the glass contained wine.

At this time, Indira Gandhi, who had been written off the political screen by now, was trying to get back into Parliament from an entirely different part of the country—the South of India. I thought it would be interesting to interview *her,* as I had been predicting her political resurrection in my columns, against the grain of received wisdom at the time.

From her office in New Delhi, there was an instant go-ahead. "She *will* meet you, if you go down to Chikmagalur" (Mrs. Gandhi's newly chosen constituency). I Telexed Independent Television News (ITN) in London (as the BBC already had a resident correspondent). After a great deal of hassle, I got permission. For a free-lancer this was a considerable achievement.

So the TV crew was assembled and we headed for Chikmagalur, in the depth of darkest South India. After a thousand miles on the plane and a six-hour ride by car, I was told that Mrs. Gandhi had decided not to give *any* interviews at all. I also discovered that there were twenty other TV crews (including the three American networks) from all over the world, who were after the same thing.

I had told ITN that we had been firmly promised an interview, we had traveled over a thousand miles with a crew of four, and now my credibility in London would be totally destroyed. I was desperate!

The crew was not told the disappointing news. They kept asking, and I continued evading their questions. After three days and nights, when we had pursued Indira Gandhi over six hundred miles of hilly terrain, waking up at three in the morning and never retiring till well after midnight, my senior cameraman said, "I think we should pack up and leave."

During this time, we had been following Mrs. Gandhi and her entourage assiduously. She stopped at a guest house each night, and her bedroom light never went off till after twelve. Every morning it came on again at four, punctually. We knew, because we kept vigil, between the four of us.

The woman was sixty-one at the time, and she could not have been sleeping for more than three hours a night. During the day she traveled at least two hundred miles by car in non-airconditioned discomfort. She addressed at least twenty meetings a day for fifteen to twenty minutes each, and was fresh as a daisy the next morning. At half her age, we were exhausted.

At the end of the three days, I decided that enough was enough. A promise had been broken. I would probably have to pay for this entire trip. My credentials in London had been reduced to zero. But I simply couldn't take any more. So, I went to Mrs. Gandhi's election headquarters and told the lady at the desk that my crew and I were leaving. When, with a gentle tap on my left shoulder, someone whispered in my ear: "Follow that car!" Just like in the movies.

For two hours we drove through winding mountain roads. All sorts of ghoulish thoughts flitted through my mind. *What if . . . ?* We had woken up at three in the morning and had been on the road till six in the evening. On that particular day, we could not have traveled anything less than two hundred miles. It was now ten at night, the road was as black as a whale's belly, and sinuous. The car ahead of us disappeared round the bend every so often, and I began to wonder . . .

Just before midnight, we arrived at the house, in the deepest forest, where Mrs. Gandhi was supposed to be spending the night. At temperatures sweeping over 100°F during the day and with very little food in our stomachs, neither my crew nor I were in a very good mood. I asked the host if we could have a wash before the interview. "No, no, of course you can't!" he replied brusquely. "Mrs. Gandhi has been waiting for half an hour. You must go to her immediately."

My cameraman's hands were shaking. I was nervous as hell, the sound man was having trouble with his wires. The room was vast. When we had set up the equipment, the host inquired, "Is it all right if I ask her to come in now?"

I nodded.

Indira Gandhi made her entrance through the door as if she had been born yesterday. She wore a white cotton sari, deftly decorated at the edge. Her face was bright and sparkling, but she had a scowl on her face, as much as to say: "What is all this nonsense about?"

I had made a list of twenty-six fairly aggressive questions I wanted to ask her. But, very unprofessionally, they all went out of my mind.

"You do realize," she said, before we began, "you are the only one to whom I am giving this interview." Whatever hostility I had ever felt for this woman dissolved in a second. Instantly as the camera started rolling, the rough schoolmistress frown vanished. She smiled with the radiance of a spring dawn. "In India we do things differently," Mrs. Gandhi declared on film.

From that ten-minute interview with me, her professed archenemy, she got more publicity than anything the twenty other crews would have given her. The sixty-second clip, shown on ITN in London, was syndicated throughout the world. Even the BBC bought it, because it was an exclusive. In India the interview did not go down too brightly, because the questions were not the kind of pointed ones that any other journalist in the same position would have asked. It was even rumored in some quarters that she might have paid me handsomely.

I wonder if either Lyndon Johnson or Richard Nixon ever knew, when they confronted her in the Oval Office, what kind of a woman they were dealing with in Indira Priyadarshani Nehru Gandhi, the late prime minister of India.

Soon after Mrs. Gandhi was returned to Parliament (in 1978) by the voters of Chikmagalur, she was sent to prison for twenty-one days by the government of Morarji Desai (the new octogenarian prime minister), on the charge of "contempt of Parliament." Just over a year later, on January 6, 1980, when the seventh general elections for the whole country were held, Indira Gandhi roared back to power on a landslide victory at the polls, in an even more astonishing political resurrection than Nixon's in 1968.

If not quite by divine right then certainly by electoral magic, the First Family of India were back in the saddle. The previous thirty-four months of *Janata* (the Hindi word translates as "the people") rule seemed more like an aberration than an assertion of democracy—the sacred symbol that Jawaharlal Nehru, father of Indira Gandhi, held dear to his heart.

Soon after the resumption of the Nehru-Gandhi hegemony, it was widely believed that son Sanjay would ascend the throne after mother. But on June 23, 1980, Sanjay crashed to death in a Pitts aircraft that he was piloting himself.

Instantly, New Delhi began buzzing with rumors about the likely successor. Some people suggested that it should be the young and pretty widow, Maneka. But they were not allowing for Mrs. Gandhi's astute perception that Indians will wear a Nehru or a Gandhi, but not someone from another bloodline. The mantle was to fall on Rajiv Gandhi, the elder son with whom I spent two long sessions in 1981, talking about the future of India.

Although presenting a more acceptable image than his late younger brother (who was considered a bit of a thug in most circles), and politically untarnished by the excesses perpetrated during Emergency rule (1975–1977), Rajiv Gandhi owed his political ascension to his mother, Indira Gandhi—easily the shrewdest politician India had produced after Mahatma Gandhi (no relation) himself.

Mrs. Gandhi calculated that, contrary to the inclinations of native ideologues molded in the Western liberal tradition, dynastic rule is precisely what the people want. They respond in obeisance to those who are used to issuing commands.

In rural India, where the majority of the population lives, the Congress party is still seen as a symbol of Mahatma Gandhi and Jawaharlal Nehru, and then Mrs. Gandhi. When she erred, as she did in 1975, by declaring the Emergency, the people turned away and with the first opportunity, in 1977 (when elections were called), they banished her to the corner of the classroom.

She lost her own parliamentary seat and her party was decimated. But in less than three years, the people forgave her and she was back in Sir Edwin Lutyen's Delhi as the de facto empress of India.

By ensuring that powerbrokers and political handymen gravitated toward Rajiv Gandhi, her only surviving son, Mrs. Gandhi was only following her family precedents. When I put this point to Mr. Gandhi himself, he replied with a question: "Do you mean that just because someone is related somewhere, he should be barred from politics?" Which was not really an answer, but a clever evasion.

In June 1981 he was elected to Parliament (before that he had been an airline pilot with no apparent interest in politics) with an overwhelming majority from the constituency left vacant by the death of his younger brother. "It was the people who forced me to stand," he told me.

From that point on, Rajiv Gandhi acquired the status of a crown prince. With opposition parties in total disarray, there were any number of Mrs. Gandhi's camp followers who willingly gave a full-throated ovation to the impending Rajiv era. As the editor of the *Indian Express* put it in a signed column: "For them [the people] it is axiomatic that the Nehrus will rule India for eternity."

Educated at Cambridge (England) and Imperial College, London, Mr. Gandhi approaches politics with refreshing pragmatism: "I don't have any objection to foreign investment provided we are not blackmailed afterwards with the threat of withdrawal," he said.

Softspoken and reflective by temperament, Mr. Gandhi listed the achievements of his country since the departure of the British. He said that his grandfather's (Jawaharlal Nehru) greatest contribution was to "send down strong democratic roots." India has been the only stable nation in the developing world. Nearly every other country solidly backed by the West has been a dictatorship, while India has come through the last decade with two major changes but with no bloodshed in the process of transfer.

Mr. Gandhi said that Westerners were perpetually comparing India with China, but it was always forgotten that India was a democracy, with all its faults, while the Chinese lived under a dictatorial regime.

Talking of his constituency, which is one of the most backward in the whole country, Mr. Gandhi remarked, "Ten years ago most people were underfed and scantily clad; today the ill-clad is the exception. Every village has at least half a dozen transistor radios, and people's expectations have risen."

Referring to his image as "Mr. Clean," Rajiv Gandhi told me that "corruption has become a part of life in this country," and that no single individual could be blamed.

"We in India do tend to have a feudal mentality," he went on. "But was Britain any better only four decades after she adopted democracy? To judge fairly, the Indian experiment should be given another thirty or forty years before a verdict can be pronounced."

It was in Mrs. Gandhi's garden, where she was shot, that her son last spoke to me. His Italian wife, Sonia, wearing a sari, brought us both a cold cola in a jug, and said softly, "Rajiv, you really should change! Those jeans are filthy." The future prime minister of India simply smiled.

Rajiv Gandhi's detractors say that he is much too "nice" to succeed in the wheeling and dealing of politics. One prominent journalist even went so far as to announce that the late Sanjay had possessed a certain criminal skill that was essential to control the state apparatus. Since Rajiv is reputed to lack this quality, he would ultimately flounder. We shall have to wait and see.

Jawaharlal Nehru's international outlook and Indira Gandhi's patrician imperiousness contrived to lend an air of regality to the most mundane act committed by any member of the clan. Being the scion of this "noble" family has not hindered Rajiv Gandhi's chances in the inheritance stakes.

It is doubtful, though, if royal blood alone will suffice in ensuring dynastic rule forever.

Mr. Gandhi seemed to be aware of this when, a little over two years before Mrs. Gandhi was killed, he reflected about the possibility of becoming prime minister. "It will be a challenging job. But we shall have to wait, maybe five, ten, or even fifteen years."

At the time, his words were less than prophetic. He could not have envisaged his mother's cruel and untimely death (she was only sixty-seven). When I talked to him, Rajiv Gandhi seemed to be preparing for his future with patience but firm resolve. In timeless India, a decade and a half was hardly a long stretch. But events were to take a bloody and unpredictable turn, much sooner than the soothsayers had predicted.

Just as Nehru's rule, over the first seventeen years of independent India, does not look as glittering today as it did two decades ago, Indira Gandhi's legacy to her country may not appear quite as disheveled and creaky to a future historian as it does just now, in the immediate aftermath of her assassination.

There are points to be made here. Indira Gandhi was indeed killed by her bodyguards. She *was* murdered for political reasons. So were Lincoln, Mahatma Gandhi, and John F. Kennedy. But it was *not* a coup. The transfer of power took place within five hours of her death, without anything like the acrimony that Lyndon Johnson had to face on Air Force One after Jack was shot in Dallas (if we are to believe the reconstructed tales of instant Macaulays). There must and will be debate about the paradox of a self-professed democracy willingly subjugating itself to the yoke of dynastic rule. But for the country at large, and certainly for the stability of the region, the smooth transition could not have been better organized.

Let me not give the impression that I am an apologist for a feudal oligarchic system masquerading as a democracy. Certain things that appear offensive to the Western temperament may be just the kind of *modus operandi* that nations like India need at a particular stage of their development.

I am a voluntary exile from the country of my birth because I find its fundamental ethos disagreeable. Which does not mean I condemn it. Indians like to vote, to express their preferences, as well as obey dictatorial commands. To the liberal mind, this is a contradiction.

Rajiv Gandhi was returned to Parliament by an overwhelming

majority from his own constituency, and his party won the largest-ever share of the popular vote in the country's young democratic history. There were pundits from all over the world observing the Indian elections with psephological microscopes. They reported misdemeanors here and ballot-box disappearances there, but not *one* person from the international team came back with a verdict of guilty. Professor David Butler from Britain wrote in *The Times* (London) that "the Indian elections in 1984 were conducted as fairly as any election I have ever observed."

In the West it is usual to make dismissive remarks about events in the so-called Third World, especially in the reactionary atmosphere of Reagan in America and Thatcher in Britain. I must confess I fall into the same trap myself, more frequently than I would care to admit. But the enormous advances that have been made in some of those countries, which one comfortably disparages at the high table of an Oxford college, almost always go unobserved.

I had always been a severe critic of Mrs. Gandhi while she was alive. There were many things she did that were manifestly inept and some actions she took brought about her overwhelming defeat in 1977 as well as her untimely death at the hands of her own trusted guards on October 31, 1984.

It is too early to make an assessment about her achievements and failures. But as Grub Street has already been at it, I shall not disdain an essay. There were several crucial points of contrast between father and daughter, as well as a few similarities. Mrs. Gandhi did not become prime minister in the automatic, unopposed way that Nehru did in 1947 as the protégé of Mahatma Gandhi.

When Nehru died in 1964, Mrs. Gandhi had held no ministerial post, and although she had been president of the Indian National Congress (the ruling party) for one term (one year), she was not even an elected member of Parliament at the time of her father's death.

Again, unlike Nehru, Indira Gandhi had never played in the live political arena. Except for a flamboyant few months in prison under the British in 1942 (a kind of pilgrimage that had become almost obligatory), she had been her father's social and political hostess (Nehru was a widower), admittedly with unique access to the sole repository of power in independent India, but never in the front line of political feuds and electioneering armies.

She met all the world's leaders and many international celebrities, but only as her father's daughter rather than as a person in her own right.

At the age of twelve, Indira Gandhi set up a children's group called *Vanar Sena* (monkey army) and aspired to help the adults in their fight against the British. She also burned all her English-made dolls in a bonfire to indicate her distaste for all things foreign. (Strangely though, she was happy to be sent to Badminton, an elite fee-paying private school in England for girls—where she met and became lifelong friends with Iris Murdoch, the novelist—and subsequently spent one term at Somerville, Oxford. So much for the much-vaunted anti-Britishness!)

After Nehru's death in 1964, Mrs. Gandhi was given a minor ministerial post (information and broadcasting) by the new prime minister, Lal Bahadur Shastri, more as a gesture to the Nehru family than for any real political clout she may have possessed or with any consideration of her competence for the job. In India, degrees and paper qualifications count a lot: Indira Gandhi did not have any.

When Shastri died prematurely in 1966, the power brokers within the Congress party could not agree on any of the three or four political heavyweights who were contending for the throne. So they chose Indira Gandhi as a compromise candidate. With the Nehru name behind her, she was uncontentious and evoked no hostility from any of the fighting factions at the time of her accession to the prime ministership of India. The kingmakers reckoned that she would do their bidding—an amiable and docile puppet behind whom the real power game would be played.

They were drastically incorrect, just as the pundits are likely to be wrong-footed once again about her son Rajiv.

Indira Gandhi's frail and pliable demeanor, her apparent feminine grace and diminutive stature, concealed an iron will and an aggressive political mind that far outwitted the men who installed her at the helm. By 1969, she had disbanded the troop of old fogies (freedom fighters with her father), split the Congress party down the middle, recruited a whole new team of Young Turks, and renamed the party "Congress (I)," the *I* standing for Indira. Her victory was complete. The old men did not even know that their *dhotis* (a long piece of cloth covering the male anatomy below the waist) were being ripped off them while they were happily snorting away on their *hookahs.*

Only a few percipient observers remarked at the time that a personality cult was about to be launched in full fury. But those solitary voices (including mine) were drowned by the general euphoria that welcomed a visible change from the ancien régime. Mrs. Gandhi had all the right slogans (*Garibi hatao*—Abolish poverty), made all the correct progressive noises, and her detractors could not compete with the idol-worshipping addiction of the Indian masses. Mrs. Gandhi was the goddess incarnate.

While her father was a visionary, though ineffectual and bumbling at the best of times, Mrs. Gandhi was a supreme strategist, with a cruel streak of Machiavellian ruthlessness. The obvious question in the Western mind is: Why, then, did she die?

The answer is both very simple and exceedingly complex. As I wrote in a New York paper at the time, "Indira Gandhi died because she was afraid to be afraid." She was trying to do two disparate things simultaneously. She wanted to be *secular* and *international,* and at the same time she was well enough in touch with the Indian pulse to know that any appearance of weakness at the center, the governing core, had always led to the disintegration of the nation. She was strung up on the horns of a violent dilemma. Do we give in to extreme factionalist demands and bow down every time we are threatened? Or do we assert our *central* strength and declare to the nation that we are still the rulers here in Delhi?

It must have been a difficult decision. But when she sent in the Indian army to storm the Golden Temple in Amritsar (the holiest of holies for the Sikhs), she must have known that she was literally staking her life.

Unlike Jawaharlal Nehru, Indira Gandhi was not averse to playing communal politics. Though she projected herself as the secular, noncommunal leader of all India, when it suited her, she stoked the incipient fires of religious and communal rivalries. There was no Machiavelli to advise her on how to contain the very conflagrations that she had set alight. On the night before she was killed, when Mrs. Gandhi said, "If I die today, every drop of my blood will invigorate the nation," she was speaking more truthfully than ever she had in her life. The Sikh separatist cause has suffered the most severe setback as a result of her death. The old, crusty, time-serving coterie has been dismissed by her son, as new prime minister, and India has once again shown to the rest of the world that she can soldier on, even when Armageddon has been imminently predicted.

What then of her record? Indira Gandhi was a lonely child who had more than a dose of *folie de grandeur* in her personality. She started ruling India in 1966 and converted the nation into a virtual one-party state. Although elections were held, she maneuvered, with the inexorable power of incumbency, to keep all opposition parties at bay. She disregarded Parliament in a way her father never did.

During the eighteen years she ruled India almost autocratically (from 1966 to 1984 with a thirty-four-month gap between 1977 and 1980), she sundered Pakistan in two, establishing a new nation called Bangladesh. Indira Gandhi will go down in history, to coin a cliché, as the first woman to have triggered an atom bomb (in 1974). The country she led became the ninth biggest industrial nation in the world under her tenure. Mrs. Gandhi redefined the concept of nonalignment and made India the fulcrum of East-West dialogue once again. By the gory manner of her death, she almost certainly ensured the dynastic succession of the Nehru-Gandhi line.

It is tempting to speculate as to how and why, as a result of Indira Gandhi's death, Rajiv Gandhi may be drawn closer to the West. Will his fads about computers and management techniques bring his country nearer to the way Reagan and Thatcher think? Though these questions appear absurd to me, I am reliably informed that they are being given serious consideration at the foreign desks of the respective governments.

Of course, Americans find it hard to understand the country's cussed reluctance to come out openly and say on which side, in the battle for good and evil, India stands. Since the Soviet Union is the devil incarnate, surely . . . ? The fact that Indians don't quite see it that way causes impatience and sometimes outraged fury.

But Indians don't look at life in the same black-and-white, either/or terms. The predominant religion, Hinduism, accepts passivity as a virtue; the *Bhagavad Gita* specifically instructs its adherents *not* to seek the rewards of their own endeavors—a far cry from the Protestant work ethic in the majority of the Western world.

If the Westerner finds the Indian occasionally fascinating, but more often pathetic, he may be surprised to discover that the object of his condescension feels enormous sympathy for his Occidental afflictions—too much reliance on material comforts, an obsession with time, a total neglect of the "meditational" aspects of life.

No wonder, then, that youngsters have flocked to the East. Grass and acid have replaced earlier yearnings for success and rat-race prizes. Yet, just as fashions fade, rise, and fall in the West, from drugs to alcohol and back again, Indian youth turns to *bhang* (grass) and coke, and wonders what the fuss is all about. Living within a culture where astrology and being high is no big deal, youthful counterparts from half a world away now confront each other, by extolling the virtues of the opposite camp. The American tells his friend how computers and fast cars are the bane of Western civilization, while the Indian electronics graduate patiently tries to explain that the power to reason is the highest faculty of the human mind.

But things do change, and sometimes for the better. More urban Indians now speak English than ever before. The Western tourist has much less trouble making himself understood. The hotels provide boiled water, the food can be as unspicy as any fastidious stomach might want, but also as exotic as any adventurous palate might seek.

India is still teeming and far-flung, noisy and filthy. But it is also challenging its own past for the first time, and stretching its powerful limbs toward the future. As an American journalist put it recently, "India is the *most* exciting place to live in at this moment."

At a party in Bombay once, I asked a vivacious young lady out to dinner the next day. She agreed, and I picked her up from her parents' place at seven. We then spent a stimulating evening together, with the conversation ranging freely from politics to sex to literature. I then invited her back to my hotel room for coffee and liqueurs. It was not till another half hour or so, when we had been sitting around and chatting convivially and nothing particularly intimate had occurred, that my companion began to sound distinctly edgy.

When I inquired whether there was anything bothering her, she mumbled an embarrassed apology and asked if I would mind opening the door of my room and leaving it ajar. Mistakenly assuming that she might be feeling claustrophobic, I did as I was instructed and discovered to my utter amazement that two burly youths were stationed outside. My date answered my puzzled glance by saying that her parents had agreed to let her go out for the evening only on condition that her brother and cousin could stand guard outside my hotel room, as I was bound to suggest that we have coffee there after dinner, rather than in the restaurant downstairs where we had just had dinner. (A word of explanation here: "Foreign liqueurs" are inordinately expensive in Indian restaurants because of the very high taxes imposed by the government—a single drink may cost as much as three times a meal for two.)

The woman was twenty-nine years old, came from an "emancipated" Indian family, and had been educated at Syracuse University.

It is not only in personal encounters of this sort that contradictions prevail. On the banks of the Holy Ganges, men and women bathe openly in near-nudity, but ask the average middle-class husband if he has ever seen his wife totally naked, and his eyes will curl into his forehead as if you had suggested that he was a manic rapist—since the idea is totally unthinkable and implies disrespect for a woman.

An assistant to the editor of a national newspaper will tell you in confidence that her boss does not like her divorced status to be revealed to the world because it might reflect upon the "good name" of the organization. Ask her out for coffee, and you will find a female eager to spread her wings but terrified lest the scorching winds of social ostracism burn her in flight, like Icarus ascending to grasp the sun.

At fashionable parties in Bombay, Delhi, or Calcutta, that woman you will see in Western clothes, with slightly paler skin than the rest of the company, and with ravishing blue-gray eyes to go with her succulently curvaceous figure, is not quite the sought-after bronze goddess that she may appear to you. Almost always, she will be "half-caste," meaning her lineage is not quite *pukka* and there is European blood in her veins. Sexually, she will be regarded as "easy," though her personal morals may win the approval of the pope. The lady will be typecast, not because of who she is, but due to the accident of her birth.

Western permissiveness is decried in India in the same way that the fox who couldn't climb to the green grapes on the high wall declared they were sour, without having tasted them. Indian men who visit Occidental cities go berserk in their attempts to build up a head count of white women they have bedded, not because they necessarily enjoy the experience, but because they can't do it back home.

One of the most perverse and fascinating aspects of Indian society is this schism between its ancient traditions of sexual liberality and its contemporary obsession with moribund repressive codes that combine male chauvinism and excessive romantic prudery in equal measure.

Women's liberation has struck India late and hard. In a country where divorce occurs in one out of a million marriages (if that), where virginity is still highly prized in a prospective bride, where the concept of "damaged goods," as far as women are concerned, still plays a determining role in a man's choice, the assertion of female autonomy and independence is both an incidental irritation in male consciousness as well as a real and frightful challenge to the so-called emancipated urban woman.

The vast majority of Indian women in villages and small towns neither resent their apparently subservient role nor feel any need or desire to change the status quo. Only in urban, cosmopolitan India, perhaps in no more than a dozen cities or so, where women read books by Germaine Greer and Kate Millet, can stirrings of potential rebellion be discerned. But even here, in the hothouse enclave of affluent Westernized womanhood, there are ambiguities and doubts. There is no general concensus about what a wife or daughter should do about the easy, unquestioned assumption of male feudal overlordship.

I remember asking a woman in her early seventies who had been a protégé of Tagore (the Indian poet who won the Nobel Prize for literature in 1913) what she thought of women's lib. She had been a widow for over a decade, but a nascent *joie de vivre* still lingered on her face. She wore a white cotton sari with a narrow, colored border, no makeup, and no vermilion powder on the center parting in her hair. These were the only concessions she made to her widowed status. Besides thin gold bangles on her left wrist (widows are not meant to wear ornaments of any kind), there were rings on her fingers, and she ate with the rest of the house instead of being confined to the once-a-day regimen of vegetarian, saltless food that husbandless women are required to adopt according to orthodox custom.

The phrase "women's lib" sent a tremor of amused nostalgia pulsing across her face. She smiled openly for a moment, and then said in her slow, soft voice: "You young people are obsessed with what are called *ideas*. We didn't ever need any. In the West, you have this expression, 'The woman's place is in the home.' Well, so it is. But not in quite the same way as you might take it to mean. I have never had any difficulty in doing exactly what I wanted, wherever I wanted, with whomever I wanted. And I suspect I had a great deal more freedom than any number of your Western women."

She paused for a moment, and I sensed that she was allowing the tape of her memory to wind back to past points of rapture and ecstasy. "*We* had power over our men, not the other way round. And we didn't have to go out and work. We did not have to do any of the mundane and vulgar things that these 'modern' ladies have to put up with. We were looked after. In a way, I suppose, we were *kept women*. But what delicious freedom! What fantastic power without responsibility!"

I caught her allusion and queried, "So, you were happy to be a harlot?"

"Who wouldn't be?" she retorted. "Words have different meanings in different settings. Yes, we were harlots, if you like, but with one very sharp distinction. Our children were legitimate, they inherited property."

"You were happy!" I said, sealing a discussion that had already gone far beyond my ken.

"Yes, we were," the old lady replied. "And we did not let the men know. They *thought* they were masters, and we let them go on deluding themselves. But in fact they were puppets. *We* pulled the strings. I know *I* certainly did." Then there was that flashing smile that could have been on the lips of a twenty-year-old, and I knew I had witnessed *resurrection*.

Although most of this conversation took place in Bengali, sprinkled with a few English phrases, the mind that motored the dialogue was certainly not a parochial one. There was always a mischievous twinkle in her eyes, even when she made the most outrageous assertions. To a contemporary Western audience, her sentiments might sound dubiously reactionary. But to me she seemed to be making a different point. I think she was trying to say that value systems cannot be grafted from one society to another, that a particular mode of operation may be regressive in one culture, and perfectly progressive in another.

The dialectical clash, the avalanche of sparks, of steel meeting fast-turning stone wheel, occurs when women are no longer able to operate within an atmosphere of affluence and leisure. When the frictions of daily living are lubricated by hordes of servants and palaces and the longueured elasticity of elaborate siestas in fountained garden houses, there is no cause for explosion or alarm. Male does not confront female, they merely elude each other.

When the twentieth century intrudes, when couples once accustomed to living in palatial establishments with no less than thirty or forty rooms are suddenly compelled by economic necessity to inhabit two-bedroom apartments in city tower blocks, where servants (all three of them) have to sleep on the landing at the top of the stairs, and the wife has to go to work at nine every morning, it is then that women's liberation comes into sharp focus and refuses to vacate the screen.

We come bang up against adjustable theory confronting irksome reality. Who makes out the shopping list for the servants? What happens if one or the other partner decides to stay out for a drink after work? Who examines the telephone and electricity bills? If the woman works in advertising or journalism, and the man is a scientist or an academic, *whose time is more precious?*

None of these questions would appear particularly startling either to a female liberationist or to a male progressive in the West. The contrast is that the upper-class Indian woman is being catapulted from a secure eighteenth-century environment to the turmoils of the twentieth century within the space of ten years. She is being made to question her role in a manner that neither her mother nor any Occidental may even begin to comprehend.

Phrases such as "I need space" or "I want to find myself" or even "I want to break the mold" sound borrowed, as indeed they are most of the time. Because it is hard to give up the womblike security of being "provided for" and "guarded against." If the male always assumes that his peacock feathers are best displayed when his wife is seen wearing the biggest diamonds in town, it is not easy to forswear "the girl's best friend," in lieu of a nebulous quest with no precise goal.

Mahatma Gandhi once told a visiting European journalist that he would learn more about the subcontinent by talking to a real Indian woman for a few hours than by reading a roomful of books. That cryptic prescription holds up as well today as it did nearly half a century ago.

The role of the woman in urbanized, intellectual, affluent India is perhaps the most difficult to define and perform. That these people constitute a minute fraction of the total population of the country does not invalidate their own very pressing and unique problems.

In New York recently, I met a long-standing friend of mine who had come away from India on an instant impulse, when her marriage had seemed to be on the rocks. One fine morning, the woman had suddenly announced to her husband over orange juice and cornflakes: "I want to go to the States." The man had adjusted his glasses, cleared his throat and replied: "Fine! Do tell me when you want to go, and I shall make all the arrangements."

The woman was taken aback by such immediate acceptance of a role she had never asserted before.

"I had tried, and I think I succeeded in being the perfect Bengali wife," she confided. "But I did not want to remain confined to being *Mrs.* Somebody all my life. I wanted to find out what I could do. At the same time, I knew I was an Indian woman. I could never become American or English. When I saw that rose in your garden in London, for the first time in many a year, I knew how beautiful it was to see and smell a big old-fashioned rose, which one had to use both one's hands to cup together. I knew then I had begun living again."

The woman was neither crying nor smiling as we walked down

University Place in Greenwich Village, my old haunt from far-off days.

"You know," she continued, "I still can't believe that I am walking hand in hand with you, here in Manhattan, New York—I, a happily married Bengali woman, with a husband and child back in Calcutta."

"Why not?" I asked.

"You know, it just wouldn't be done. All this afternoon, you have never made a pass at me, and I wouldn't consider reciprocating, even if you had. But we have held hands and hugged each other, without a retinue of onlookers. We have just been ourselves. That's what I shall miss most when I go back to India."

Sadly, very sadly, I reflected that she was saying more than she knew. Hypocrisy is an impregnable barrier. And in cities like Bombay, Delhi, or Calcutta, it is compounded with a self-righteous aura that says, as in the Bible, "He that is not with me is against me." Natural demonstrations of affection and love are not only frowned upon, they are punishable by law. Two British friends of mine were locked up in jail for a night because they insisted on going on "kissing in public" (in Connaught Circus, the hub of New Delhi) when a policeman had told them to stop.

The other side of my friend's dilemma was the acute awareness that her daring odyssey of self-discovery, which had made her come to London and New York, was only possible because she *was* Mrs. Somebody. She could never have done it on her own, not traveled first class and had all her reservations meticulously worked out, if her husband had not been the successful industrialist he was.

I was born in a large (twenty-six-room) house in Calcutta some two months before World War II broke out. My father was fifty-six and had already established a very successful miniempire in industry and commerce. My mother was forty, and my parents had been married for twenty-seven years at the time of my birth. Although they had both come from lowly financial backgrounds (villages, in what was then undivided Bengal under the British), the blood stock was from the purest pool of Hindu Brahmin lineage.

By the time I was about six and old enough to draw upon conscious memory, I was aware that my father was both rich and famous. We had a resident smithy in the house, some four full-time carpenters who made all the furniture to order, a deaf-mute house painter who worked a nine-to-five day, and a whole host of servants, cooks, and chauffeurs, including one gatekeeper who lived in.

At the same point in historical time, no child of six from an identical socioeconomic setup in the West could have had even a remotely similar upbringing. Yet, materially, I did not ever feel that there was anything unique about our family. Most of my friends, both in school and later on in college, were from roughly equivalent environments, give or take a servant or two. Where we differed was the way in which orthodox religious rituals were imposed and practiced in daily life. And the rigid system of patriarchal authority that my father exercised over the entire household. I can still recall, in all its awesome vigor, the thundering voice of my old man as he castigated either his wife or a servant or even my eldest brother (twenty-two years my senior), sending shivers of fright down the children's spines.

It was to break this parental domination that I lopped off the family name, Chakravarti (which means, in exact transliteration, "suzerain of the realm"), from my own, and thus ensured that no one would know what caste or family or geographical region I came from. (Names in India provide direct clues to all three).

To the external world, my father was a totally Westernized man. He spoke and wrote English fluently. His clothes were tailored at the best British establishments in Calcutta. In the last quarter of his spectacularly successful life, he had various honors and fellowships heaped upon him by several royal societies in England. His personal habits were impeccably Occidental. Yet, other than to visit relatives and family friends, he never went out with my mother. Whether they were Indian or foreign, he never entertained his business associates at home. None of his sons or daughters (except me) were allowed any say in the choice of their careers or their marriage partners. He brooked no opposition to the *ex cathedra* manner in which he laid down the law to the minutest detail. I remember being particularly irked when, at the age of thirteen, during vacation from boarding school, I was taken along to the barber's by my father, and made to accept a center parting in my hair, when all my chums had graduated to a left-side parting.

When an intellectual commitment to individual freedom and autonomy is pitted against a psychological yearning for domination and dictatorship, which does one choose? When in theory,

India opts for a democratic structure, but in practice yields to an authoritarian, dynastic regime (as during the Emergency), where does the true loyalty lie?

It is this quandary, this endemic intellectual ambiguity in the personal constitution, that makes the average middle-class, educated Indian so different from his or her counterpart in the West. In her own way, my mother was a far more powerful influence on the development of the clan than all the "raging bull" activities in which my father indulged. What she did and how she thought continues to control the behavior of the second and third generations.

My mother was a small, frail woman, no more than four foot eight in height. She had translucent skin, a very fair complexion (a tremendous asset in a country where dark skins are considered congenitally inferior), and large, dark brown eyes. She was exceedingly attractive. There is some uncertainty about her age, since there were no birth registers in the villages of Bengal at the time, but the general consensus seems to be that she was born in the year 1900. At the age of twelve or getting on to thirteen, she was married to my father, who was thirty. They had never seen each other before the day of their wedding, and neither of them found this extraordinary or impossible to accept. He was handsome and successful, she was pretty and came from a good Brahmin family. That was all.

She produced her first child in the village when she was barely fifteen; he was in the city, and did not hear about either the arrival of his firstborn or its death ten days later, for another year, when he returned to visit his wife and family during vacation. Without going into the details of subsequent developments in their lives, let us simply state that my mother and father produced thirteen more offspring, of whom nine died, and I was the last surviving issue.

My mother accepted her husband as the sole lord and master. He, in turn, conceded the total governance of domestic affairs to her. She chose the servants, she handled the housekeeping money, she decided what presents to give at weddings. More than this, she was the sole selector of wives for her sons. Theoretically, it was the man who chose. But in practice, it was the other way round. Though she deferred to him in public, in private she always had her own way. The most vicious fight I witnessed between my parents was when they had to decide on a bride for my second brother. My father was screaming and shouting in his usually bellowing voice and my mother was soft and steely, holding her ground. They threw pillows at each other, the female throw as fierce as the male one. All of a sudden they subsided, and I remember my father saying, "There is a child in the room, woman." "All right," my mother replied, "it is decided then. I choose." Imperiously, she walked out of the room. It was the only time in my young-adult life that my father had come and hugged me close. "Don't take any notice of these women, my son," he had whispered as he held me in his arms. "They are different from us." Then he paused, laughed a big laugh to himself, patted me on the cheek, and declared, "But you will learn soon enough."

For years I did not know what he meant. But now I think I have a vague idea.

My mother was as severe and ruthless a dictator in her own domain as my father was in his. But she had wholly different methods of enforcing her diktat. The strange and sad thing is that her regime still holds good today, while his has crumbled to dust. On her daughters-in-law, she imposed the most punishing routine. They were made to cook, not allowed to go out to the cinema more than about twice a month, and intimate verbal dialogue during the day between husband and wife (we all lived in a large communal house where the concept of privacy was totally alien and doors were never either shut or locked) was strictly forbidden. The wives of her sons chafed at the leash. But there was nothing they could do about it. Both my elder brothers obeyed my mother as if she were the goddess Durga incarnate. They would never have dreamt of defying her.

What happens when children decide to defy matriarchal authority is an altogether different story. It is my purpose here to try and explain what it means to live under the awe-inspiring shadow of a woman who virtually controlled your destiny.

Mother was the quintessential Indian, more than any man from that subcontinent can ever be. She was not torn by doubts. She had no intellect; she was, I think, simply fiercely intelligent. As the youngest daughter-in-law in the house when my father married her, she had been subjected to ferocious indignities. She had put up with it, and decided that in her time she would do the same. She did not question the system. Emotionally, she accepted male over-lordship, but she also believed very firmly that men were basically babies. There was no need to challenge them in their own territory; there were other ways of exercising one's sovereign will.

One very important thing I remember about my mother is her absolute refusal to speak English. It is a superstition in orthodox Brahmin homes that women who speak "foreign" tongues become widowed in early life. It is not often stated in public, due to the usual Indian habit of institutionalized hypocrisy, that Nehru's mother did not speak English. I suspect that this superstition arose from the male desire to keep the woman in *purdah* and so prevent her from participating in public life.

When my mother died in 1971, my senior-most sister-in-law assumed command over the household. She had married my eldest brother in 1941 and had grumbled and complained about my mother's rustic and authoritarian ways all through the thirty-odd years of her married life. She had been the first woman in the family to wear rouge and powder, use cleansing lotion on her face at night, and put on lipstick. My mother abominated these modern intrusions, but since she could not directly control the personal habits of her daughter-in-law, she got her own back in other wily ways. This "modern" woman was not permitted to accompany her husband to official business functions. She was made to cook, order the servants, prepare breakfast for my father, and a whole host of other menial tasks besides. My mother knew how much my sister-in-law loved to go to "the bioscope" (the cinema). This was therefore forbidden, except on special occasions for which permission had to be sought (by my brother) weeks in advance.

After my mother's death, when my sister-in-law's son had been married for more than three years and had already produced a male child, the regime that was imposed upon the new and younger daughter-in-law of the house was exactly the same as the one that the new lady governor had once complained about so loudly. My nephew had to ask his mother's permission to take his wife out for an ice cream. If there was a movie they both wanted to see, the mother had to be consulted first. As it says in the Old Testament, "the sins of the fathers (and mothers?) will be visited upon the third and fourth generations." Remember, we are talking about a man who was twenty-eight at the time, and his wife twenty-three.

Remarkably, male dominance in the Indian family is rapidly becoming a thing of the past. My father's bullying habits would not be tolerated by even a minute fraction of progenies (of either sex) today. While women still hold sway. Let me illustrate.

The contemporary Indian marriage I am about to describe took place between my twenty-five-year-old nephew (my late second brother's son) and an eighteen-year-old girl in May 1984. It was a wedding in a typical middle-class, educated urban milieu, and helps to sharply focus on the insuperable gulf that divides the usual Occidental assumptions about male-female relationships from those of the Indian.

The boy had graduated with creditable honors in mechanical engineering some four years previously. He then did an apprenticeship with the Dunlop (multinational) company and got himself a much-coveted job as a junior executive. He was bright and handsome, and was considered a very desirable catch by parents of single daughters. The family line from which he descended was also fairly impressive. And though his mother was a widow, the inheritance, both from his father's insurance money and the legacy left to him by his grandfather, was sufficiently robust to provide very well for his future wife and family.

The girl came from a similar though somewhat lowlier financial background. She was studying for her English honors final exams, which were due to be held at the end of May. She was pretty, if slightly plump, which satisfied the average Indian male's craving for "plenty to hold on to." Both families were Brahmins and the two horoscopes had been examined and compared in detail to establish that the match would be a propitious one. The middleman who had brought the two parties together expected to do handsomely from the transaction, as there was to be a lavish dowry from the girl's side and the festivities planned by the boy's family were not to lack in opulence. As the go-between gets a percentage cut out of both items of expenditure, the prospective wedding would be fairly lucrative on either count.

Some three months before the actual marriage, when "talks" had just started, I happened to be in Calcutta. As a senior member of the Chakravarti household, I was asked to accompany the "in-

specting team" from the groom's family to have a look at the prospective bride. I declined the invitation, and made a quip to the
effect that the other members of the family should report back to
me as to whether they had found the piece of meat or cheese they
were about to buy worth the market price.

The inspection ceremony, which precedes any conventional
wedding, is the most grotesque and hilarious drama that can be
imagined. A group of some ten or more people from the groom's
family descends upon the house of the would-be bride. She is then
presented on stage as a cross between a humanoid doll and a man-
nequin. Often she is required to sing and dance, display her han-
diwork (if she has any) in embroidery and clothes-making.
Frequently, the parents announce that all food being served to the
visiting party has been entirely home-prepared by their daughter.
She may also be expected to read out a page of printed English
text so they can check on her locution and accent. In other words,
this is an examination of all those characteristics that are thought
to be desirable in a wife or daughter-in-law. The prospective husband is almost always absent at this initial stage. Only if the girl
passes the preliminary tests, set to her by such disparate and de-
manding quarters as her future mother-in-law, the male elders of
the family, and junior female members of the entourage, does she
get a chance to see her would-be husband at a future meeting. At
that most fateful encounter, there are again some ten or more people present. The prospective groom is allowed to ask a few questions, the girl none. The implicit assumption is that she is being
tested, not the other way round. If he approves, and the horoscopes match, and the dowry is agreed upon, then the wedding
plans go ahead. If not, the whole process starts all over again with
different parties.

My remark about cheese or meat was meant to indicate an ap-
proximate congruence between the mental and emotional dispositions of a shopper in the marketplace who prods and presses the
goods on the display counter before making a purchase, and the
altogether more onerous business of selecting a bride. But the
comparison was severely criticized as being in bad taste, a symp-
tom of my incorrigible conversion to the barbaric attitudes of
the Western world. My joke splashed like a boulder in a pool of
sewage.

· On this occasion the girl rode over the hurdles and passed her tests with top marks from every quarter. The other mundane items on the agenda were duly discussed and a wedding date was fixed—exactly three weeks before her Bachelor of Arts examination at the university. But this last fact was given the least consideration among all the other matters of moment that are pondered before a wedding.

Prior to describing the actual ceremony, let me relate two conversations I had—the first with the groom himself, the second with his widowed mother. Knowing my nephew to be a bright and cultured boy, I was curious to find out why and how he could surrender himself to such a situation without demur. One wanted to discover how, in 1984, an educated man of twenty-five could consider spending the rest of his life (divorce, you might recall, does not figure in the calculations as a realistic or plausible alternative to the compulsory or volitional servitude of marriage) with a woman he had barely seen for ten minutes, and that, too, in the company of ten other hawk-eyed adults from both sides of the camp. His reply was intriguing.

"Well," he said, "marriage, like everything else in life, is a gamble. Even if you have known a woman for years, there is no guarantee that things will run smoothly for the rest of your married life. It is better to let *them* [his elders] take the decision. Then, if things go wrong, I can never be blamed for having chosen the wrong person. Besides, I am not the most important figure in this whole affair. The vital factor is my mother, because my wife will have to spend a great deal more time with her than with me. So it is absolutely crucial that the two of them get along together. After all, I can always adjust."

It was not only startling to hear a twenty-five-year-old talk with the world-weary air of a man of seventy. What unnerved me was the total absence of individual assertion, the resigned acceptance of a flaccid fatalism in a bright young man who could have opted for a different course. His confident and succinct answer to my question also assumed that the girl he was about to marry had no choice in the matter at all. Nor did the notion of sexual compatability or its reverse enter the discussion. For someone who was speaking in the tones of a much-married male of advanced years, it was amusing and sad to remind oneself that this young man had never even dated a girl in his life, let alone slept with a woman. As became a dutiful son, his main concern was for his mother, who had come to live with him since his father died, and would go on doing so when he was married. The control of household affairs would be entirely in his mother's hands; his wife would be expected to act as an obedient but unpaid domestic, and adjust to her new life under the strict supervision of her mother-in-law, just as the older lady had done in her time to the mother of *her* husband.

What my nephew said not only reflected his individual attitude to his own marriage. I believe it hinted at a value system that affected all kinds of other areas as well, and represented fairly typically what young men from middle-class families think and feel in India today. For a Westerner to understand the kind of person he is dealing with from India, be it in New York, London, or New Delhi, it is essential to remember that beneath the scientific, literary, and cultural sophistication, there lies a bedrock of beliefs and assumptions that are precisely antithetic to those of the Occidental.

The conversation with the mother was even more revealing. She saw no reason to feel squeamish about asserting that the marriage was mainly a matter of her own convenience. Certain other incidental considerations did intervene, such as the physical needs of her son, the necessity to produce heirs for the family line, and so on. But the principal function of the impending wedding and the bride who would come with it was to provide her with a servant who would execute her commands in the house. It was vital, therefore, that the girl was not headstrong and self-willed, that she should not be the kind of person who would wish to control the son to such an extent as to make him discard his docile and sweetly obedient nature. "Never know about these modern young women," the mother had said. "They have such strange notions about what their husbands should do."

When I reminded her about the time when she herself had been a new young bride and had desperately wanted her husband to be less servile to his mother and more caring and attentive to the wishes of his wife, my sister-in-law replied that it was futile to think about what we may ideally desire. "We may want many things, but do we ever get them? I did what I was told to do, I had no option."

The implication was clear. She had paid her dues, now it was the turn of the next generation to do the same. There was no question of changing the system. My mother's iron will continued to rule from regions beyond the crematorium.

About sex she was equally adamant. Marriage was a serious business in which a myriad social considerations had to be carefully pondered. Sex was an incidental parameter, young people were far too obsessed with it nowadays. It was not the be-all and end-all of life. When I asked as to what would happen if the woman found her husband sexually incompatible in bed, she replied vehemently, "Whoever heard of a wife not liking her husband? Anyway, liking has nothing to do with it. If she respects and obeys her husband, then everything else follows automatically." The implication was that as long as the man was able to satisfy himself, and thereby procreate, there was no further need to consider any other factor in the sexual domain.

She was saying this about an eighteen-year-old girl in 1984 who was expected to graduate soon with an honors degree in English. The couple would be living not in some small village outpost in the Styx, but in a major metropolis like Calcutta, once called the Second City of the British Empire.

Sexual incompatibility was a newfangled notion that had no connection with the real and important things of life. And suddenly I was reminded of that Victorian injunction to a new bride: "Lie back and think of Queen and Country."

In fact the analogy is frighteningly precise. Indian marital morality and social ethics are a fairly faithful replica of Victorian England at about the turn of the century. If the woman didn't like it, she simply had to lump it. To contemplate the possibility of choice in these matters was a repellent heresy.

The wishes and the welfare of the two people least considered at an Indian, Hindu wedding are those of the bride and groom. Each of them, in their own different houses, are woken up before sunrise (at about 4:30 A.M.) and given a public bath with turmeric and mustard oil. These two ingredients are supposed to act as cleansing and invigorating agents, according to religious symbolism. They are then fed a plate of curd and popcorn, on which they have to subsist for the remainder of the day, till they are joined in holy wedlock after an elaborate pageant that does not usually finish till the early hours of the next morning (all "propitious" wedding hours occur well after sunset). In effect, they are made to starve for over twenty-four hours on the day that is meant to be the most significant in their lives (other than birth and death, of course, over which, normally, they don't have any control). The purpose of this exercise is to prepare the respective bodies (and empty stomachs) to be in a state of "holy grace."

For the rest of the day they are pretty much left alone while others in the household (visiting relatives, friends, cousins, aunts, and sundry other hangers-on) go about eating and drinking and generally making merry in an atmosphere of gay abandon. Loud music blares out from amplifiers so that the whole neighborhood is informed that a wedding is in progress.

After sunset, the wedding party from the groom's house begins its stately progress toward the abode of the bride. The boy is invariably clad in an outfit that makes him look like a cross between a clown and a surrogate princeling. He has a papier mâché crown stuck on his head, and the gaudier the clothes, the more affluent his family is reckoned to be. Depending on the area of country in which the pantomime is being performed, the mode of transport (for the groom only) can be a horse or an elephant or even a camel. In urban (so-called sophisticated) India, it is usually a car. When animals are employed—and they really do look spectacular because they, too, are dressed up in silk and satin with gold and silver embroidery—the procession is headed by a band of trumpeters, flautists, and drummers. Frequently, there are tubes of neon light held by slow-moving footbearers on either side of the road, through which the parade passes. There is always a riot of color and sound, firecrackers explode, petals of roses are scattered, till finally the "lucky" man arrives at the bride's house.

The bride has been well titivated by sandalwood paste on her face and all kinds of ornamental designs (in herbal dyes) on her feet. She is wearing at least one or two pounds (avoirdupois) of gold jewelry on her body, starting with a gold and pearl band on her forehead, large earrings, and chains of pearls and rubies lower down her face. In affluent surroundings, she might even be sporting silver and gold anklets which tinkle as she walks.

There is incense in the room, the thick overpowering odor of religiosity permeating the atmosphere. The ceremony starts with the oldest member of the groom's clan blessing the would-be bride in a language (Sanskrit) that no one understands, but that the priest recites and the blesser repeats in parrotlike fashion. Since I was a "senior," I blessed the bride with the following words in English: "I hope you have a happy marriage. I pray that you live your life to the fullest, in freedom and autonomy, not in servitude." The Sanskrit ceremony for each of the other senior blessers took ten minutes; mine was over in less than thirty seconds. My English words were not appreciated, especially because everyone in the room understood what I said. (Perhaps there is a point to linguistic opacity.) The eighteen-year-old girl looked up at me (prospective brides are supposed to keep their heads well bowed down), startled, and then smiled.

In the next hour or so, the groom, who has been stripped of his pantomime attire by now and made to put on a five-yard-long piece of fine cotton cloth *(dhoti),* leaving the whole of his body above the waist totally exposed (What if the man had a naturally depilated chest? What a letdown for macho hirsute humanity!), is taken to the holy place where the ceremony is about to be performed.

It is not quite a tabernacle or an altar, but a piece of raised ground, about eight feet square in area, which has been liberally sprinkled with liquid cow dung. This sanctifies the place and makes it fit for religious ceremonies. The groom is then required to recite a huge host of mumbo jumbo (in Sanskrit), not a word of which he comprehends. The bride is ushered in only at the point when the priests declare that the prospective husband is in a fit enough state of "religious grace" to receive his prospective wife. She is brought in with her head totally covered by her gold-brocaded sari and attired as before in all her jeweled refinery. She is seated in the lotus position on a wooden plank, which is carried at a height of some seven feet above the ground by robust male members of her own family.

There are several points to be made here. The first is about her covered head. The reason is that in days gone by, neither bride nor groom were expected to have seen each other before the sacred moment of their wedding. So the ritualistic pretense goes on. The modern convention of a ten-minute encounter at least (what if it is under the invigilating stares of a score of other people?) is ignored, an assertion is made that it never did happen.

When bride and groom finally meet, look at each other eye to eye, a silk canopy thrown over their heads, with the girl still ridiculously supported by seven sweating men, she sitting, he standing with exposed hairy chest, it is then and only then that they are supposed to have first set eyes on each other. The occasion is called *shuva drishti*—auspicious eye-gazing.

My tone of amused cynicism about the whole agenda of religious ritual and symbolism stems from a conviction that perhaps new wine cannot be poured into old bottles without cracking the skin, that conventions that were once perfectly valid have now outlived their utility.

When girls of twelve or thirteen were married to boys some five or seven years older, when they had never ever ventured out of their homes on their own, when young men did not even speculate about selecting wives of their own choice, it may have been an efficient and adequate social mechanism to marry them off when they were young, suiting the convenience of their families and elders.

Today, the old-fashioned joint family is cracking up. There are no longer large houses with twenty-six rooms to accommodate sons and daughters-in-law in vast profusion. Girls are going to high school and college. Whether their parents approve or not, they are seeing boys. Economic necessity is beginning to dictate that women go out to work. More often than not, the environment is no longer segregated along sexual lines. If they don't actually have "affairs" in the Western sense, women are starting to develop crushes. The old tabula rasa has ceased to exist. Would-be wives no longer come to their husbands in a state of wide-eyed innocence. If, if general, they have not had sexual experience, they have at least heard about it and seen it in action in one or two instances.

Over a hundred years ago, my own aunt (my father's eldest sister-in-law) was married at the age of three to my uncle, who was then nine years old. The boy died four years later and my aunt became a widow when she was seven. Since that point, she lived a life of total celibacy, shaved her head once a month (widows are not allowed to have hair, which is considered an adornment), ate one vegetarian, saltless meal a day, and acted as a menial domestic in our extensive joint household. She finally died at the age of ninety-four in 1970, having had absolutely no contact with any man, emotionally or physically, throughout her whole long life. She not only did not complain about this, she was proud of it. I know, because she told me.

No woman in contemporary India would put up with this kind of subjugation. Yet, the structures that regulate social life have changed very little. So, we have a situation where ritual and custom are at wide variance with practice and reality. Confrontation, therefore, impends, and a social explosion may well result.

What is intriguing and unique about Indian weddings, certainly Hindu ones, is the interwebbing connections they have with all sorts of other areas. They reflect not only the dispositions of one man to one woman. They reveal that individuality is at a severe discount, that aspirations toward the possibility of human happiness are regarded as anathema, that fatalism is a lacing thread that runs through the whole tapestry of society. Indian weddings tell you a whole lot about why old folk are relegated to "homes" in America and England, while they are prized as the sole source of wisdom in the mystic East. Since "boy meets girl" seldom occurs in real life, kissing is forbidden on the Indian screen. Even the word *romance* means totally different things to someone in London or New York as against a man or woman from India.

Values from a wildly different era still prevail. The paradox is that so do computers, microchips, satellites, and video games. If you can imagine one single American family, in which one son is an aeronautics engineer, another a farmer who uses a bullock cart to till his fields, the third a polished debater in the halls of Congress, and the fourth a professional reader of tarot cards, you would begin to have an idea about contemporary India. Superstition and science can and often do exist side by side, frequently in the same person. What is totally incomprehensible to the Western mind is the fact that diametrically opposed concepts reside in the same mental container.

After the "auspicious eye-gazing," the marriage ceremony continues in two, almost wholly separate parts. While priests go to work on the couple in front of a raging (holy) fire, and the groom and bride sweat profusely, guests (some four- to six hundred, at an average middle-class wedding) are being fed and feted by the bride's father and other male elders. The food is always esoteric, rich, and profuse. There are several sittings, each of them for a hundred or so and lasting for over an hour. Guests are seldom interested in observing the actual ceremony to the bitter end—which, in this case, dragged on till about two in the morning. When the meal is over, the new husband and wife continue to chant endless Sanskrit *mantras* and consolidate their bond under the stern control of priests and holy men, who know they will earn more the longer the pageant continues. No one understands what is being said. The important thing is that ritual is being rigidly observed. When the six-hour marathon of *pujas* and holy offerings is over, and the priests paid off, the couple are finally allowed to eat.

They are then escorted to their "wedding room," and the torture starts again in a totally different guise. Junior members of the girl's family are encouraged by elders to plague and pester the newly married couple. I remember being asked to hide under the bed at my second brother's wedding (when I was ten) and told to spring on them after they had shut the door of their room on their first night together.

My nephew told me afterward, in his usual precocious manner, that there was a point to all this. It was to inject a vaccine into the male system that would prevent him from ever contemplating going through *that* experience again. Perfectly po-faced, he announced, "Why do you think there are so few divorces in India?" I was glad to see that he did have a sense of humor.

There is no way to figure out how many marriages are actually consummated on the night of the wedding, since market surveys are not conducted on these subjects in India. But given the circumstances, I doubt if more than 1 percent of couples really copulate on that occasion. My sister-in-law told me (many years later) that her husband did not make love to her till over a year after their marriage. Which would not be surprising, since she was fifteen at the time and my brother was all of twenty-two. I am reasonably certain that neither of them had had any experience with the opposite sex until they were married. People can be and often are very timid and shy about these matters.

Immediately after sunrise on the next day, the couple start for the groom's house, once again in stately procession. On arrival at her in-laws', the girl is thoroughly dunked in holy water and made to undergo a purification and bathing ceremony in front of some thirty-odd female onlookers. The symbolism here is that she is being cleansed of all the impurities that may have clung to her body (and soul?) when she was living with her parents. Now that she is in her husband's territory, she must be stripped bare of any erstwhile leanings and loyalties.

Although most of this is done as token gestures to past codes and values, it is not impossible that lingering remnants of what they mean continue to agitate the minds of both parties. In effect, the girl is told that all her previous life with her mother and father and siblings must now be forgotten, that her new and only concern should be for her husband and his family; that her loyalties are now being severely reprogrammed. For a virginal and wholly inexperienced girl of eighteen, this must be a matter of deep psychological upheaval, especially when the girl has been launched into a house in which she knows absolutely nobody, but where she is expected to perform as a virtual slave.

How does one contemplate the significance of such a formative experience when one meets that "ever so charming and sophisticated Indian lady" at a cocktail party? In all probability, the woman has had to live in two or three utterly disparate worlds and value systems within the span of two decades. If she seems incomprehensibly gauche or stubborn at one moment, and delightfully self-assured and refined at another, how does one know that she is not one, but several different people, all in one body? If she appears mysterious and inaccessible, could it be that she is aware of these conflicts, and much too private yet assertive to reveal the source of her personal duality?

In a sense, this business of "reprogramming loyalties" is what modern India is all about. Past history and culture, over five thousand years of the collective unconscious (to borrow a phrase from Jung), press heavily on the contemporary individual psyche and force a confrontation with modern modes of thought which, in almost every sphere, generates a fierce dialectic from which there is no escape to the Hegelian haven of synthesis. Thesis exists in all its profound and antecedent glory; so does antithesis, in satellites and cyclotrons. But synthesis proves elusive. Mrs. Gandhi used to set her election dates and launch wars on neighboring countries only after consulting her resident astrologer. She was both a democrat and a dictator, but never the two at the same time. Men are feudal in their homes, but progressive at work. Women claim to be feminists, but expect their menfolk to support them. Scientists will probe the secrets of fundamental particles and pay unqualified homage to Heisenberg's uncertainty principle, yet expect and demand determinism from their wives. Brilliant young executives will introduce a regime of cybernetics in the office, but will violently repudiate the new math that their sons are taught at school.

Perhaps the contemporary Indian is more typically a symbol of the last quarter of this century than any other human being on earth. If Erich Fromm's thesis of "collective insanity" is to be given a respectful audition, it is necessary to reflect that the Indian mind has been forced to live in a state of schizoid tension for the past half-millennium. The intellectual "barrow boy" solution of taking the *best* from East and West, the cerebral cop-out in attempting to integrate elements from diametrically opposed camps, is at best pathetic, at worst explosively dangerous. The only point at which negative and positive meet is zero. No transition from the one to the other is possible without crossing the Rubicon—a "test by fire."

A totally different kind of wedding took place between Diana and her Indian husband in 1974. She was from Boston and had met Balraj (nicknamed Bob, for American convenience) at a party in Cambridge, Massachusetts. She had instantly fallen head over heels in love, and had followed him back to India after he got his Ph.D. Two years later they were married in his hometown, Patna, Bihar, in as indigenous a fashion as a foreign woman was allowed.

I gathered all this information when I met Diana at the dining room of my hotel in Khajuraho (in 1984). As the Indian Airlines flight on which we were both booked was canceled, we traveled together from there by car (for five hours) and then took a late-night train (2:30 A.M.) back to Delhi. I had a fair amount of time to talk to her.

Diana still used her old Indian surname, even though she had later married an American by whom she had a child. She was working for the State Department in Washington, and lived a few miles away from her office.

When I asked what she *now* felt about her first (Indian) husband, she replied in a single word, "Pity!"

Apparently, the man was a brilliant student at MIT. Diana had been enamored of his good looks (she was not particularly pretty herself) and his air of effortless confidence. By her own admission, she had chased him back to India and the two of them had married in native style (at her own insistence) in the city in which he was born. Diana was naïve, romantic, and committed enough to overlook all kinds of lapses of social etiquette, both in her man and in his relations. She was absolutely determined to marry this man, with whom she felt she was deeply in love.

What made her come back to India again and again was, I believe, a quest to understand why that idyllic partnership broke up. After the wedding, the couple had gone up to Gujarat (a backwater state), where he had landed a "good" job. She told me she had been wholly willing to fall into the role of "a typical Indian wife" (sans the supervisory eagle eye of mother-in-law watching every operation), without any reservations.

If the marriage had lasted, "I would have been perfectly happy to spend the rest of my life in India." Clearly, she was not a normal American female, because she added, "All these things that outsiders complain about are really nonessentials." (Like hot water in the tap, a working telephone, some sense of hygiene, even a car?) But Diana was adamant. She asserted, "There is absolutely nothing unacceptable in being an Indian wife to a real Indian husband who loves you."

There were several variables to her statement. So I queried. How would one distinguish between a "real" from an "unreal" Indian husband? What is an Indian wife? Are Indian husbands the only kind of people who love a woman one day and cease to do so the following year? Is there a commonly accepted definition of "love" about which both Indians and Americans can agree?

Her replies were profoundly revealing.

Diana said, with total calm in her voice and an amused expression in her eyes, "You are missing my point. I thought that Balraj was really Indian, that's why I wanted to marry him. It turned out that he was neither Indian nor American nor anything else for that matter. He had come to the States, got his Ph.D., and had made a great impression on everyone. All the time he was *there,* he gave out this total Indianness, which made him so attractive. When we came back to India, he started speaking with a strange accent, which was neither American nor Indian, but a kind of hodgepodge. By speaking in that way, he wanted to impress his friends. But it felt funny to me, at first, anyway, then it got boring. We started having rows. He insisted that he spoke with a fluent American accent. After a while I had to tell him that no American I had ever heard spoke the way he did. This set him flaming."

Clearly, the woman was using me as a touchstone, so I let her continue.

"I didn't mind that he pretended to his friends. But I thought he shouldn't try to pull that one on me. After all, I did not marry him for the way he spoke. I couldn't really care less whether his accent sounded Indian or Japanese. It was a shock for me to realize that *he* cared very much. And that he expected me to be part of his charade."

Diana paused, wiped her lips, and continued, as if she were giving a dissertation (State Department training, no doubt!). "A good deal later, it dawned on me that he wasn't kidding at all. Balraj actually believed that he was talking like an American, and every time I told him he was not, he felt I was doing it out of spite."

"You mean, he was hung up about his accent?" I asked.

"That, and much more besides. All the time he was in Cambridge, he wanted to show everyone how Indian he was. One of the first things that struck me about him was how gentle and considerate and understanding he was—in fact, how totally unlike an average American male. But here in India, after we were married, he was trying his best to put himself across as the kind of American I most detested. I couldn't understand this transformation."

"What were those things you most detested that Balraj wished to project?" I queried.

"Well, it gets very personal here. But you know what I mean. The macho image. The woman being the little miss who sits at home cooking meals. No preliminaries before lovemaking. Having a beer with the boys till all hours of the night."

By this stage I think I got the message.

Balraj insisted on coming back to the States, despite Diana's repeated and futile requests to stay home. At the job he took in Philadelphia, he was not a spectacular success. For this he blamed his wife. Whenever their only child (a son, who had been born in India), did badly at school, it was *her* fault. He began drinking heavily and raged at her for having trapped him into coming back to America, when in fact she had suggested the exact opposite course of action. Frequently, in his bellicose mood, he would beat her up.

All the qualities that Diana had so prized in her Indian began to be turned on their heads. Where she had thought he was gentle, he became rough, trying vainly to imitate his friends at the bar. Balraj's "understanding" and "consideration" gave way to a species of red-neck bullying that was unappetizing, to say the least. His attempts to copy American manners in speech and gait began to look sadly pathetic, instead of cute and endearing.

He had become a "nowhere" man, with the poisoned worst of both worlds simmering in his heart.

At least, that was Diana's story to me.

The woman is now apparently happily married to another State Department official in Washington. They have two children (including the one from Balraj), and the couple live in an elegant suburb in Virginia. Diana feels she is at long last well and truly rid of her "Indian bug." Not I, but the reader, must decide as to what really happened between those two people. And whether Balraj's Indianness was crucial and germane to the explosive fracture of their marriage.

One story that Diana told me would appear to cast some doubt on her assertion that she would have been perfectly happy to live the life of a typical Indian wife, if only her husband had been a "real" product of his country, and continued to "love" her.

After their marriage, the couple had moved to Ahmedabad in Gujarat State (western India), where Balraj was employed as a highly paid research chemist by a large industrial outfit. Although the job was lucrative and provided status, Ahmedabad was not a city where there was a great deal for an American woman to do. There was no expatriate Western community (as in Delhi or Calcutta or any other major metropolis), which could provide a sense of belonging for an exile in a foreign land. Wives of other executives in the company were polite and friendly enough, but they never showed any desire to become really intimate with Diana. Social life was restricted to evenings at the club, an occasional movie or two. But the place simply did not provide the kind of amenities that Diana would have taken for granted back home in the States. Art galleries, theaters, concerts—the bric-a-brac of civilized life, which would be on offer in the big cosmopolitan cities of India, did not exist. A car ride into Bombay would take ten hours over bumpy roads; train connections were poor and highly uncomfortable. So Diana started to get restless.

Within a year of their wedding, she decided to take a job. As she was fluent in Spanish and Balraj's firm was negotiating a big deal with Argentina at the time, Diana wheedled herself into the operation as a translator-cum-secretary for the project. But the deal fell through, and once again she was left with a mountain of time on her hands.

It is pointless reflecting that large masses of Europeans and American women found themselves in an identical condition some thirty years ago. Diana was not a product of that era. She was an articulate and intelligent woman who needed to have things to do besides going to the market every morning and ordering around a bevy of servants.

So she tried her hand at social work. But here again, Diana came up against a barrier. People resented an American woman trying to play "lady bountiful" among the city's wretched poor. They questioned both her motives and her manner.

"I knew I couldn't change the whole of Indian society overnight," she told me, "but I wanted to do what little I could." Neither her husband nor her few Indian women friends could understand Diana's urgent need to be able to tell herself that she was not sitting there doing nothing, or her desperate craving to make some kind of personal gesture that would relieve her of a feeling of callous indifference in the face of the immense gulf that visibly separated the poor from the rest of India.

This is a problem that very few Indians, even highly educated and sensitive ones, seem to comprehend. That to a Westerner, to throw up one's hands simply because the sharp inequalities and obvious injustices appear so vast and intractable, is to accept moral self-indictment. Doing nothing about such grotesque poverty as exists in India is a way of condoning it, especially if one reaps the benefits of a system where a small few prosper while the masses continue to live supinely with hunger, destitution, and disease.

But Diana did try just one more time. The maid who worked for her had a daughter of eight who came along with her every day. Diana fed the little girl and bought her clothes, and finally got her enrolled in the local school, paying the fees herself. If she couldn't do social work at large, Diana felt that she could at least help the one person who was directly under her own control. The maid's wages were higher than what other servant girls got, and this set the neighbors clacking their tongues. Diana, with her foreign ways, was spoiling the market for everyone else. It was all very well for her, she with her fancy accent and fair skin. If one maid was paid such ridiculously high wages (about twenty dollars a month for a six-day week), then all the others would start to get ideas. Obviously, the money must be coming from her rich parents back in the States. All Americans were wealthy and they just couldn't understand how difficult it was to make do with meager Indian salaries.

In vain Diana tried to explain, when she was given a chance, that she was paying the maid from the housekeeping money she got from her husband. There was no subsidy from anywhere else. Besides, her parents were not rich! Everyone else in the company complex in which they lived earned about the same as Balraj. If they wished, the other women could afford to pay as much as Diana did. But that would mean they would have to spend less on their saris and their once-a-month visit to the jeweler's. It was preferable to believe that Diana was just being her extravagant, indulgent American self, rather than accept that she did not want new dresses and gold ornaments every other week.

Eighteen months after the maid's daughter started her education, the woman came up to Diana one morning and tearfully confessed that she had had to take the child out of school. The little girl was betrothed to the washerwoman's son (who was eleven), and as he was being taken out of school to join the family workforce, his parents had threatened to break off the engagement, if the prospective bride continued with primary school. They could not have a daughter-in-law in the house who was better educated than their son. No wife should ever outstrip her husband in learning.

Once again, Diana had come up against an Indian institution that foiled her best intentions. There was no way of persuading the mother of the girl that engagements broken off at the age of nine do not constitute the collapse of all hope for a child's future.

*   *   *

If Diana was fighting a losing battle in modern India against ancient customs, then my visit to Madras set the tone for an experience that was cast in an altogether different mold. But before I relate the most massive collision of cultures I have ever experienced, let me talk a little about a city that is not often the topic of contemporary Occidental discussion.

Madras is situated on the east coast, halfway up the left thigh of the Indian subcontinent. It is the oldest city of the British Raj, and was founded by a man named Francis Day in 1639 according to instructions from his bosses at the East India Company in London to build a fort "to facilitate trade." Much of the city's character comes from its official buildings, which are in the nineteenth-century mode of architecture known as Indo-Saracenic—a unique blend of Western and Indian styles. It was here that Robert Clive, the founder of British India, first arrived in 1743 as a menial clerk, and from where he went on to become the Commander in Chief of the British forces in India. It was in Madras that the seeds of the wealthiest and most powerful empire the world has ever known were first sown.

But if Madras is a colonial city, with its wide avenues, gracious gardens, and stately buildings, it is also the nucleus of a host of temple complexes, which date as far back as the pre-Christian era. In this region of India, the temple is as much a place of worship as a mainspring of art, music, dance, sculpture, and, even today, an integral and vital part of social life. At sunset, hawkers sell their wares, from shimmering silks and colorful ribbons to shiny vessels and fragrant flowers. Women meet at the temple, exchange family gossip, consult horoscopes, and arrange marriages. Youths flirt with evanescent glances, wise men recite stories of the time when rich traditions flourished, when maritime commerce was establishing itself in this land as its people explored new nations and welcomed traders from China and Rome.

Indians who come from Madras regard themselves as the original inhabitants of the subcontinent, predating the Aryans. They are usually very dark-skinned, with shiny, glistening faces, white (as against yellow) teeth, and partially Negroid features. Tamil, which is the state language, claims to be as old as Sanskrit, though most scholars dispute this. The people are intensely relious, and vegetarianism is the generally accepted norm, not the exception.

If India is divided between North and South, with Caucasians (Aryans) above the center and Dravidians below, Madras can legitimately claim to be the pivot of southern culture. Madrasis are intensely nationalistic, family oriented, and devout. More than those from any other subrace in the whole country, the men from Madras are acutely chauvinistic. In general, they tend to be very clever, and capable of keeping their several lives in separate, sealed compartments. Scientists who direct vast research centers will offer *pujas* to gods before starting the day. Young men will consult priests and astrologers before setting out on a foreign trip to Frankfurt, Germany, or Princeton, New Jersey.

In a sense, this is the heart of orthodox, Hindu India, where idols of gods exist in abundant profusion at every street corner, and men and women dress in long cotton cloths, as if they were about to perform penance and prostrate themselves before a deity any moment.

On a sweaty, sweltering day (105°F in the shade) in May 1984, I set out from my hotel in Madras to visit the temple that attracts the largest Hindu crowds from the whole country. The area in which it is situated is called Tirumala and the shrine itself is named Tirupathi.

The site, which is a huge complex with its own municipality and civic corporation, is some 120 miles from Madras, about six hours by car. The temple houses the idol of a deity that is regarded as the most "alive" (*jagrata*) in the whole country. People by the thousands flock to it every day of the year to offer their prayers, heal their sick, bless their marriages, invoke fertility in childless women, inaugurate auspicious ventures, terminate feuds, claim protection from enemies, and a million other things besides.

The idol is reckoned to be over a thousand years old, though the temple itself cannot have been built more than three hundred years ago. The stone figure is the representation of an incarnation of Vishnu, one of the holy Hindu Trinity: Brahma, creator of the universe; Vishnu, governor of the immortal gods; and Siva, governor of the mortal world. But as in all things (like dates) in India, no one is quite certain about the actual figures, and one scholar's hit is as good as another layman's miss.

On the way up to the temple, we drove through flat green

country. On my right were deep-watered paddy fields, where women were bending down under the fierce summer sun to plant seeds for next season's crop. Bullock carts wafted past my window as if they were tableaux from another age. Creaky old ladies, carrying bundles of firewood on their heads, fleeted by.

All of a sudden, I saw a huge bus on the left side of the road, and I stopped the car to find out what was happening. The vehicle lay in a ditch, like a brown beetle on its back. There were bodies scattered all around, and massive gunnysacks of rice and lentils, splitting at the seams. Bystanders had come to watch and gesticulate. All the attention was paid to the goods the bus was carrying on its rooftop: The dead lay there inert, unmoving, pitilessly speechless.

My chauffeur got back into the car and drove on. For a whole hour we did not talk. Then he said, "Sir, I know you are upset. But things like that happen every day in this country. You can't let yourself get worked up about this. We are going to the temple."

I couldn't answer. There was a frog in my throat and death and annihilation on my brain.

"You know, sir," my chauffeur pursued, generously trying to distract me, "the place we are going to visit has the second richest god in the world." As he was saying this in pidgin English, laced with Hindi, I became intensely curious.

"What do you mean by the second richest god? Which is the first?" I also wanted to know what kind of a creature "a rich god" was.

Speeding along at thirty miles an hour, the driver replied, "Well, there is another more rich god, in Rome. I think it is called *VAT CAN,* but I do not know for certain. In that place there is a richer god . . ."

I was aroused.

How could a god be rich? What the hell was he talking about? Had all that death and destruction finally driven him out of his mind?

"No, sir, I know these things for a fact. In the newspapers they said that on the first of January this year [1984], Tirupathi got twenty-five *lakhs* of rupees [roughly a quarter of a million dollars]. That was in one day. You just think what they make in a whole year!"

(Remember that the average Indian earns less than two hundred dollars a year!)

Soon the scenery began to change as we crossed over to the adjoining state of Andhra Pradesh. Tall palm trees gave way to shrubs, the road undulated over hillier terrain. By midday, the heat had become oppressive, as heavy as a blast of steam in a Turkish bath.

Approaching Tirumala, the picture altered again. Costumes became more colorful; buntings in red, blue, and yellow littered the narrow streets. The throb and pulse of festivity sang in the air. My chauffeur stopped the car and said I should have lunch before going up to the temple.

As we had arrived at the place already, I couldn't see why we should have to waste precious time. After all, I was not making a pilgrimage. I was here strictly in the line of duty, and visiting Tirupathi, "the second richest god in the world," was no different for me than a glance at the Taj Mahal or a spin over Manhattan island in a helicopter.

But the man insisted. "You will see, sir, it takes time."

I checked my impatience and yielded to his superior local knowledge. Only later did I realize that the driver was right. It took over an hour to climb from the bottom of the hill to the top, where the god was ensconced in his holy shrine. It was a slow, tortuous ascent (about ten miles) along a winding mountain road, though the view was spectacular. When we reached the peak, it was only the beginning of my ordeal.

What amazed me was the sheer size of the complex that surrounded the temple. The comparison with the Vatican was apposite. There was a small railway station, a bus company, a whole host of hotels ranging in price from two dollars a night to thirty. There were living quarters for the men who ran the outfit, shopping arcades, market stalls, and priests peddling holy stones and religious artifacts. The place was run like a tourist resort, with a sharp eye for profit. But as it was a *Devasthanam* ("God's abode" in literal translation, meaning a religious trust), it was exempt from tax.

The message from all the literature was unambiguous, and blared loud and hard to the gullible and superstitious, the weaker vessels of vulnerable humanity who need a faith in the face of oppression and poverty. If you pay your mite, you will be released from earthly bondage and attain *mukti*—the cessation of the endless cycle of birth and rebirth. Poor today, and heaven tomorrow! But you *must* put your two cents in the kitty first.

The temple itself is on slightly higher ground than the rest of the minitownship. As you approach, the shining gold dome glinting in the sun assaults your eyes. A sea of swirling bodies engulfs and sweeps you into a narcotic haze from which there is no voluntary escape. Men and women with totally shaven heads go about chanting holy *mantras,* and you are driven along, as if by an unseen force over which you have no control.

When I asked the driver to come along with me to the temple, he was reluctant. I was surprised at his pusillanimity, since he had just been telling me how devout and religious he was. Soon I discovered why. The queue to the entrance, visible at a distance of about five hundred yards from the gate of the shrine, was quite literally some two miles long, winding round and round the quadrangular building at a depth of about six people to a line.

Looking at the awesome spectacle, I said to my chauffeur, "Well, now that I have actually seen the temple, I don't think there is any real need to go in! We can take a leisurely drive back to Madras."

The man smiled, sensing my discomfiture, and replied, "No, sir, you cannot go away without a *darshan* [auspicious audience] of the god, once you have come to Tirupathi. But you must not worry. There is a shortcut. These people have been waiting in line since the morning, before sunrise, because they have no money. For you, there will be no problem."

Once again I was startled and bemused, having to concede that even as an Indian by birth, I knew very little about the vast country that spawned me.

Innocently, I queried, "How can I get in? With all that lot in front of me?"

My driver burst into a boisterous laugh and replied, "You don't have to go there. With money, you get a shortcut. I told you."

As if in a trance, I took off my shoes and socks, deposited them at the entrance to the complex, and started walking. It was just before two in the afternoon and the stone slabs leading up to the temple had been roasted to a fierce hot plate. The undersides of my feet burned. Every time I jumped, my driver held me by the arms, protective assurance cascading out of his eyes. I felt both insecure and vulnerable, but there was no exit on this road. I knew I had to go on.

At the entrance, he said firmly, "You wait here." And making a gesture that every stallholder knows, he rubbed his fingers together and demanded, "Give me some money!"

I did as I was instructed, with the stinging heat scorching the soles of my poor unshod feet. Fifteen minutes later, my driver came back with a piece of paper (I still have it) and announced, "You see, there is always a way. This is your shortcut ticket." It had cost twenty-five rupees (about two dollars and fifty cents), and my man was mighty proud to have proved his point. This little paper token would enable me to run ahead of the queue, see the god, and make an exit, quickly. Or so I was told.

On entering the precincts of the shrine, no longer escorted by my driver, I discovered once again how words have different meanings in different contexts. What was a shortcut to my man was a very long cut indeed for me. True, I had managed to get within the compound without standing in line. But from here on in, it was a contest between equals. The "free" standers had been waiting all day merely to get in, but once inside the walls, there was no further hierarchy between the fee-paying, shortcut ticket-holders and the rest. We simply stood in different queues. At the gate to the temple proper, the two lines met. After that it was a battle of bodies—whoever could push in ahead with the greater force and pressure got in first.

It took an hour. Sweaty bodies pressed and bullied each other, women were given no more quarter than elderly men or even children. The odor of perspiration, rotten food, flower petals, and human spittle hung in the hot humid air like an invisible cloud. On the ground, there was a constant flow of pumped water to clear the constantly accumulating mess; I waded through this mass of congealed humanity, inch by inch, ankle deep in slush.

Marshals of the temple, both men and women, kept pushing people on, lest the caterpillar motion of the line be reduced to an even slower pace. When I finally came before the god, with incense choking my lungs, I was allowed a bare thirty seconds to stop and pay homage before being violently moved on. In front, within a cordoned area, there was a mound of rupee notes—offerings by devotees for favors the god might care to do. Someone told me that a money mountain of that size (about three feet high and four feet square) built up roughly every five minutes, before the priests cleared it away and started afresh.

After the *darshan,* pilgrims are accosted at various points in the exit queue, for further donations—holy food, sacred stones, gold armlets, horoscopes, and quick predictions are insistently on sale at every turn. It took another forty-five minutes to get out. Within the temple itself, there was more gold than I have ever seen, even in James Bond's *Goldfinger.* The doors, the throne on which the god was erected, the latticed windows, the massive altar—they were all made of solid twenty-four-carat gold. The dome on top, the archways leading in, and every bit of ornamental decoration were also cast in the precious metal. Yet, there were no security guards, no police. No Hindu dares steal from such a holy god. And any non-Hindu would be lynched alive if he was foolhardy enough to set foot anywhere near the place, let alone attempt to pilfer the sacred booty.

It was a sight and a phenomenon I shall never forget, not only for what it was but for what is symbolized to millions of Indians all round the country. When I got back to the car, shoes on again, my driver asked, "Did you offer *puja,* sir? And make a prayer?" I kept sullenly silent. "All Hindus who come to Tirupathi ask for something from the god. And he never refuses. That is why he is so rich!"

The drive back to Madras took some six hours. We wandered through a different part of the country this time, and by dusk farmers were weaving their way home from the fields. The slow, soft dark clung around the car like a shroud, a bridal veil cleft asunder by the glaring headlights and the hooting horns. I was sticky with sweat, my feet hurt, my mind felt numb with thoughts of that rich gold god, sitting up there at the mountaintop, drawing devotees across the length and breadth of the land, like the call of those Sirens in ancient Greece. I did not wish to see any more bodies strewn on the roadside during the return ride, so I dozed.

Tirupathi is an emblem that cements Indian diversity by the potent, unifying factor of one faith: the synthesizing, adhesive, and absorptive character of Hinduism. India uniquely embodies and represents Hinduism in a way no other country in the world represents and embodies any other religion.

If one thinks of Protestantism, one conjures up Britain, Holland, America, even the countries of Scandinavia. If one thinks of Catholicism, there is Italy, Spain, Ireland, and South America. Judaism is not only professed by the people of Israel; there are more Jews in New York City than there are in the whole of that newborn nation. Islam is not represented by any one single country. But if one talks of Hinduism, with a following of over six hundred million people, there is only one country that comes to mind.

But then Hinduism is not a "religion" in the way in which Islam, Christianity, Judaism, or even Buddhism are. It is a way of life, an attitude to mortal experience that pervades the thinking of even those who profess a different faith within the country.

The strange mixture of passivity and arrogance that characterizes the Hindu mind can also be perceived in a Muslim or a Jain or even a Sikh. The *sadhu* (holy man) sitting on the roadside does not think of himself as a Hindu, and the Westerner does not see him practicing a particular religious faith. He could well be a Muslim or a Buddhist, but meditation is a Hindu phenomenon which transcends the barriers of a particular body of doctrine.

What Westerners see as fatalism, a resigned acceptance of misery, is in fact a much more active belief in the theory of *Karma*. It instructs its adherent not to be concerned about the immediate rewards of his earthly deeds, but rest content with an absolute conviction that every act of piety will bring its due reward in an afterlife.

Man is born again and again in different forms and guises, and his ultimate goal is to be released from this endless cycle of birth and rebirth, from the travails of earthly tribulations, and merge with the Brahman, the universal timeless being who has no form.

This notion of reincarnation produces an apparent passivity that the foreigner frequently interprets as supine acquiescence. Occidental notions of human dignity come into violent conflict with the surface servility that is often displayed by the Indian.

In the holy city of Benares (modern name: Varanasi), there are men who predict the future by the diverse "sciences" of palmistry and astrology. If you insist in changing your destiny, various stones and talismans will be prescribed, for a fee. When you ask how predestination can be reconciled with the idea of tampering with the future, these men will patiently explain that though the story of your life is already written in the stars, you can nevertheless change bits and pieces by propitiating the gods.

Yet, in the same city, on the banks of the Ganges, bodies are cremated with no notion of aesthetic or human dignity. In the poor *ghat* (riverbank), where the paupers come to burn their dead, bodies are left half-roasted, as there is not enough money for firewood, and I have seen dogs fight and scramble for human flesh. But if you attempt to take a picture, you will be violently manhandled and told not to invade private and holy territory.

A Brahmin priest once confessed to me that he knew he was in for a hard time in his next life because he hadn't performed enough *pujas* in this one. When I asked him why he didn't rectify the present situation as there was still time (he was not yet fifty), he insisted that it was his fate to be a nondiligent member of his vocation (something like a lapsed Catholic).

How else could he explain the birth of six daughters, each of whom would require a fat dowry, and not one single son, who might have brought a small fortune into the house? When I floundered in incomprehension, he explained that he had to spend a much larger portion of his time than Brahmins should in earning money for these dowries. And this prevented him from doing holy deeds. In his past life, he must have committed many virtuous acts, so that he had been fortunate enough to have been born a Brahmin. But in the next incarnation, he was in for a kick down the caste ladder, as there weren't sufficient funds invested in this life to produce good dividends in the next one.

The servant who bows to his master may be inwardly feeling vastly superior, but he accepts his *Karma,* which has put him in that particular role at that precise moment in his ceaseless evolution. Allowing the master to horsewhip him on the back or even kick him in the face may be his due atonement for sins he had committed in his past life. The host who surrenders his last scrap of food to his guest is doing so with a shrewd eye to the reward he will receive hereafter. Selfless action is an investment in future gain, though not necessarily in this existence or the one that follows.

To the outsider, Indian hospitality may appear unworldly and selfless, but it may not be quite as uncalculated as it looks. Grace and docility may hide an insurgent arrogance; self-righteousness may come packaged in a humble mien. No Indian really thinks he can learn anything from another culture, but very few will be brash enough to say so to a foreigner.

Because Hinduism is not a religion in the sense that an Occidental understands the term, because it is in the blood and pervades the very air that an Indian breathes, it shows itself in odd and unexpected ways. A nuclear physicist at the Tata Institute of Fundamental Research in Trombay may lecture persuasively on his subject at an international seminar, assuming postulates from scientific determinism, and yet he will be perfectly unfazed in asserting that everything happens by predestination. Divine plan and human effort will be seen as supplementary, not exclusive, modes of controlling mere mortal destiny.

A scientist will tell you that atoms may be fused to produce enormous energy, yet quite firmly assert that if God had not charted the course of this discovery in minute detail, no man on earth would have been capable of unleashing such awesome power. What may appear crudely superstitious to the Western mind, will be accepted as preordained. My brother-in-law, who has something of a reputation in fuel technology, does not eat meat, practices Yoga, and prays for supernatural guidance, while educating his students in the subatomic mysteries of coal and oil.

What looks like inert acceptance is often a camouflage for a firm belief that, beyond a certain point, there is nothing that can be done by human endeavor alone. What is destined *will* happen, so it is fruitless and foolish to expend energy in trying to deflect the ordinations of fate.

This results in a very convincing rationalization of inactivity, because one can never be sure whether further action will be useless or not. Or at what precise juncture God has taken over the steering wheel. The best one can do is watch the road ahead, and pray there is no head-on collision. Laziness becomes sanctified, and the work ethic of the Western world is treated with superior disdain. The reason why the ruling class in America and elsewhere are wary and apprehensive about drugs is that under grass or acid or any of the other chemical stimulants, this is precisely the mental state that is induced.

But then is indolence a characteristic Indian phenomenon? Depends where you look and how. Go to a bank and try to cash a check, and you will find rows and rows of quiescent empty desks with men behind them chewing betel-nut leaf, and talking garrulously about the enormous strain of work, how things have been going from bad to worse, how the bosses simply do not understand the hard slog that underlings daily perform. You will get your money in the end; everything works out in a Panglossian manner, but it takes hours. If you have scheduled an appointment for later, on the assumption that the simple transaction of writing a check and cashing it in your own account should take no more than ten or fifteen minutes, you will be in for a shock. That appointment will have to be missed, and the person you were to meet will fume at you, because at the bank or anywhere else there will be no telephone; and even if there is one, it will not work—meaning you will get an "unobtainable" tone or continuous busy signal.

Like a dead city frozen in aspic, every resemblance of life will be there: banks, buses, telephones, post offices, markets, ice-cream vendors, et al. But they will be surface facsimiles of the real thing. Your mistake will be to assume that they work like those anywhere else in the world.

Yet, with all this said, go to a hotel like the Taj or the Oberoi, and you will find that the lifts function with a fluid efficiency. You may not be able to get a number in Calcutta on the telephone, but try to get Tokyo or New York, and you will be talking within minutes as if to your next-door neighbor. Room service will be prompt and gracious. You will have flowers in your room, with compliments from the manager. Housekeeping will be immaculate and unobtrusive. For the money you pay for an average dinner for two in Manhattan, you will be living in palatial splendor.

Try the Holy Ganges, for instance. Hire a boat for the princely sum of 150 rupees ($15) and you will be rowed to Howrah Bridge and back by two oarsmen in less than two hours. You will see washerwomen and *sadhus* bathing in the thick chocolate-colored water, the large round sun scattering scarlet freckles on the rippling river. If you have a foreign friend with you who is overwhelmed by the "romance" of India, you will not have either the courage or the effrontery to tell him or her that those four bamboo poles enshrouded by thin gauze is in fact a lavatory, where people from "superior" backgrounds defecate, while next door, devout men dip their heads in the same foul fluid and pray that their sins will be washed away.

Does this mean that India is uncivilized, primitive, and barbaric? Is the country ever going to emerge from its dark and sluggish past and confront the twentieth century? Is there nothing but poverty and filth, snake charmers and *sadhus,* bullock carts and constipated telephone systems?

The answer must be a resounding YES to the last two questions, and an emphatic NO to the first. But for very different reasons from what the Westerner might imagine. Just as the scientist believes in predestination, so does the whole country display a startling schizophrenia that leaves the foreigner bemused. Industrialization is proceeding at a pace unparalleled anywhere else in the developing world. Sophisticated technology is being imported and developed at a speed that still stuns visiting professors and World Bank economists. Video games and computers have started creeping into the homes of the wealthy. India is being press-ganged from feudalism into the microchip era in a way that looks like a prewar film being played back at double speed.

The mind of the Indian technocrat is as sharp and fine-tuned to the nuances of late twentieth-century life as any in the world. Surface paradoxes of behavior and belief often cloak the most urgent conviction in material progress. Space satellites may be a far cry from hand-woven cloth, but it is precisely because both phenomena coexist in the same country that Westerners are perplexed. They do not know what to make of a nation with one foot back in the dark ages and the other aggressively kicking forward into the world of nuclear fusion and computerized factories.

Nothing is quite what it seems, and magic might well explain what India is all about. Here you have a nation that produces the most brilliant scientists and astute politicians, yet the late prime minister used to decide dates for her travels and national elections on the advice of her astrologer who told her about "auspicious" times.

Sixteen-year-old brides are burned for lack of adequate dowries; there are occasional ghoulish reports (in *Time* magazine, if nowhere else) of human sacrifice; charlatan gurus have captured the attention of the Western media; millions worshiped Prime Minister Indira Gandhi as goddess Durga incarnate.

And yet the Indian diplomat will present himself as the most polished spokesman of Third World rights at the United Nations, Indian writers in English will sweep onto American best-seller lists, win MacArthur Foundation awards, and jostle for the Nobel Prize in literature. Modernity and medievalism will live in the same body, both metaphorically and physically.

I remember being taken along to a holy man once in a village some three hundred miles from Calcutta. With Western skepticism sown deep in my soul, I joined the group, more out of curiosity and a sense of theater than out of conviction. The man was sitting cross-legged on a slightly raised dais made of mud and consecrated by liquid cow dung painted over the whole plinth. The crowd could not have been less than five hundred, and a long queue waited to touch the master's feet and seek his blessing. He had a white beard, long hair, and wore saffron robes, as if he were made up for a Hollywood TV series.

I had been told that this guru performed genuine miracles, and I wanted to see the kind of quackery he would display. At first nothing spectacular occurred, and I was about to withdraw, boredom and prejudice equally confirmed. Then suddenly there was a deep hush all round, and a rickety little child accompanied by a wailing mother was deposited at the holy man's feet. I could see his lips move, but I could not hear what he was saying. Quite abruptly, the mother stopped shrieking, and sat staring as if she were under hypnosis. The child began to stir on the bamboo bed, and little by little, it started to move its limbs. In less than half an hour, its whole face changed from stricken palsy to healthy radiance. A while later, it actually got up and walked.

My amused disbelief was gently shaken. Though I did not know what was wrong with the infant in the first place, I did observe a profound transformation in his face during the small time he was in the presence of the holy man. But the real miracle was not what happened to the child, but when the white-bearded man called out my name and said, in perfect English, "So you want proof, do you?"

There was no way the man could have been told my name, and absolutely no means he could have read my mind except by clairvoyance or extrasensory perception. Whatever it was, the piercing power of his eyes unnerved me, and I was even more stunned to discover that this serene holy man, surrounded by ignorant rustics, was a Ph.D. from Princeton.

* * *

Miraculous or otherwise, the most visible and intense impression of India that a visitor will receive on first encounter is the teeming multitude of people that make up the country. Nowhere else in the world—except perhaps in China, which I have not visited—is there such a thick coagulant of humanity, which assaults one like rivers of molten lava down a volcanic mountainside. It is not simply a matter of population, which at the last count had hit 730 million, and looks set to overreach the billion mark by the year 2000. It feels as if one is inundated with people everywhere one goes; privacy becomes an alien concept. I have never quite understood how husbands and wives, sleeping five and six to a room with their grownup children, manage to fulfill their minimal conjugal functions. Yet fulfill them they must, since the birthrate shows no signs of declining, the population is going up by a million a month, and pregnancy has not yet become a rare medical condition.

What this means for planners and economists must be the most nightmarish dilemma of modern times. The country has just become self-sufficient in food, for the first time in several decades. Yet the paradox is that this very remarkable achievement presages formidable problems for the future. When famine and malnutrition are banished and the death rate is staunched, while at the same time the birthrate continues to rise, there are more mouths to feed and there simply is not enough to go around.

India is engaged in the Sisyphean task of trying to come abreast with the rest of the world in technology, health, and modern welfare, while every step forward is matched by several steps back because of a steeply ascending demographic curve over which no one seems to have any control.

But no description of India's "ocean of humanity" (Galbraith's phrase) can be complete without a mention of that old bogey called "caste," about which the natives, especially educated ones, are intensely sensitive. Whenever a foreigner asks an Indian about caste, the answer is likely to be in the form of a defensive question: "But don't you have *class* divisions in your own country?"

Although, it must be added, that it would be less frequently addressed to an American than to a Britisher—perhaps because the American does not carry the same colonial luggage on his or her back, and is less likely to be obsessed with the phenomenon, and would almost certainly give less offense if the original query were put casually.

I shall have a great deal more to say about caste in the relevant section of this book, because it is both less and more noxious than *class* as Europeans know it. At several points, the two phenomena intersect, but they are not one and the same thing.

Crucially, one is sanctioned by religion, while the other is a social device that regulates power hierarchies. Caste is theoretically immutable: You cannot change from the one to the other just because you feel like it. With effort, talent, and luck, you can change class, though some old families in England and America may smile wryly at such an assertion.

Yet with all her problems of caste and communal divisions, her appalling poverty and mass illiteracy, India is still a country that pulses with the possibility of a glorious future. Superstition may irritate the foreigner, corruption may eat into the sinews of the nation, politics may be a conundrum, but India challenges the imagination in a way in which no other country does in the world today.

Steering the middle path with superb acrobatic skill, India is the preeminent leader among the nonaligned nations of the world. Mrs. Indira Gandhi, with all her faults, was a world statesman whose utterances were taken seriously across the globe. Wooed by both the Soviet Union and the United States, India rejects neither while tantalizingly withholding her hand from both.

On the subcontinent, India exercises a magisterial authority, which is the envy of her smaller neighbors on the East and the West. Her military might is next only to China's, among Third World countries. Her culture and traditions are sought by hippie progenies and Fulbright scholars alike.

The Taj Mahal remains one of the the seven wonders, though acid fumes from a chemical plant across the river Jumna are eating away at the precious marble that has remained intact, impassive, and immaculately beautiful for well over three hundred years.

Kipling's adage about East and West never meeting may have been true in his time. But India is living proof that civilizations can cross-fertilize, that astronauts and *sadhus* can live on the same planet, and if not on the same street, then at least within bicycling distance of each other.

87

Barriers of color, creed, and race vanish when the human mind connects across oceans and centuries, only because there are many more similarities between Homo sapiens than there are differences.

In trying to tell the story of my country in this book, I have always remembered that I was born there while the reader was not. Yet I have not let go of the feeling that pain is always pain, wherever Man may be, and ecstasy is the same fierce flame everywhere on the planet.

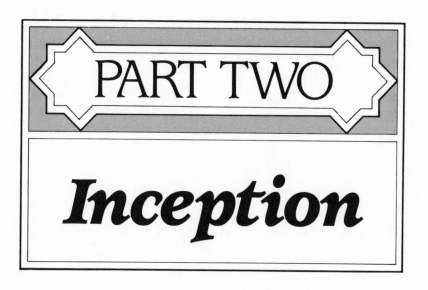

PART TWO

Inception

Black Hole and Bubbling Brilliance

Rituals at Wounded Knee

Desserts in the Barren Kingdom

Land of the Magic Carpet

2

Black Hole and Bubbling Brilliance

Calcutta is a far more extreme metaphysical condition than the notorious "Black Hole" with which it is historically associated in the Western mind. From a collection of three alluvial villages in the Ganges delta, some three-hundred-odd years ago, it has now grown into a swirling, sweltering metropolis, the fourth largest city in the world, after Tokyo, New York, and London.

More babies are born in the place than anywhere else on the planet. It is the most congested urban center on the globe. In 1963, there were over 102,000 human beings living per square mile in Calcutta, while New York contained 27,900 and Los Angeles a mere 7,800.

It is a city where 64 percent of the adult population is illiterate, where more than a million people are born, bred, and continue to die on the pavements, where the water supply is a perennial host to the most eclectic bacteria that modern medicine has yet recognized.

Calcutta does without electricity on an average of about four to six hours a day all year round; during the monsoons, that figure goes up to twelve to sixteen hours over every twenty-four-hour period. Telephones seldom work. After a particularly heavy downpour in June or July, the center of the city is laid low by four to six feet of water, and no form of transport except rickshaws ply the streets. The city is cut off from the rest of India and the world.

Undigested sewage courses through the open drains like arterial veins, collecting unseen infections and visible bandicoots by the thousand. *Bustees* (shanty towns made of bamboo poles, hessian, and cardboard boxes) litter the whole city. Ceaselessly the city sings a dirge in hopeless melancholy for the most colossal and arid overture to despair, disease, and destitution.

A British journalist, Geoffrey Moorhouse, wrote not so long ago, "Calcutta is a definition of obscenity!" Yet, within five hundred words of the same essay, he went on to declare, "Calcutta is by far the richest city in India, even though its various problems have started to turn this richness into a collapsing wealth. It is possibly the richest city anywhere between Rome and Tokyo, in terms of the money that is accumulated and represented here." And the same writer quotes Charles Stewart (1813) in saying, "The province of Bengal is one of the most valuable acquisitions that was ever made by any nation."

Less than half a century later, the whole of the London Underground would be built from revenue that came from the Indian colony, Calcutta being its nerve center. Unlike contemporary politicians who gripe at the miserly sums that Western nations dole out in "aid" (at exorbitantly high rates of interest) to Third World countries, the early British incursors into India knew when they were on to a good thing. And no wonder!

"Writers" (clerks) recruited by the East India Company in London were sent out on an annual wage varying from £3 to £7 and returned home to England after twenty-odd years of service with fortunes amounting to £20,000 (sterling) in the mid-1700s—and were able to buy themselves into the landed gentry of their homeland, with large country houses in Surrey, Suffolk, and Sussex. One begins to realize, then, why Calcutta, like Venice some six hundred years previously, provided the quickest and easiest access to a fast buck that any city in the world has ever boasted in recent times.

Robert Clive, universally acknowledged to be the founder of the British Raj in India, arrived in the country as a menial clerk on an annual wage of £3.10, and returned to England some twenty-seven years later with a fortune of £130,000. Multiply that figure by a cool thousand for contemporary comparison, and you will get an idea as to what Calcutta had to offer a little less than 250 years ago. And do remember, this was a sum accumulated by one man in one city. The eight grandees and their heirs who founded the East India Company in London in 1599, with a Royal Charter of Assent from Queen Elizabeth I, were not done out of their dues. Nor was the British empire, under Empress Queen Victoria, less than than 300 years later.

Lord Clive of Plassey (Clive the commoner bought himself into a baronetcy on returning to England) and Warren Hastings after him, acquired indecently massive fortunes and were exposed in the British Parliament because they were regarded as upstarts. There were other men who made millions, too, but they did not attract the ire of orators like Edmund Burke, because they were modest enough to build a country house or two, lease a castle, employ no more than fifty servants, and live the life of affluent country squires, away from the hub of power in London. Hastings was impeached by the House of Commons, more because he flaunted his *arriviste* wealth (at a time when the Prince Regent was seeking and had been refused the governorship of Bengal), rather than because he bled the natives white in that far-away colony.

At about this time, a nawab of Bengal was writing to the governor to describe what it meant for an Indian to be at the receiving end of this philosophy:

> And this is the way your Gentlemen behave; they make a disturbance all over my country, plunder my people, injure and disgrace my servants . . . Setting up colours, and showing the passes of the COMPANY, they use their utmost endeavours to oppress the peasants, merchants and other people of the country . . . In every village and every factory, they buy and sell salt, betel-nut, rice, straw, bamboos, fish, gunnies, ginger, sugar, tobacco, opium and many other things . . .
>
> They forcibly take away the goods of the peasants, merchants etc, for a fourth part of their value, and by ways of physical violence and oppression, they oblige the peasants

to give five rupees for goods which are worth one in the market place. If the man does not pay what is demanded, he is bound and disgraced, by your soldiers, and they do not allow any authority to my servants over my own land.

Quod erat demonstrandum!

I quote this *in extenso,* because I want to show how subtly hypocrisy can function. The Dalai Lama has been going around the world for the past twenty-five years talking about communist oppression; not for one moment have we heard about Tibetan lamas exploiting their own people to the point of total starvation and worse. I have visited Tibet and I have talked to these people, and I know.

It is also apposite to point out that when Occidentals complain about Oriental "corruption" as an institution in India, it was *they,* not the natives, who most benefited from its fallout.

When a man on an annual salary of seven pounds returns home after twenty years of service with more than twenty thousand pounds, it is accepted that corruption has been institutionalized. And this happened over and over again. When Queen Victoria's government took over power from the East India Company, one of the first things that the British cabinet did was make every serving officer sign a document that categorically insisted that "private profit" (meaning bribes and self-interested trading) would be punishable in law. If the British government did not feel that there was widespread corruption among its own officials, such an action would have been scarcely necessary. There are British reports about Indian conditions in the middle of the eighteenth century that make it abundantly clear that the natives were honest and god-fearing, and that the notion of cheating the emperor or his representative was a novel one, introduced into the country by the foreign traders. In course of time, indigenous inhabitants, observing their alien masters at work, faithfully copied their customs. And corruption was one of the nastier legacies that the Raj left behind.

We must not forget, too, that while all this was going on, His Britannic Majesty was involved in a small dispute with another part of his dominions, which was asserting that "there should be no taxation without representation," and which later gave rise to a lit-

tle confrontation that historians now call the "War of Independence." At that precise time, however, India was far more important
to Britain than what would later become the United States of
America. Here there was nothing; India existed already, with its
rich market, its raw materials, its civilization, and the enormous
potential of founding an empire on an already cultivated land.

Contemporary Calcutta and modern India are wholly inexplicable, even to the indigenous inhabitant, let alone to a visiting
outsider, without some comprehension as to how and why the city
sprang into existence. Its narrow gulleys, rat-infested lanes, open
sewers, marble palaces, maimed beggars, grandly staircased clubs,
acres of billiard-table lawns, manicured and bordered with marigolds, bougainvillaeas, rhododendrons, and gladioli, comprise a
canvas made from the woof and warp of history.

Strangely, though, it is the same history that informs us: Calcutta is the youngest of all the big modern cities on the globe.
Manhattan was founded eighty-one years before Job Charnock
pitched his tents on the banks of the river Hooghly (a tributary of
the Ganges), and Maisonneuve created Montreal half a century
earlier.

No such place called Calcutta, or indeed a country by the name
of India, existed before the British arrived. They created both these
entities. But the ferment, the chaos, the grinding, putrefying,
headlong rush into the suspended animation of total infirmity, which
everyone predicts, but which, miraculously, never seems to happen, is the result of an old civilization confronting the vital exuberant arrogance of a newer one. Posed in tableaux, teeth gnashing
in fierce acrimony, decayed and delayed on the one arm and fling-
ing about the other like a pregnant hysteric, the city survives—
continues to exist.

Calcutta, in 1911, suffered a future shock a while before Alvin
Toffler, when King George V, at the Delhi durbar, announced that
the capital of British India would be shifted from Calcutta to Delhi.
There were outraged editorials in the British-owned papers, not
least in *The Statesman,* descended from *The Englishman,* which
condemned the move, perhaps more because rich patrons would
be upset than because they were concerned for what might be good
for the imperial power.

But as usual, the British had scented a trail. India had always been ruled from Delhi. Though newcomers to the empirorial stakes, they knew how to assume the postures of imperial regality.

The British did this with a shrewd eye to the future of the colony. Calcutta's petulant hostility was to suppurate for a while and then bring about the end of an empire on which, it was once asserted, "the Sun would never set."

From a journal written by an Englishman of twenty-five in 1969, who insistently wishes to remain anonymous, here is an excerpt:

> A man of forty, he looked seventy—with a gangrenous leg—with a rag wrapped round it, we had to take him outside because of the stench to hose his leg down. The water started the blood flowing over the green flesh; bone and muscle dropped off. The foot was just a skeleton, and you could see right through his leg up to the knee. A crow came and picked up a bone that had fallen off his foot (they're hungry too). My stomach didn't think much of this and added to the mess flowing down the drain.

Both for Indians and foreigners alike, it is poignant to read firsthand accounts like this, because there is no room here for opinion. At the age of seventeen (in 1958 in Calcutta), I recall being confined in Coffee House on College Street through a long night, while furious fires raged all round and bullets whistled through the shrouded dark, and more than a dozen trams and buses were set on fire. Of course we argued, we wondered if this was or was not the solution. There was revolutionary blood in our veins then, a strident desire to change the face of the world, make it a better place for fellow humans to live and breathe.

I had just about heard of E. M. Forster and had read his *A Passage to India*. Personally, I didn't quite know what to make of the book at the time, but eons later, I came to a rather heretic conclusion: The man was both a bad writer and intensely illiberal to boot. My timid speculations were confirmed by P. N. Furbank's authorized biography of the great man *(E. M. Forster: A Life)* in which it is related that the writer employed a shotgun artist to kill a dog that had become too fond of his homosexual friend Joe Ackerley, then editor of *The Listener*. The incident is of no importance by itself, but is absolutely crucial in understanding how India has been presented to the world. Mr. Forster has always been taken as a liberal who had a deep empathy with India—at least this is how the Western literate world has seen it. Perhaps it is not entirely impossible to speculate that someone who "hated the coloured natives" was not the ideal spokesman for the aspirations of those very peoples who were beginning, at least in Calcutta, to bestir themselves into a semblance of assertive autonomy.

The vitality of the city does, of course, show itself in varied and unexpected ways. There is violence of a kind that is wholly outside the emotional geography of the visiting Occidental. The eruptions are not organized in the way in which crime is orchestrated in Chicago, New York, or Belfast. Nor does the city experience the fevered explosions of psychopathic hoodlums.

Violence in Calcutta is and has always been endemic and totally spontaneous. Regularly, bus drivers get lynched. A man driving his own car may be dragged out by a crowd because he had bruised an urchin who had sprinted across the street without looking right or left. He may be beaten to unconsciousness if the police don't arrive on time. Bombs will explode on the street, kill twenty people, and within minutes, traffic will resume in all its crushed normalcy, as if nothing spectacular had just occurred. A woman will be thrown out of a speeding taxi, facedown on the road, have a fractured skull and blood gushing out of her mouth, and a multitude will gather round her like flies, but no one will touch her or call the police or the ambulance. If you attempt to take her into a nearby house, as I once did to my enormous chagrin, a different kind of crowd will follow you to the doorstep, and pester you for money, or else threaten to multilate the children of the house if you don't pay up.

Violence in Calcutta is a dialectic mirror image of the ostensible passivity that most inhabitants of the city habitually display. I have seen buses being physically overturned and set on fire by a two-hundred-strong mob, while pedestrians and motorized traffic nimbly picked their way around the raging conflagration, as if it were just another minor domestic mess, like an upturned flower vase in the living room.

In 1946, during the Hindu-Muslim riots, bodies lay heaped on pavements by the thousands. The stench of rotting corpses wafted in the breeze as complacently as the scent of freshly cut grass permeates the air of an English baronial estate in springtime.

Indeed, the name of the city, anglicized from the original Kalikata, is an eponomy of violence. Mother Kali, the black goddess of destruction (and creation, too!), with a garland of thirteen human skulls strung round the neck, her protruding tongue dripping blood in gory scarlet, is the sacred deity from whom the city derives its critical identity. There are folktales, impossible to verify, that even within the last hundred years human sacrifice at dead of night was a regular practice at the Kali Ghat temple in Calcutta. The necks of freshly menstruating virgins were forcibly pressed between firmly squeezing wooden clamps on the ground, and then their heads were lopped off with one herculean swing of the massive steel cudgel that still hangs in the temple today.

Yet an amiable tolerance characterizes the city, both for a soothing gentleness and the most explosive aggression. And it is this stark contrast that bewilders the visitor from the West. In the early part of the seventies, when terrorists of the Marxist persuasion (Naxalites) were on the rampage, bombs would go off regularly, people would be maimed and killed, police would open fire, a few more would die, yet life would go on as if nothing dramatic were happening.

I have been in discussions with the most refined and articulate intellects who supported these atrocities at the time, their softly modulated voices halting only for a moment while the sound of an explosion on the street outside shattered the air, and then going on from where they left off, as if it had been merely the pop of a ladylike hiccup at a genteel dinner table. The *bhadralok* (civilized gentleman) in Calcutta is the most assiduously complex city man in the world. He can be both saturnine and graciously hospitable, intellectual and barbaric, civil and outrageously uncouth, in the same human frame.

Varied explanations have been offered for this incipient and endemic violence, which seems to lie just beneath the docile and acquiescing surface of a city where the average inhabitant on the street presents the most mild and resigned visage. Obviously, the extreme poverty, the disastrous lack of elementary amenities like sanitation, transport, and rudimentary medical care, sitting in aggressive propinquity with such grotesque wealth and ostentatious opulence, must provide the dry psychic powder for random revolt. No wonder Lenin declared that "the road to world revolution lies through Peking, Shanghai, and Calcutta."

But Western observers have noted that such contrasts exist in other parts of the globe, too, if not on quite the same scale. Franco's Spain, Salazar's Portugal, South America today, parts of Italy and Greece, have witnessed similar confrontations between rich and poor. Conditions during the Industrial Revolution in Britain were not altogether different from those that exist in Calcutta today.

The only distinction between the present Oriental nightmare and past Occidental barbarities lies in the sheer difference in numbers and density. One particular episode illustrates this point more appositely than any other. In 1955, when the Russian leaders Bulganin and Khrushchev visited the city, over two million people gathered on the Maidan (a huge open space about the size of Central Park in Manhattan) in Calcutta to welcome the honored guests. There were another million who lined the route from the airport to the center of town. Prime Minister Jawaharlal Nehru said he believed that this was the largest crowd that had ever assembled in one place in India.

The funny thing was that the exuberant enthusiasm of the human avalanche was so intense that the Russians had to be bundled out of their open car, secreted into a police van, and driven to the old governor's palace (Raj Bhavan), totally hidden from view of the clamoring masses. In order to get some idea about the sheer size of such a crowd, we may recall that the funerals of Mahatma Gandhi, Kennedy, and Churchill attracted vast numbers, too, but not all the people were in one place at any one time. If you can imagine the whole of Central Park, every single spot in the place including the ponds and the hillocks and the roads, occupied by men and women crushed together like commuters on the subway at rush hour, then you might get some idea about the Calcutta crowd that had turned out to pay homage to the new leaders of the Soviet Union.

There are no accurate figures of how many people died and the exact number who had to be treated in hospitals. Newspapers were coy about the fatalities, which were almost certainly in the hundreds. People were trampled to death, many suffocated. It took more than

eight hours for the crowd to finally melt away. A city that can produce such a mass of humanity for such an occasion must also contain the potential for a kind of violence unimaginable in any other
part of the world. If rats confined in congested captivity develop a
fierce malevolent psychosis, what happens to Homo sapiens?

Calcutta was born in 1690, nearly a century after that historic
launching of the East India Company in London. Job Charnock
landed in the village of Sutanati at the mouth of the Hooghly, and
pitched his tents to found a city called Calcutta and sow the seeds
of the mightiest empire the world has ever known.

The site was inhospitable in the extreme. The three villages of
Govindpur, Sutanati, and Kalikata, which finally amalgamated to
make up the future bustling metropolis, were set in marshy swamps,
the climate was ferociously hot and humid, surrounded by vast
jungles with wild animals, mosquitoes, and bloodthirsty brigands
prowling the undergrowth. Two hundred years later, in 1896, Mark
Twain would say that the weather in Calcutta was "enough to turn
a brass door-knob mushy."

Yet Charnock had inadvertently spotted a point of supreme
strategic value. Calcutta would be accessible by sea from Madras,
where the British then had their headquarters. The river Hooghly
would provide both an easy escape route in times of trouble and a
handy waterway for supplies and military reinforcements. By land,
the city would be some four hundred miles from Murshidabad, the
then capital of Bengal. Calcutta would become a place where the
declared writ of Indian rulers would be virtually impossible to en-
force. The British would be able to build Fort William, ostensibly
to protect their trading interests, but more durably to entrench
themselves in the most impregnable military bastion in the whole
country. They would do so with impunity, because the emperors
would have little power to impose their diktat on a defenseless coast,
short of marching in with an army over hundreds of miles of
treacherous terrain, on the backs of donkeys, horses, and elephants.

The next nawab in Murshidabad did in fact try to do precisely
that, and enshrined the fearsome phrase "Black Hole" in history
books across the globe. But it was an act for which the British would
exact a heavy price, and that would mark the beginning of the end

of indigenous military suzerainty on the whole of the subcontinent.

In 1756, the new nawab, Siraj-ud-daula, ascended the throne in Murshidabad at the age of twenty-five. He looked around his miniempire and decided that the British down south in a strange placed called Calcutta were getting too big for their boots. So he embarked on an impulsive attempt to enrich himself quickly by grabbing all those masses of golden coins that the foreigners were rumored to have stuffed in their vaults.

With the first sign of the monsoons, when the land lay slushed in mud like an Irish stew, Siraj-ud-daula began his march toward Calcutta, with, to quote Sir Percival Spear, "30,000 foot, 20,000 horses, 400 trained elephants and 80 pieces of cannon."

There was little that the British encampment in the fort could do. The East India Company directors back in London had been unwilling to spend money to erect a legitimate fortification. As long as they got fat dividends, their servants out there in the East could perish, for all they cared.

The story of the rout has been documented, fictionalized, romanticized, and told and retold with fantastic variations on the theme, in folklore and history books, and continues to be related on gentle evenings in mother's lap in most Calcutta households, even today.

The nawab decimated the British. Governor Roger Drake fled down the Hooghly in ignominious defeat. Anyone who could, did likewise. The conquering forces of Siraj-ud-daula imprisoned 146 English captives in an eighteen-cubic-foot underground cell with one window, when the temperature outside was over 100°F. Next morning, on June 20, 1756, when the door to the prison was opened by the warders, there were only 23 people still alive. One hundred and twenty-three men and women had died overnight, in an episode that would be forever immortalized as "the Black Hole" of Calcutta.

At least, this is the received version of the incident in British history books. Local historians dispute the veracity of the tale. Whatever the truth, it is pertinent to bear in mind that the British were slaughtering native recruits and their own white-skinned soldiers for desertion, with the kind of cold equanimity that we have recently heard about from My Lai in Vietnam. Hands and legs were cut off, heads severed from the rest of the body, cautionary gibbets lined the routes of the defending (English) army, before they turned tail, almost to a soldier. These were barbaric times, in which the foreigners played a comparably sanguinary role.

It is not impossible that we listen to such baleful liturgies about the Black Hole because the British army disobeyed while its commanders fled in vile cowardice, and achieved a low-water mark of military disgrace in the steady and purposeful onslaught into the most verdant and lucrative land that any conquering power had ever surveyed.

This is how an English journalist has described the legacy of that classic moment in imperial history:

> But today, there is merely a tablet in an arch next to the General Post Office, which the visitor has difficulty in locating; it is surrounded by crowds of pavement tradesmen in lottery tickets, suspenders, sunglasses and ball point pens; and they grin and chant "BLACK HOLE OF CALCUTTA" in the most mocking fashion.

Six months after the tragedy, Robert Clive returned from Madras with an armada of ships, soldiers, and munitions, to wreak the most monumental revenge in recent military history. He recaptured Calcutta in one short night and went on to defeat both Siraj-ud-daula and the French army captain Dupleix—who had sided with the Muslim ruler in the earlier battle. Clive contrived covertly with Mir Jafar (Siraj-ud-daula's uncle and Commander in Chief of his army) to vanquish the defending army by marching into Murshidabad after an historic battle at Plassey on June 23, 1757.

Through British connivance, Siraj-ud-daula was assassinated by his own soldiers, Mir Jafar was installed as the puppet nawab at the kind pleasure of Robert Clive, the newly appointed Commander of the British forces in India.

Mir Jafar gave in and colluded with the foreigners by selling his birthplace, and even today, the name *Mir Jafar* is used in colloquial parlance as a synonym for *traitor* and *snake in the grass*. For he was the last native titular head of Bengal before the British saw fit to dispense with hypocritical ceremony and declare themselves the formal rulers of the land.

It was in Calcutta that India was humiliated as she had never been before.

At about the same time, George Washington was unshackling his country from the British yoke.

In the tradition of classical, Old Testament Christianity, Robert Clive sought retribution and revenge for the devastating defeat that his countrymen had suffered at the hands of "colored natives."

The East India Company reaped an annual windfall of several hundred millions in today's currency. Clive was personally provided for very handsomely.

But mere money, which was astronomical even in those days, does not yet explain the subtle pervasive power that the city exercised over the Anglo-Saxon imagination at the time. From this point on, for the next two hundred years after Clive's victory at Plassey, the paramountcy of Calcutta and the British would remain unchallenged in India.

For the first time in the history of that tiny island of Britain, a mere handful of men would control the destiny of millions in a far-away land and effortlessly acquire monumental fortunes. Perennial losers and amateurs in the colonial game, always last in the queue, the British had finally discovered a haven.

Calcutta was an emblem of the resurrection of the national psyche. It helped finance the Industrial Revolution, when miners and millworkers were suffocating to death by the thousands back in England; when cigar-smoking, brandy-swilling, commercial tycoons made their presence felt in the highest councils of the land for the first time; when "trade" and "aristocracy" would marry in mutual machination.

When His Britannic Majesty had lost both his head and his North American dominions, India was to provide a soothing solace. Far, far more significant than the victory against the Kaiser and Nazi Germany, at the battle of Plassey Britain found itself, lodging its firm imperial boots in the fertile soil of Kalikata, while India lost her identity.

Here is Geoffrey Moorhouse, in the Foreword to his eponymous book on the city:

> The story of Calcutta is the story of India and the story of the so-called Third World in miniature. It is the story of

how and why Empire was created and what happened when Empire finished. It is the story of people turning violently to Communism for salvation. It is also the story of Industrial Revolution. The Imperial residue of Calcutta, a generation after Empire ended, is both a monstrous and a marvellous city.

But historically, the marvel preceded the monstrosity. In 1805, Lord William Bentinck (a street is still named after him), the British governor-general at the time, suddenly found Calcutta to be the richest city he had seen after London. In gaping amazement, he announced, "The spectacle is altogether the most curious and magnificent I have ever met with." In sharp contrast, at the other end of the nineteenth century, young Winston Churchill would be writing back to his American mother in London, "I shall always be glad to have seen it [Calcutta, that is], . . . for the reason . . . that it will be unnecessary for me to see it again."

Over one hundred years earlier (in 1795), the future Madame Talleyrand would be writing back to her sister in Paris, "Calcutta has the *grandest* balls anywhere in the world in Governor Hasting's *Palace.*"

Karl Marx wrote six learned articles in the *New York Herald Tribune* in the middle of the nineteenth century about the proletarian explosion that would imminently take place in the British colony. He did not mention that almost a hundred years earlier, the first governor-general to rule in Calcutta was paid an annual salary of £25,000, approximately three hundred times the current emoluments of the president of the United States. No wonder that George III's son was hunting after the governorship of Bengal while his mad father was busily giving away America to George Washington's armies.

Although Rudyard Kipling spent a week at the Great Eastern Hotel in Calcutta, and called it "The City of Dreadful Night" in a series of jingoistic essays, Lord Curzon, the most aristocratic viceroy that India ever saw, had a different opinion. Curzon established the Archaeological Survey of India, and we owe the preservation of the astounding caves at Ajanta to his foresight and acumen. In 1903, these were the words he spoke to a group of businessmen in the city:

To me Calcutta is the capital, not merely of a Province, great as that Province is, but of the Indian Empire. As such it appears to me to fitly symbolise the work that the English have done, and are doing in the country. For though of the enormous population that make up the city on both banks of the river, not much more than 30,000 are returned as Europeans and Eurasians, yet a glance at the buildings of the town, and the river and the roar of the smoke, is sufficient to convince the onlooker that Calcutta is in reality an European city set down in Asiatic soil, and that it is a monument—in my opinion, one of the most striking monuments, for it is the Second City to London in the entire British Empire—to the energy and achievements of our race.

Strong, stirring, chauvinistic stuff that, frequently quoted with irony by the present incumbents of Curzon's legacy, the Indian governors of West Bengal who still live in the same palatial establishment that imperial viceroys inhabited just over seventy years ago.

Unlike most other viceroys, or any other British subordinate ruler for that matter, Curzon was an aristocrat. He stood out. Recently, his *Notebooks* have been published in England, and this is what an anonymous reviewer in *The Observer* (London) had to say about it:

Head and shoulders above almost everything else, Indians salute style; and it was style that made that most superior person, George Nathaniel Curzon, the most admired of all the Viceroys, allied to the fact that he had studied their history and preserved their monuments.

India, and not only Imperial India, was the great romance of Curzon's life, and stiff-necked though he could be or excruciatingly facetious in the *Punch* manner, it shines through . . .

It is difficult for Americans, molded in the tradition of the frontier psyche, to understand that Indians may complain about British depredation yet appreciate that a single individual was sensitive enough to attempt to preserve a heritage. Members of a race are not all alike, generalizations are the most abominable travesties to intellectual perception. The British in India were far and away a plundering and philistine tribe of incursors.

This does not mean that every individual Britisher must carry a personal burden for his country's actions. It is equally true, however, that if the member of any nation tries to defend his government to the last letter ("My country, right or wrong"), he will almost always land himself in the position of an intellectual pantomime. I have seen this in journalism as well as in the media at large. It would be a mistake to assume that all Britishers behaved the way Curzon did in India.

But here is another picture of the same city by the most impressive local English historian, H.E.A. Cotton, in 1909:

> Ten minutes' walk from Dalhousie Square will land the seeker after sensation in a labyrinth of narrow, unpaved, winding lanes, polluted with odours and swarming with humanity, where the scavenging carts are the rarest visitors and the ghostly glimmer of an occasional and inadequate gas lamp furnishes the solitary illumination. Not a thousand yards from Government House [Curzon's legacy, once again!], troops of jackals may be heard after sunset sweeping through the deserted streets and making the night hideous with their fearsome howls.

Those winding unpaved lanes still exist in conditions of filth and stench, far worse than they ever were in 1909. If jackals no longer sweep the streets at night, in the radiance of the full moon today, you can see hundreds of men and women huddled under rags not far from the same Government House, sleeping away the unproductive agony of their existence on pavements.

But no city in which one is born can ever look the way others see it. There is no other place but Calcutta that can quite invoke the same love and despair in my heart.

For even when it is at its most degrading, Calcutta pulses with an intellectual and cultural exuberance that does not exist in any other Indian city. Young children may be deliberately maimed for beggary and deposited on street corners in the early morning by a syndicate lorry (Bertolt Brecht got the idea for *The Threepenny Opera* after reading a report on the organized mendicants of Calcutta), nude kids with swollen, malnutritional bellies might frolic in the slush of open roadside gutters, garbage from the plush restaurants may be picked clean for scraps of food, yet Calcutta will mount the most sophisticated and professional productions of Sartre and Beckett, Shakespeare and Pirandello, both in translation and in the original.

Concerts of Indian classical music, under huge canvas tents, will begin in the late evening and go on till dawn, attracting audiences in the thousands. Heated discussions on politics, art, and philosophy will endure for hours on end, both among the student rabble in Coffee House, as well as in the refined, Scotch-drinking environments of old anglicized institutions such as the Bengal and Calcutta clubs.

College Street will boast of being the physically longest secondhand bookstore in the world, with stallholders huddled together like migrant salesmen in a Western flea market, where you might pick up a first edition of Gibbon's *Decline and Fall* as well as the woodcut drawings of Gustave Doré. Everyone, but everyone, will have an opinion on the most abstruse to the most mundane subjects. Bengalis in Calcutta will talk and talk and talk, till the words battle in homicidal cacophony, leaving the Western visitor baffled and weary by the inexhaustible energy of verbal typhoons.

For it was here that West and East first met in that complex and extended battle of wits and intellectual dialectics that would finally bring about the fall of the empire. Calcutta would soak up the liberal humanist philosophies of Kant and of British thinkers like Locke and Hume, and use those same cerebral tools with which to beat the imperial conquerors at their own game. By introducing English education into Bengal in response to Thomas Babington Macaulay's condescending call to "train a nation of clerks," the enterprise would rebound like a boomerang. It would produce such ferocious forensic minds as C. R. Das and Surendranath Banerjee, who would hold their own in any debate against representatives of the foreign rulers.

Calcutta would show up the hypocrisy of asserting one set of standards at home and practicing a totally different ideology in the colony. With merciless brilliance, the Bengali leaders of the Indian National Congress would demonstrate the logical heresy of conquest and domination of one nation by another, and the inevitability of the end to military hegemony.

In addition to this nationalistic ferment that the city initiated in the Indian psyche, Calcutta is also directly linked with the only four winners of the Nobel Prize that the country has produced. First, it was Surgeon Major Ronald Ross of the Presidency General Hospital in Calcutta, who discovered that the bite of the menial mosquito was the cause of malaria. Then it was Rabindranath Tagore, the Bengali poet, who won the Nobel in literature. Later, Sir C. V. Raman got it for physics, working in a laboratory in Calcutta. And finally, there is the Albanian Mother Teresa, who arrived in Calcutta in 1928 and got the Peace Prize for reasons that are not altogether flattering for the city.

Such figures who have attracted international attention in the past ninety-odd years are not the only glittering stars on the Calcutta firmament. There were giant personalities and minds who were sowing the seeds of potential revolt against foreign rule way back in the mid-eighteenth century.

Although specific demands for British withdrawal and greater autonomy were not made till the beginning of this century, there were men like Raja Rammohun Roy, who were calling for an end to superstition and dependence in the 1700s. Roy was a polyglot, fluent in seven major languages, ranging from Persian and Arabic from the Middle East, to French and German from Europe, as well as Sanskrit, Bengali, and English. He founded *The Arya Samaj* in Calcutta in an attempt to return to authentic ancient values by purging Hinduism of its fungus-ridden addiction to ritual and multitudinous deities. A fiery reformer who preached the abolition of the caste system, Roy spearheaded the "New India" movement, heralding an epoch to be later known as the "Indian Renaissance."

Some twenty years after Raja Roy's death in Bristol, England, and long before the suffragettes had been heard of in England, a Sanskrit scholar from Calcutta by the name of Vidyasagar (in literal translation, "Sea of Learning") campaigned for women's rights, and successfully agitated for legalizing the remarriage of Hindu widows (forbidden up to that time) in 1856.

Then in 1893, another son of Calcutta, Vivekananda, would grip the attention of "The Parliament of Religions" in Chicago (where no representative from the Hindu religion had been officially invited!) by introducing his speech with the simple, stirring words, "Sisters and brothers of America . . ." Vivekananda would go on to establish Ramakrishna missions (after the name of his guru) across the whole of the United States, and following the triumphant return to his own country, these missions would spread all over India.

But it was in 1858, a year after the famous Sepoy Mutiny, that Calcutta formalized itself as the capital of the British Raj. With Queen Victoria's taking over the governance of the country from the East India Company and announcing herself as the "Queen Empress of India," Calcutta became the jewel in the crown and the first city in all the dominions of Her Imperial Majesty.

It was a cunning move, motivated largely by Disraeli's astute perception about the queen's megalomaniacal inclinations, and her manifest dislike for his rival Gladstone, the Whig. It is an unnoticed irony of history that what was essentially a domestic *political* move became in retrospect a profound act of statesmanship in preserving the empire for as long as it lasted.

The British could not have remained in India after the turn of the century—if that long—if there had been no British monarch to whom the Indian people could pledge their loyalties, divorced from their anger and frustration against the political apparatus imposed upon them by the East India Company and an alien race.

Viewed from this perspective, the Delhi durbar held by George V fifty-three years after Victoria became empress was not an exercise in pure ostentation. It diluted the vitriolic feelings that were then brewing against the British, and lubricated the passage of several awkward pieces of legislation. The procession that welcomed the king-emperor and his wife on their arrival in Bombay was spearheaded by ". . . the Imperial insignia and a herald proclaiming in the *vernacular,* Long live Emperor George! Long live the King of Kings! Long live the Great Power!"

In his speech of welcome to the king and his spouse, the city father of Bombay (an Indian) said, "His Majesty's determination to announce his coronation in person to his Indian people is a demonstration that the Crown is the living bond uniting many different races in different climes under the flag which stands for the ideals of justice, toleration and progress."

If this was merely the feeling of a fawning minority craving favors from the foreign paymasters, then it is somewhat surprising that over a quarter of a million people burst into tumultuous applause at the end of the speech.

This is how the special correspondent of *The Times* (London) described the durbar:

> The ceremony at its culminating point *exactly typified* the Oriental conception of the ultimate repositories of Imperial Power. The Monarch sat alone, remote but beneficient *[sic]*, raised far above the multitude, but visible to all, clad in rich vestments, flanked by radiant emblems of authority, guarded by a glittering array of troops, the cynosure of the proudest Princes of India, the central figure in what was surely the most majestic assemblage ever seen in the East. [Italics mine.]

To see the prolonged period of British rule in India, and particularly the shifting of the capital from Calcutta to Delhi, as a direct function of both the mystique of monarchy and the Indian temperament is neither pleasant not intellectually fashionable. But the special correspondent of *The Times* was not quite so off the mark when he wrote that the durbar ceremony exactly typified an Oriental conception of the ruler to the ruled.

It has been argued that the servile and obsequious aspect of the Indian personality, which so grates upon the visitor, was the *result* of an era of oppression imposed by an alien conqueror. To attempt to turn the argument on its head has always seemed sacrilegious to anglicized Indians and Western liberals. But history shows that Indians, except for pocket minorities, were bowing down to their lords and masters for well over a thousand years before the British arrived on the scene. And it was only when the ruler failed to typify the Oriental conception of his person that empires broke up and internecine strife between rival factions ensued.

The British Raj was finally consolidated when Queen Victoria became empress of India, as she then symbolized in the Indian mind an extraterrestrial writ to govern mere mortals, the deus ex machina, hand of God in human affairs, an incarnation.

The idea is not as farfetched as it appears at first glance, for Gandhi, apart from being clad in the mantle of the Mahatma—great soul and father of the nation—was widely regarded by the masses as an incarnation; I once saw Nehru angrily *kick* a man out of his way—as he was walking down the aisle of a public meeting—because the man wanted to pay homage to the Lord Vishnu in human form. The head of the only remaining Hindu kingdom in the world, Nepal, is even today worshipped as the incarnation of the creator of the universe; husbands are still held to be miniature gods by their wives. When I was a child my mother used to recite a Sanskrit couplet whose literal translation would be:

Worship thy father and thy mother
For they are the human forms
Of gods who reign high above.

The whole fabric of Hindu society is permeated with the belief that the only sanction of authority is a divine one, that truth is *revealed* rather than the end product of an analytic quest, and that the individual is less important than the community. Western parliamentary democracy is notionally irrelevant in India, and it was adopted in the country to salve the consciences of Western Oriental Gentlemen who sought the applause of Western liberals—perhaps unconsciously—more than for the good of their own people.

The British successfully exploited this conceptual commitment to divinity through their monarchs, and so established the strongest-ever colonial empire. There is a belief floating around in certain quarters that the Raj was essentially a grand collection of fuddy-duddies who enjoyed their *punkah* and sherbet, displayed a gross insensitivity to the feelings of the natives, and bungled their way through two hundred years of imperial history. This notion is nothing but a result of wishful thinking by people who cannot see human events other than in terms of white and black.

The British in India were in fact neither demons nor saints. They displayed more insight into the psychology of the native population than any other imperial power that did not integrate with the conquered people. As a legacy, they left behind an excellent civil service, railways, a postal system, the basis of an industrial economy, a far-flung country unified for the first time in many a century—even with partition in 1947—and the seeds of the Western empirical analytic apparatus.

And all this was accomplished principally in the last hundred years of British rule, the period over which the monarch was also the head of the India dominions. I do not believe that this was mere coincidence. For even at the fiercest point of India's struggle for independence, neither Tagore nor Gandhi—surely the two most widely revered Indians—ever disavowed their loyalty to the crown.

I am not making a value judgment. Or perhaps I should. Whatever *good* might result as a by-product, it is always morally wrong to exploit, to govern by force, to buy a slave so you can improve his or her standard of living. The British did all these things and they were morally wrong in doing so. But actions that are morally repulsive do not always produce a complete spectrum of undesirable results.

It is exactly the same ploy that Indira Gandhi pursued in free India. The vast majority of the population do not and will not respond to the abstruse ideal of democracy. But put that idea in human form, let India be incarnated as Indira, and the masses will worship and obey without a whimper.

It is unpleasant for Indian intellectuals to accept this thesis. But it is precisely because of this craving for the deification of an idea in mortal flesh, the ceaseless Hindu search for gods in human guise, that the paradox of Western-style democracy and dynastic rule continues to exist in such precarious equilibrium in India.

Mahatma Gandhi was a god, and he used his celestial authority to the hilt. Jawaharlal Nehru was a god, too, but he felt intellectually uncomfortable in the divine, while relishing his earthly regal role as much as any Caesar ever did. Indira Gandhi had no such ambivalence. At a gathering of international journalists, she once angrily remarked, "My father was a saint who had strayed into politics. I have grown up with politics in my veins." And she was right. Mrs. Gandhi knew the pulse of the Indian people far more intimately than any living politician. She knew that they wanted a Goddess Durga incarnate on the throne in Delhi, and was only too willing to provide them with their favorite idol. If her eldest son, Rajiv Gandhi, succeeds in metamorphosing himself into a deity drawn from the pantheon of Hindu gods, the Nehru-Gandhi hegemony will continue to rule India till well into the next century.

But here again our city might cast a shadow on events yet unforeseen. West Bengal, with Calcutta as its capital, has been the only ruling ministry headed by a Marxist chief minister popular enough to have withstood the late Mrs. Gandhi's insidious and persistent attempts to topple all state governments that did not belong to her party. Although the credit for electing the first Communist government goes to the state of Kerala (just over twenty years ago, Kerala had the first ever Communist party in the world returned to majority power in a free democratic election—neither the Soviet Union, nor China, nor Cuba can boast of such a dubious privilege, simply because they do not have "free elections" as the term is defined in the West), West Bengal has enjoyed a longer period of uninterrupted Marxist rule (with other splinter parties in coalition) than any other state in the union.

Jyoti Basu, the chief minister, is an England-trained barrister whose lackluster performance on the public podium belies a sharp mind and astute political awareness, which have won him the unswerving loyalty of the business community in a city that has always regarded capitalism and communism to be sworn enemies.

Very shortly, Calcutta will have the first underground train system in the whole of Asia, excluding Hong Kong. And it has been designed and built by local engineers and architects, against insuperable geographical and financial odds, with minimal advice and help from foreign technicians. The Calcutta Metro, as it will be called, is reputed to be the first of its kind in the world, built as it is on alluvial soil where the waterbed is dangerously near the surface all year round. Apart from the cyclotron (again, the only one of its kind in Asia, outside China), Calcutta's greatest showpiece will be the Metro, when and if it starts functioning in the not-too-distant future.

But as usual with self-congratulatory hosannas, Calcutta does trip itself up in uproarious hilarity at times. Inhabitants of the city will proudly quote an aphorism (usually attributed to the nationalist leader Lok Manya Tilak): "What Bengal thinks today, India thinks tomorrow," implicitly claiming that the city is the intellectual hub of the country, if not the whole world. What few such braggarts seem to know is the fact that the quip is a not very subtle adaptation from Kipling: "What the *bandar lok* [monkey people] think today, the jungle thinks tomorrow!" Hardly a eulogy, whichever way you look at it.

Again, I have heard grave discussions within the august premises of the Bengal Club on the various legacies that Calcutta has bequeathed to the world, including the title of a long-running London musical. Sedate middle-class visitors have been known to take their wives to see *Oh! Calcutta!* in London as a gesture of patriotic pride in their hometown, only to witness to their intense embarrassment a ribald show bearing no connection to the Second City of the Commonwealth, but which will live, if only as a footnote in theatrical history, as the first revue ever to have presented full frontal nudity onstage in New York and London.

In fact the name of the show was invented by the late Kenneth Tynan, once the drama critic of *The New Yorker,* as a literary pun on a painting by the surrealist Clovis Trouille, called *Oh! Quel Cul T'as!,* the English translation of which ("Oh! What an arse you have!") refers to the massive posterior displayed by the lady on the canvas.

Calcutta today is a Janus-faced city. It is modern and cosmopolitan in the sense that New York is, while London and Paris are not. Yet the place draws its inspiration not from the well of poverty and destitution in which it currently finds itself, but from a vivid and regal sense of history, whose implications often escape the outsider.

Ian Jack, a British journalist, recently wrote that "Calcutta is a wreck, haunted by culture." What he failed to perceive were the myriad of echoing tales resonating in the wreckage. There is an absolutely devastating story by Tagore that ends with the manic declarations of the hero: *"Sab Jhut Hai, Sab Jhut Hai!"* ("Everything is lies, everything is lies!") He is complaining about reality not matching up with fantasy.

What Ian Jack and a whole host of notebook-carrying visitors to Calcutta cannot possibly know is that culture is something every Bengali assumes as his birthright in the here and now, not as an heirloom hidden in the cobwebbed attics of his atavistic mind.

For if there is squalor, there is grandeur, too. Walk into the Marble Palace of a summer afternoon, and you will find paintings by European masters of the late eighteenth and early nineteenth centuries, massive chandeliers in hand-cut glass, marble halls and colonnades, peacocks, fountains, and grand pianos right there in the middle of the most putrefying filth.

A city that contains the largest number of people who live fathoms below the poverty line also accommodates the house of Birla: a single family whose wealth can only be comprehended if one talks of Woolworths, Gulf & Western, General Motors, *The New York Times,* and a host of other subsidiaries in jute and steel, owned by the sons, in-laws, and immediate relatives of one man, the late Ghyanasham Das Birla.

Of course Calcutta has its regular planeloads of doom-watchers, report-makers, television crews, and pontificating pundits who fly into town swathed in air-conditioned comfort, do a tour of inspection, and hurry back home to their havens in the West with news that makes the Occidental listener feel at once superior and a tiny bit nervous.

For it was just such a report in 1967 by nine Anglo-American town planners, that focused world attention on Calcutta:

> A city in a state of crisis. We have not seen human degradation on a comparable scale in any other city in the world. This is one of the greatest urban concentrations in existence, rapidly approaching the point of breakdown in its economy, housing, sanitation, transport and the essential humanities of life. If the final breakdown were to take place, it would be a disaster for mankind of a more sinister sort than any disaster of flood or famine.

After that, the great cities of the West, particularly New York, began to feel uncomfortably close to the same sense of megalopolitan collapse about which there was so much film and print emanating from Calcutta. But the response in the West was a curiously self-hugging one, as much as to say there are worse places than here.

Once again Calcutta had acted as a forerunner, if not for an entirely worthy cause. For it was from this place in India that warning signals first came: that it is possible for a city to choke itself in its own smoke, drown in its own sewage, reduce itself to a standstill in its own congested traffic, have its own homeless rise up in fevered rebellion, and witness the horrifying spectacle of newborn infants screeching their way to instant death for want of adequate medical facilities.

But if nearly two decades after that ominous pronouncement,

Armageddon has not yet occurred, it is not due to the lack of recurrent announcements of final doom that reverberate on television screens and newspapers throughout the world. Calcutta still receives its regular quota of cameramen and tape-recording journalists, who do not always fare kindly in the hands of street mobs, any member of which earns less in a month than a couple of rolls of color film in our photographer's Pentax.

People turn to communism for salvation—not because they choose between good and evil, but because the highfalutin phrases of democratic demogagues begin to sound furiously irrelevant. When poverty does not mean being on welfare at a minimum of fifty dollars a week, but having to scavenge for food for a family of five, to feed them once a day with a pound of rice and a handful of lentils, lectures about "our glorious way of life" can often provide the spark for explosion.

When "home" is a six-foot ring of concrete to be used as a sewage pipe at some future date, it is an affront to human dignity to begin a discourse on "the value of freedom in democratic societies." The dramatic invocation "Let them eat cake!" did not generate the French Revolution, but the attitude embedded in those heartless words had a great deal to do with the storming of the Bastille.

Look at a vulgar imitation of the Taj Mahal in the Victoria Memorial Hall, go to the National Library in Alipore and see where the British governors once lived, climb the dirty fetid stairs to the Asiatic Society, and you will find a Calcutta of many-faceted dimensions. Walk into the Grand Hotel (the most expensive in the whole of Asia), and gaze in astonished delight at Desmond Doig's sketches of old Georgian and Victorian buildings that remain. And always remember, the city is everything you see, and much more besides.

It is the Bengali mind above all that sets the city apart. Like arterial veins branching out from the heart, Calcutta pumps out life-giving fluid to the rest of the country. Having sustained the national ethos for the past three hundred years, the city invites attack and opprobrium in the same way that brickbats get thrown at parents by growing adolescents.

Bombay tries to assert its riches, yet cannot compete with the unassailable fact that Calcutta produces 40 percent of all of India's wealth. Delhi insists on being the center of power, yet does not know how to deal with wayward Bengal and Marxist Chief Minister Jyoti Basu, who recently spent three weeks in Peking as an honored guest of the Chinese government. Everyone talks about the poverty in Calcutta, yet there is hardly a discussion in the whole country where the exuberance and vitality of the city are not vigorously asserted.

Here we come to the Bengali mind and the pivotal reason why Calcutta must be the central source of Western comprehension about India. It is the city that first came into contact with the West, rose to fabulous prominence for a couple of hundred years, and then sank into the most squalid degradation. During this process it managed to produce a vibrant culture that was both more refined than that of the British predators and more authentically indigenous than anything that had gone before.

Calcutta is the only city in the whole of India that has a direct historical link with events in the past. Every other place is a mausoleum. There are palaces in Rajasthan and Hyderabad that boast of "living traditions," but they are isolated relics rather than whole urban conurbations. Infinitely younger than Delhi or Agra, Calcutta has not yet suffered rigor mortis, while every other city in India, except perhaps Benares, has sunk in and out of life and death, in cyclic resurrections and recurring burials, for the past two thousand years.

The mind of the Bengali, the original indigenous inhabitant of Calcutta, is a perverse and fascinating mixture of old and new. It admires the empirical rationalist traditions of the West, while despising its material fixations. It will aspire to argue on equal terms as long as legitimate parity is conceded, and suddenly give up because the rules in the game are not being followed.

The Bengali from Calcutta will burst into furious flame when a point of principle is being carelessly desecrated, yet he will subside without a whimper if a totally puerile attack was made on his motherland. He will sigh with a shrug of disgusted superiority if someone talks about Calcutta's sewage, electricity blackouts, or transport problems. At least 1001 examples will be cited to demonstrate that Calcutta's quandaries are not unique.

But just as James Joyce had to flee Ireland to write so memorably about Dublin, most prominent sons of Calcutta have sought refuge in exile. Rabindranath Tagore received news of his induction into the Nobelity (Nobel Prize–winner for literature in 1913), while on a visit to the United States. His first published work appeared under the pseudonym Bhanusingha (a clever Bengali pun on his own name), because readers in Calcutta were not prepared to accept the raw colloquial parlance *(chalita bhasha)* of an innovator of genius. Nirad C. Chaudhuri, author of *The Autobiography of An Unknown Indian* and perhaps the greatest Indian writer in English, lives at Oxford, England, in the ninth decade of his life, having been shabbily neglected by the province of his origin. Only Satyajit Ray, the most original filmmaker that India has produced and winner of numerous international awards, cussedly goes on living in Calcutta, battling even now against snide hostility from a city that does not know how to honor its brilliant progenies.

While gathering material for this book, I happened to be in Calcutta during the Christmas-New Year recess in 1983. As a visitor, I organized a party to which I invited friends from my graduating class of '59, Presidency College, my alma mater (once called the Balliol of India). There were some ten of us men, each of my erstwhile colleagues with their exquisitely beautiful wives. We talked.

One was a high-powered diplomat who read Goethe in German in his spare time. Another was the manager of a British bank. The third, a powerful stutterer, was considered by the World Bank the most respected economist about Third World affairs. The fourth was a physicist who managed the business of the cyclotron. The fifth was a presiding politician in the state, the sixth was an industrialist of national repute, and so on. I was the only odd bod out, merely a writer.

But in that one assembly on that single evening, there were discussions about "structuralism," "the thermodynamics of volatility," and "the inescapable effulgence of Keats," among many other things. The man who spoke the least was a fully tenured professor of geophysics at the University of Texas. An absent colleague, who now lives in the States, was Gayatri Spivak—the internationally acclaimed structuralist philosopher who translated Jacques Derrida's *Of Grammatology* into English.

My host, who did not go to Presidency College, remarked at the end of the party: "What a bunch! Is there any city in the world which can boast of such a galaxy of stars?"

Of course he was overplaying his chauvinism, but the message was clear.

The mind of the person from Calcutta is a complex and ambiguous one. Most Indians resent Bengalis for no better reason than that they are unfathomable. If you can imagine the garrulity of the Irish, married to the argumentative dispositions of the Jew (Leopold Bloom, where are you?), and throw in some Italian, for fierce gesticulation and hot temper, and ice it over with upper-echelon WASP sophistication, you might get to the kind of explosive confection that makes up a Bengali.

Calcutta is an exact epigraphy of this fascinating and ambivalent terrain.

3

Rituals at Wounded Knee

*T*he rituals of "birth, and copulation, and death," to borrow a phrase from Eliot, reveal the methods by which a society functions and transmits its values to the next generation. Just as Calcutta is a key to the understanding of India, not an emblem of the country nor its representative city, so also are the customs and practices associated with each of our three main acts in the human drama.

The birth of a boy in a middle-class Hindu home in Bengal occurs under wholly different circumstances from those which would herald the entry of a male heir to a Bombay industrialist. Villagers in the North have altogether different ways of treating a pregnant woman compared with the way in which she may fare in the tribal (aboriginal) regions of central and eastern India.

There are connecting threads as well as wide divergences in each sacred and secular ritual. And sometimes the congruences strike the foreigner so forcefully that the dissimilarities are overlooked.

If one talks about a birth in the West, there are certain reflex images that instantly come to mind, irrespective of the class or color of the mother. We think of a hospital, antiseptic smells, doctors, nurses, pre- and postnatal care, and so forth. The essential picture that forms in our mind is unlikely to be altered, whether the mother is a Kennedy or a domestic from Harlem. Surroundings might differ, the luxury and accouterments might vary in vast degree, but the minimal mechanical aids to the delivery of a child in the Western hemisphere, whether it be natural childbirth or any other new-fangled craze, would remain the same for Jew, Christian, or pagan, from the lowest class to the highest. This is not so in India, and it profoundly influences the attitude of the society to the newcomer, as well as the child's subsequent conscious perception of the universe in which it finds itself.

For a start, the vast majority of Indian babies are not born in a hospital or anything resembling a medical environment. The statistics are not at hand, and even if it were possible to collate all the figures from the far-flung regions, they would be wholly unreliable, anyway. But I would hazard a guess that of more than one million births that occur every month in India, over 90 percent take place in conditions that would not meet with the approval of a health inspector visiting a Manhattan restaurant.

Much as in Victorian England, the midwife rules the roost. Often it is the oldest woman in the family, having presided over many other entries, who delivers the child. A bowl of hot water, a couple of rags or handmade quilts, and a kitchen knife may be all she has at her disposal. In villages across the whole land, a woman may be working in the fields right up to the point her labor pains begin, take herself away from prying eyes, squat on the ground, deliver her own baby, clean the slimy mess in a nearby pond, hand it over to an elderly female relative, and resume her toils under the merciless sun on the same day.

In middle-class homes, like the one in which I was born, a particular room is usually set aside for childbirth. Among the more affluent, it would also adjoin a bathroom, but in more menial surroundings, buckets of water and a minicanal dug into the stone floor acts as a drain to carry both excreta and fetal slime into the street below. As births are frequent, the delivery room is in constant use. In our house, my own bedroom was the one immediately next to this chamber of horrors, where more than thirty babies came into the world. From the age of three to the time I was sent away to boarding school at ten, every few months I would hear those ferocious and earsplitting screams of women behind closed doors and later wonder why they made such a happy fuss about the newborn infant when it had caused so much pain during its arrival. I would reflect that I might have done the same thing to my mother, and feel wretched and guilty about having had the audacity to enter the planet.

The image that recurs persistently in my mind is of a woman, merging into a myriad, laid out on the floor (not on a bed), covered by enormous swathes of cloth, a tiny bundle of pink-red flesh by her side, screaming out its lungs, an enveloping smell of incense, and a large iron bowl with glowing coal being fanned into flame. Years later I was to discover the purpose of that fire in the middle of a Calcutta summer: to heat pads of toweling, which were then placed on the abdomen of the mother.

These customs were not unique to our house; they were and still are universally practiced. The female who goes into the hospital to have her baby is the exception, not the rule. And we are talking about middle-class homes here, not the villages, where the amenities simply do not exist and there is no choice.

Several crucial elements remain similar. Except in the highest socioeconomic strata of society, a female newborn is regarded with disfavor, while the male receives special treatment. This is because the girl will one day have to marry, and her father or guardian will be required to provide a dowry for her. Although in small scattered enclaves throughout India where the aboriginals still live, matriarchal values prevail, in general the subservient status of the female infant is accepted, sometimes covertly, often openly. We shall discuss dowry in a moment, but first let us look at how certain social mechanisms originate in response to malign factors.

There is a phenomenon called *ashauj* (unclean), which is observed in all Hindu (the majority) homes. This puts the immediate family members behind a veil, precluding their participation in any auspicious or celebratory occasion. Significantly, a family comes under *ashauj* both when a child is born and when someone dies. But even more fundamentally, the period of *ashauj* is only seven days for a male infant, and thirty for a female.

The reason is clear. The new mother will be treated with a certain cordiality if she has produced a baby boy, and maltreated if she has given birth to a girl. So religion intervenes to protect the mother from being abused by enforcing a longer period of convalescence for a female progeny, and by implying that *she* is unclean and dirty and could not be employed for household chores. The onus is deftly shifted.

Ritual is playing a subtle underhand game. It is telling her mother-in-law and other members of the clan that we are not trying to protect *her*—rather, the contrary. You will become *unclean* if you make use of her as a servant-maid during this period. Religious ritual is not concerned with *her* rights, because if it were to do so openly, they would certainly be ignored. It is protecting the new mother by subterfuge, by putting the self-interest of society at an apparent premium.

And since religion is so powerful and pervasive, its dictates work, while any number of social, hygienic, and moral exhortations would simply be laughed away.

This shows itself even in the way the presiding priest insists on separating cleanliness and dirt after the child is born. It is never implied that if you enter the "delivery room," you might contaminate and infect the infant. Once again religious ritual insists that anyone who enters the place where a birth has just occurred becomes *unclean*. So, if you do wish to go in to cradle the baby, you have to disrobe completely and indulge in a purifying bath before you are permitted to emerge again as a clean and wholesome person, fit to be accepted by society. Since this whole business is rather tiresome, very few people decide to pop right into the room to touch and feel. A safe distance is maintained between the possibility of contagion and the vulnerable immune system of the screaming infant. Superstition is consciously used to obtain results that countless lectures on medical hygiene could never accomplish.

Social custom, ritual, and religious practice are so closely interwoven in India that it is difficult for an outsider to figure out where religion ends and simple social custom begins. Most Indians find themselves in a quandary if they are asked whether a birthday ceremony, which begins with incantations of Sanskrit *mantras* in a Brahmin household, is a social function or a religious one.

There is such intense osmosis between religious precepts and almost every other sphere of life that to disentangle the separate threads is not only an impossible task; the very endeavor is based on assumptions that are contrary to the Indian way of life. This does not apply only to people who are orthodox. It is valid across the board.

An Indian will be taken aback when asked by a foreigner whether touching the feet of an elder is a religious or social custom. Since it is such a universal practice among Hindus, most Indians do not give these things a moment's thought. But if they pause to consider, they will grudgingly concede that the custom is based on premises that originated in religion. In treating any older person as an object of veneration (hence the token symbolism of touching his feet and talking the dust off his soles and putting it on one's head), the Indian is subscribing to an ancient mystique of age that derives directly from the *Mahabharata*. Although the person who is doing it may be as fiercely secular as any Western skeptic, he is unwittingly performing a ritual that is deeply imbued in religious precept.

The same is true for the rituals associated with the birth of a child. From the lowest to the most lavish households, there will always be a priest in attendance. According to the gradations of orthodoxy to which the family subscribes, there will be *pujas* offered to gods in all their multiple dimensions. Sometimes beggars will be fed in opulent establishments. Gifts will be distributed to Brahmins, bells will toll, cymbals sounded, conches blown. Incense will be burned, visitors bearing presents for the newborn infant will be feted with garlands of flowers and treated to sweetmeats and tea.

Not all these things will happen in every house, nor will the minority communities such as the Muslims, Christians, and Jews follow identical rites. But if they have lived in India for more than two or three generations, some subtly tailored version of the same ritual will be observed everywhere in the country, except at the most elite and refined layer of Indian society.

At its moment of entry, the child's exact time of birth will be recorded and sent off to the family astrologer. The priest will chant some holy texts to make the time propitious. If it is an unholy hour, sacred stones and talismans will be tied to the infant's arms and neck to ward off evil spirits.

When the astrologer sends back the horoscope, which often runs into hundreds of yards, handwritten on a scroll, the resident priest will be asked to interpret. Depending upon the socioeconomic status of the family, the horoscope may deal with whole years in slabs, or else split them up into months, weeks, or even days. The more detailed the listings, the more expensive will be the services.

But one of the things about this extraordinary piece of paper is that no average person will be able to comprehend a single line. Having looked at my own horoscope, I have been completely befuddled by it, consisting as it does mostly of circles and crosses in different colored inks, with all kinds of lines drawn across them, sprinkled with a few words and phrases in ornate Bengali.

For contrary to popular Western conception, a person's horoscope does not predict anything. It merely charts the course of the planets and their precise conjunction at any given moment with those that ruled at the time the subject was born. From this data, it is the priest, or the translator, who comes out with a comprehensible version of what the likelihood of such planetary confluences might be. Quite obviously, a great deal depends on interpretation. If Saturn is evil in general, is the presence of Venus likely to soothe its malign glare? And so on.

It is not a concept to which I personally subscribe. For astrology presumes predestination, which vitiates any scientific notion of free will. But every Indian I know from a Hindu background does have a horoscope, a fact that must influence the way one looks at the world in later life, in however direct or glancing a manner.

Out of this intimate and unavoidable indoctrination in religion and ritual, from the very moment of birth, springs another facet of Indian life whose impact is far more ominous and modern in its implications.

No one knows precisely how fast the population is growing. It is generally accepted that life expectancy has gone up and stands in the mid-forties at the moment. The death rate has gone down, and so has infant mortality. Famine and disease no longer kill as many people as they once did. So the demographic curve is shooting up at a fierce gradient.

The reason for this is traceable to two interrelated factors that owe their origins once again to religion and ritual. When infant mortality was the norm rather than the exception, people deliberately created large families to ensure that some children survived, allowing for a few casualties to disease and famine along the way. The fact that the situation is totally different today has not radically altered the psychological landscape. Parents, especially from the vast village populations, still feel that without a family of six to eight children, there is no guarantee that at least two or three will survive.

And since the mystique of age is so thoroughly ingrained almost since birth, it is taken for granted that no child will dare rise up against its parents. In a country where there is no state-run social-security program of any sort, the survival of some offspring is absolutely essential for parents in their old age. For laborers and farmers, children are the only insurance against the prospect of dying in dire penury when they are no longer able to work.

If city kids rebel, and we hear of youth being in revolt against the older generation, it is the luxury of educated, Westernized, affluent young men and women who comprise less than 1 percent of the 750 million people who currently live in India. The overwhelming majority still believe that parents must be worshiped, that age is unselectively venerable, that old men and women must be provided for, however poor one may be oneself. Even today, lowly migrant laborers in America, Canada, Britain, and Germany, send substantial checks back to their parents and old relatives in the villages and small towns of India.

The most urgent and devastating problem confronting the country at the moment is the population explosion. Poverty, corruption, superstition, even famine and disease, can be directly related to this absolutely fundamental malaise. After all, it is not as if poverty does not exist in Britain or in the United States, though admittedly in relative terms. Corruption is not India's monopoly; recently, Japan, Belgium, and a few other countries scattered across the globe have shown themselves quite as proficient in the art. The difference lies in the extent to which it infects the body politic, and the economic capacity of some nations to shoulder the burden of endemic internal exploitation.

The only serious attempt to control the birthrate was made during Mrs. Gandhi's notorious Emergency regime (1975–1977). Her late son, Sanjay, initiated a scheme called *nashbandi* (vasectomy) for villagers and poor townspeople. Incentives were offered to men who voluntarily submitted themselves for the operation. Mobile vans toured the villages, blaring out the message from loudspeakers. Transistor radios and cash prizes were part of the inducement.

But as usual with all such well-meaning enterprises enforced under a dictatorship, it turned sour. Since Indira Gandhi's government during those two years was virtually unaccountable to anyone but herself, the scheme misfired. Zealous underlings began to use coercion to fill up the required quota of vasectomies in order to achieve promotion or a royal pat on the back. As there was no recourse to law, and as the press was totally censored, the devastation continued unabated.

Rumor, one of the strongest opinion-makers in India, began to tell of young unmarried men forcibly tied and gagged while the doctor in the mobile medical van cut off the seminal duct. Other versions hinted at impotence and worse. In a land where there is very little entertainment other than copulation and resultant procreation, this was really bad news.

When she called an election in 1977, Mrs. Gandhi was disastrously defeated at the polls for this one single thoroughly progressive measure that Western-oriented Sanjay had initiated. Uncharacteristically, the lady had gone along with a scheme that went against the grain of Indian tradition. She had touched the raw, fundamental nerve of fertility and birth.

Contrary to sophisticated interpretations of that electoral rout, I do not believe that the Indian masses would have cared a damn whether Indira Gandhi had respected the constitution and behaved democratically or not. If only she had left them alone to go on copulating and procreating, her dictatorship could have continued to the end of her life and beyond, without an interruption.

Since that apparently progressive but horrendously ill-conceived endeavor, no serious attempt has been made to control population growth. The health minister in the government that took over from Mrs. Gandhi in 1977 told me at the time that "abstinence" was the best method.

On resuming power in 1980, Prime Minister Indira Gandhi did nothing other than put up a few billboards in the principal cities of India, advertising the benefits of a two-child family. In more than five hundred villages I visited or traveled through while gathering material for this book, I did not see a single billboard advocating birth control. Apart from the fact that the problem is most acute in villages, where 85 percent of the population lives and literacy is often below 10 percent, billboards do not a population policy make.

Babies are being born in India at a more explosive rate than in any other comparable country in the world. Ominous and violent warning signals lie scattered everywhere on the landscape. While Apocalypse threatens!

Birth does not occur without insemination, but in India the two phenomena are more than physiologically linked. There is a whole host of religious and social rituals that connect them in such intense symbiotic ties that sex and procreation are often treated as one process—a sentiment with which the present Holy Father in Rome has much sympathy.

But if "sex for pleasure" is held to be a modern and permissive concept, then it surely finds its apotheosis in third-century India, when a *rishi* (holy sage) by the name of Vatsyayana composed a book called the *Kama Sutra,* probably the most famous erotic-sex manual in the world. Translated into English, it is a treatise on "the lessons of sensual pleasure." *Kama* is a difficult word to get across, but sense and sex blend into it without mutual disharmony, and *sutra* is a learned exposition on the noun that precedes it.

When I first read it at the age of twenty-four in England, the book made me laugh. On second thought and somewhat more serious consideration, I realized it was an exceedingly portentous volume. One is led to expect one thing and is served up with something totally different. There is nothing remotely erotic or pornographic about the *Kama Sutra*. It is a detailed how-to book based on a profound perception of sociosexual mores as they existed at the time. It tells the reader, without a flicker of humor or a sniggering inflection in the lecturing voice, how to seduce your master's wife, what to do with the servant girl, how to increase the girth of your penis, the various gradations of phallic sizes that are compatible with the corresponding vaginal dimensions, the methods that should be employed to bring a frigid woman to orgasm and so forth.

It is as much a social document as a sexual-instruction manual; indeed the sex is often subsidiary. The book inadvertently describes what went on in third-century Hindu India. If we are not too prurient, we may take lessons in how to deal with the kind of laissez-faire sexuality that appears to be the current norm in the West, without making obviously rigid comparisons.

From Vatsyayana we have to make a steep descent into the erotic temple architecture of Hindu India, from about the tenth century onward. If the *Kama Sutra* is sociological in the most pedagogic sense of the term, then phallic, vaginal, and any number of other figurations that are scattered in riotous abandon on the walls of temples in Khajuraho and Konarak, are the most uninhibited ex-istential celebrations of sexuality that may be found anywhere in the world.

But one should sound a note of warning here again. I have been to these places and they did not appear to me to be the kind of erotic turn-ons that they might sound in the brochures. It is the English-speaking guide who will leer and snigger as he drops his voice a pitch and whispers the word "suck" or even the other one that rhymes with it.

There is a great deal of evidence scattered all over these temple configurations that suggest that any form of repressive puritanism was wholly absent in ancient India. We see birds pecking at wom-en's nipples; a stallion copulating with a female; extended orgies of one single male with several females; large phalluses doing their work; sucking, caressing, pullulating with a fierce zest that leaves one dazed and wondering about the regal temperaments that com-missioned such works and the lowly artisans who executed those commands. But these ancient stone carvings are not incentives to erotic arousal. At least not to me.

If you pick up a ten-cent guidebook, however, you will find the following sentence about the erotic sculptures at Khajuraho: "From our own superior modern perspectives, we may find these works, especially on the walls of holy buildings [temples], to be totally disgusting and displaying lax moral standards. . . ."

It is pointless to ask for an explanation of these vivid and stir-ring graphic portrayals of sexuality in all its flamboyant variations, because no written records exist. Even dates are notoriously un-reliable. One scholar will say that these sculptures are meant to "bring out the contrast between the serenity within and the sen-suality without." Another will assert that they occur at the base of the temple to demonstrate how Man may climb upward to spiri-tual salvation. Yet another school will claim that they belong to the *tantric* sect, which employs sex to achieve *mokhsha* (release from the endless cycle of birth and rebirth).

No single opinion is any more authoritative than another. These temples in Khajuraho were built over a period of some two hundred years. Twenty-five (out of a total of ninety) still survive today in various states of preservation. It is safe to assert that the kind of social and sexual life they so intricately and graphically illustrate in stone must have existed in the world outside the temple complexes, since they are not hidden away in a cupboard, but spire into the sky with tall majesty and gothic mass. Personally, I simply respond to their incandescent glory and concede to them the same status as Mallory's dramatic declamation about Mount Everest: "Because it is there."

Due to the profusion of erotic scenes on the external walls of the temples in Khajuraho and the single massive monument at Konarak, the Westerner is likely to get two very misleading impressions. The visitor might well conclude that these are the only two sites in India where such sexual "aberrations" occur. And that would be wrong. There are quite literally thousands of temples scattered all over the country where equally graphic stone portrayals of sexual activity can be seen. The difference is that they do not exist in such abundance in one spot for the tourist guidebooks to make a song and dance about them. Nor is their sculptural quality as magnificent.

Khajuraho and Konarak are not isolated pimples on the smooth, decorous surface of an otherwise sexually reticent universe. Hindu India was an absolute riot of uninhibited sex, and the stone figures of *lingams* (phalluses) and *yonis* (the female pudenda) that occur in well over a million Shiva temples, are a witness to the fact that whatever else the country might have been up to over a thousand years ago, copulation occupied a fairly important and assertive place on the agenda.

In one South Indian temple, I remember seeing a single stone carving (over ten feet in height) of Shiva and Parvati in such a fiercely close embrace that the two figures looked as if they belonged to one body—half male and half female. This concept is enshrined in the Sanskrit word *ardhangini,* implying a total equality and fusion between the masculine and feminine elements. No other religion in the world accepts this kind of physical and psychic integration.

The creator is both male and female, quite unlike the patriarchal attitudes of Judeo-Christo-Islamic traditions. If you worship Shiva, you also worship his wife, Parvati. If you bow before Vishnu, you are doing homage to Lakhshmi, too. With Krishna, you genuflect before Radha as well. The significant feature is the fact that the female principle is always mentioned first: *Radha*-Krishna, *Lakhshmi*-Narayan (another name for Vishnu), *Sita*-Ram, and so on. This is unique to Hinduism and the resultant perceptions of male-female sociosexual relationships.

It is significant, too, that the only recorded instance of polyandry sanctioned by institutionalized religion occurs in the *Mahabharata,* the great religious epic, when Draupadi marries the five Pandava brothers, and produces a child by each of them. There is no other historical or literary document in the world that sanctifies a woman taking on more than one legitimate husband at the same time.

Promiscuity, as defined today in the West, does not get short shrift either. Krishna, an incarnation of one of the holy Hindu trinity, is recorded as having had affairs with 120 milkmaids; his wife, Radha, was seduced by the youthful god while she was still married to his uncle.

The upshot of all this mythology, ritual, and sculpture is a single anguished cry of incomprehension from the Western onlooker: If all this was so, how come the Indians we meet and read about today are such a sexually repressed lot? Why is *kissing* not permitted on the Indian screen? Why do Indians sometimes appear so sexually grasping and uncouth to the point of barbarism?

The answers lie both in the accident of history and in the propensity of the Hindu mind to absorb, integrate, prostrate itself to a greater power. With the incursion of the Muslims some seven hundred years ago, and later the British, the Islamic-Christian lid of repressive puritanical patriarchalism was clamped tightly down on the spontaneous, effervescent sexuality of Hindu India. And like James Watt's steam engine, it created enormous pressures within— from which the country has not yet recovered.

The Westerner mostly meets anglicized Indians who have absorbed a great deal of Occidental mores. Although the tensions are concealed just beneath the surface, the projected persona is usually one of grace, sophistication, and an acceptance of those very norms that the Indian's deep atavistic yearnings have taught him to spurn.

The histrionic farce lasts for so long, and no longer. Then he explodes, because he does not know how to deal with the turbulent subterranean churnings of his own "collective unconscious."

The natural inclinations of his psyche push him one way, his borrowed clothes and his adopted Western mannerisms shove him in another. In moments of stress or unwary abandon, what the Westerner finally observes is a flood of violent vomit, because the authentic stomach has refused to accept the foreign food that has been injected into it.

When I first arrived in London in 1961, an Indian friend who had been living in the country for some time advised me: "You really should do it, as soon as you can!" As I wasn't quite sure what he was talking about, he helped me out: "The first time I slept with a white English girl, I felt the British empire melting in my arms." He was wholly unaware that he was being wildly hilarious as well as sadly pathetic. He was trying to teach me the ways of the world, as best he knew.

If he had been talking to a Western visitor in India, he would never have uttered the words he spoke to me. My friend would have tailored his remarks to suit his audience. But his torn and lacerated soul would have remained just as afflicted. And sooner or later the volcano would have erupted, in ways that neither he nor his Occidental companion would have dared to anticipate.

Western incursions into the sexual mores of India reflect themselves in many ways. The most hideous Hindu custom of *suttee* (anglicized from the original Sanskrit *swati,* meaning a chaste and faithful woman) was outlawed by Lord William Bentinck in 1829 because it was supposed to force newly widowed women to jump onto the funeral pyres of their late husbands.

Yet again, it is ironic and not entirely insignificant that Job Charnock, the founder of Calcutta, snatched an exceedingly attractive Indian woman who was just about to throw herself on the funeral pyre of her dead husband, and married her instantly in a Christian church. History is strewn with such absurd ironies, we know, but it does not make them any the less startling.

There was yet another ritual called *jauhar,* and I shall let a British historian called Tod describe it:

> When further resistance seemed impossible, they preferred death to disgrace [i.e., the certainty of being dis-

honoured by rape, and performed that horrible rite, the *jauhar,* where the females are immolated, to preserve them from disgrace or captivity. The funeral pyre was lighted within the great subterranean retreat, in chambers impervious to the light of day, and the defenders of the Fort beheld in procession the queens, their own wives and daughters, to the number of several thousands . . . The fair Queen Padmini closed the throng, they were conveyed to the cavern, and the opening closed upon them, leaving them to find security from dishonour in the devouring element.

This particular event occurred at the turn of the fourteenth century in Rajasthan when the Muslims invaded, but residual impulses in that direction still remain some six hundred years later.

The other ritual connected with Hindu marriage, which even today occasionally creates sensational headlines in both the national and the foreign press, is the notorious practice of dowry. This is a custom in which the bride's father is required to pay a certain amount in cash, and often in goods, too, at the time of the wedding to the groom or his parents.

The sum of money is negotiated in advance, and the actual figure will depend upon several variables, which will be determined by the market value of the would-be husband. At the top of the scale will be a "foreign-returned" boy (usually a graduate from a British or American university), who may command as much as $45,000 within an average middle-class milieu. Lower down the scale will be members of the prestigious foreign or civil service (as their jobs will be secure, even if they don't earn a great deal), then an ordinary graduate from an Indian university, and so on. If the man is wholly uneducated but runs a little stall in a village or small town, he may still demand and get as much as $1,500 to $2,000.

Several other factors may determine the size of the dowry: the skin complexion of the groom (the fairer he is the higher the price), his job status, the social standing of his family, and finally, the bargaining power of the middleman who brings the two families together.

Attempts are now being made to eliminate the services of the go-between by advertising in newspapers; there are whole pages devoted to husband- and wife-hunting in the English and native press. A typical ad might read:

WANTED—FOR HANDSOME, ENGLAND-RETURNED, FAIR-COMPLEXIONED BOY, 26, WITH BRILLIANT PROSPECTS, A REALLY BEAUTIFUL VIRGIN FROM RESPECTABLE SOUTH INDIAN BRAHMIN FAMILY, WITH WELL-TO-DO BACKGROUND AND ECONOMIC CAPACITY

That last phrase, "economic capacity," is a coded signal, indicating that a fairly fat dowry is being demanded, since it is against the law to do so openly. The Dowry Prohibition Act of 1961 expressly forbids the giving or taking of dowries. But the law is more frequently breached than observed, because when the giver and the taker are in collusion, it is almost impossible to prove that an illegal transaction has taken place.

The practice of dowry is as often condoned as condemned. It is motivated by greed, a craving for the ostentatious display of social and economic status, and ultimately underlines the implicit assumption that a woman is a burden. It is the girl's father who pays for the wedding, however lavish or modest it may be. It is he who is the supplicant to the groom's family, it is he who has to beg, borrow, or steal to scrape up enough cash so that his daughter may have a suitable marriage.

Supporters of dowry make sophisticated pleas about the facility of social mobility that the practice of dowry affords. A beautiful girl from a lowly background may climb several steps up the social ladder if the boy is less than handsome but comes from a high-class family. A boy who has done brilliantly at the university but does not have the economic backup to mix on equal social terms with his colleagues may be given a head start in life with the right sort of dowry. The trade-offs are not exclusively financial, either: If a boy is handicapped while the girl is healthy as a rose, the dowry demand will be correspondingly low.

But as in all such specious arguments in favor of the myriad evil practices that sully the Indian landscape, dowry enthusiasts overlook the darker side of the ritual. A man may pawn his life away in trying to marry off his daughter. If he has more than one, and he is not rich, a good half of his earnings may well be mortgaged for more than thirty years. The father of a marriageable boy will sometimes contend that sending his son through school was an expensive and exhaustive business for which he justifiably expects a return, quite forgetting that educating a girl costs money too, and not too many of those "foreign-returned" products will settle for uneducated wives in contemporary India.

The point at which the custom produces a cascade of horror stories is when commitments made before the wedding cannot be kept, or when demands continue to pile up in a never-ending stream, even after the marriage has taken place. A new bride might be so harassed by her in-laws, sometimes even by her husband, that she might decide to take her own life rather than endure further torture.

The phenomenon is largely, though not exclusively, confined to the lower-middle and peasant classes, but no less gory and horrendous for that. Recently, a judge in Delhi sentenced a mother and her son to seven years' hard labor for pouring kerosene over a seventeen-year-old newly wedded woman while she was asleep, setting fire to the bed, and letting the girl burn to death in the flames. This was not an isolated instance. In 1983, there were five hundred such cases reported to the police in the capital and its immediate surroundings alone. And thousands more occur in the rest of the country.

Sometimes girls hang themselves with their own saris; elsewhere, a murder may be made to look like self-immolation, with forged handwriting to pass off as a suicide note. Because of the immense difficulty in procuring suitable firsthand witnesses (as these incidents mostly occur within the house, where other family members are hardly likely to squeal), and because the custom of dowry is covertly condoned by society, the police often turn a blind eye. They argue, not always heartlessly, that the time and effort it takes to solve one bride-burning case is enough to tie up a whole village or small-town constabulary for weeks on end, without any guarantee of a guilty verdict at the end.

Trevor Fishlock (the London *Times* correspondent in India at the time) relates how in 1982 a case came to light in Delhi in which a businessman was discovered to have had three wives in seven years and they had all died of burns. This was the incident that provoked the *Hindustan Times* (Delhi's most widley read English-language daily) to publish a cartoon in which mom and dad are shown looking through the "Grooms Wanted" columns in a newspaper with a can of kerosene and heap of ashes by their side, while the caption announces: *"Don't be upset, son, we'll find the right girl . . . even if it means burning a few more!"*

Deaths are necessary in the dowry stakes because neither banishment (to her parents' house) nor divorce quite fits the bill. A divorced man is worth considerably less than a widower. And polygamy, apart from being an imprisonable offense, does not fetch any kind of market price at all.

Outside marriage, however, sex occupies a highly ambiguous place in contemporary urban India. It is not regarded with the healthy neutrality to which post-Freudian Western culture has tried to aspire. Indian society, from top to bottom, is currently fighting an imposition of moral and sexual mores that are alien to its fundamental nature. Except at the very top anglicized crust (less than 1 percent of the metropolitan population), there is no such thing as "dating."

Even in middle-class homes, there is no opportunity for boys and girls to mix openly. In colleges and universities, furtive dating does go on to a certain extent, but never with parental or social approval. A single woman who is known to have gone out with a man is invariably stigmatized in the marriage market—hence the stern hawkeye with which her movements and meetings are supervised by elders and parents. The only opportunity for the most modest intersexual contact occurs on celebratory occasions such as a wedding or even a funeral, but never in normal surroundings.

Foreign films are permitted to show kissing on the screen, but not much more, while indigenous productions are prohibited from showing anything other than a chaste embrace. In order to bring out the liquid curves of a woman's body, filmmakers resort to dousing their heroines with water, so that the thin silk sari clings to the flesh, thus achieving a partial effect of nudity.

Soft-core porn is available in abundance in cities like Bombay or Calcutta, where pictures are pilfered from foreign magazines and indigenous stories are stitched in to add local color. An old issue of *Playboy* or *Penthouse* might fetch as much as fifteen to twenty dollars in a middle-class milieu, while more graphic and open depictions of sex would raise the price as high as a hundred dollars.

This moribund repression of sex in any form results in violence and crime. The sudden eruptions of mob frenzy in metropolitan centers are directly connected to this complete absence of any normal sexual outlet for the unmarried man. In general, Indian women do not regard sex as a pleasure, but rather as something to be endured, much as in Victorian England. Recently, a Bombay magazine ran a series of articles based on a survey that showed that 90 percent of married women who were questioned did not know about "tongue kissing," and all of them confessed that the notion of foreplay before lovemaking was totally foreign to them. Conversely, a man in his late twenties or early thirties may enter the bridal room on his wedding night wholly virginal and totally inexperienced in sexual play.

In May 1984, Khushwant Singh, a journalist of national repute, caused a furor by announcing that "Indians have sex in their heads instead of in their groins, where it belongs." Yet you will see men openly fiddle with their genitals in public, to the intense embarrassment of Western visitors; the Indian will be wholly oblivious to the fact that the masturbatory movements he is making with his hand in his trouser pocket or through the long shirt over his *dhoti* is causing the lady from the Occident to blush.

I recollect one recent New Year's Eve in Calcutta, in the land of the *Kama Sutra,* when I was dancing with an American friend in a fairly exclusive club, where the room was dimly lit and the music was a slow, soft number. Suddenly, the entire proceedings were abruptly called to a halt by the disc jockey, who announced on the microphone: "No *snuggly* allowed on the dance floor. Will the gentleman please detach himself from the lady."

I had been holding my friend no closer than you would an acquaintance at a party in New York, and we were certainly not writhing in delirious ecstasy. But I had dared to kiss her on the cheeks in public, while dancing alongside more than a hundred other couples on the floor. What was even more galling to the onlookers was the fact that my friend was white-skinned and foreign, and ravishingly attractive to boot. A subconscious equation was instantly made between the lascivious mores of the Occident and the kind of behavior in which men indulge with harlots—certainly not permissible within the respectable environs of an exclusive club in Calcutta!

So how do men, and women for that matter, manage? Of course, prostitution exists, but only for the lucky few—those at the very bottom and at the very top of the socioeconomic ladder. A cheap whore in the most unsanitary brothel may cost as little as $2, while a call girl with an English-speaking mien may sting you for as much as $150. There is nothing in between.

Since the salary of an average middle-class man in his mid-twenties is about one hundred dollars a month, he cannot afford, even if he wished to, the luxury of those manicured ladies who are available to well-heeled foreign gentlemen in the five-star hotels of Bombay, Delhi, or Calcutta. His background will revolt against going into a sleazy house where some twenty women are locked up in little rooms, where the pimp is a betel-nut-chewing, potbellied, slimy specimen of humanity, and where he is likely to be blackmailed for the price of a pair of rayon trousers.

I do not know what people do for sex, if anything. But there is an ingenious theory (to which I personally do not subscribe) that asserts that because Indians do not eat beef or any other kind of meat with any regularity, their sex urge is minimal. They do not require the same degree or frequency of gratification as Westerners seem to expect as a matter of course. But it begs rather than answers the question.

What has always intrigued me is the phenomenon of domestic servants in every middle-class Indian home. These are males who come from the villages into the big towns and cities, work for pitiful wages (about $2 to $7 a week, seven days a week, twelve hours a day, with food and lodging paid for, and nothing else), and return home once a year on unpaid leave for a month. For the rest of the time, they sleep three or four to a room or on staircase landings in modern apartment buildings, and have absolutely no means of indulging in sexual activity within normal circumstances.

Naturally, they resort to the brothels, and often catch infectious diseases, which remain untreated for extended periods. And these are frequently transmitted to the children of the households in which these menials work.

The other side of the coin is the recruiting program of the brothel owners, who seek information about maidservants in the house where a male client may be working, and using suitable inducements, are sometimes able to persuade such a servant to leave and join the agency, where she might earn as much in a day as she did slaving away for a month as a domestic.

* * *

But prostitution also has another and more startling face. There is an area in Delhi, in the old part of town, called the G. B. Road, where certain ancient traditions are still maintained, admittedly in threadbare conditions. The Great Moguls were famous for their patronage of talented "courtesans," and even today on G. B. Road you will find women with silver anklets and cheap jewelry dancing to the tune of classical *ghazals* and singing the night away. This they do in front of grotesquely fat businessmen, who rest their bulbous behinds on matted floors and toss rupee coins onto the middle of the tiny dancing ring, crying "Toba! Toba!" (Marvelous! Marvelous!) in pathetic imitation of the grandeur and glory of days long gone by.

The tout outside will fix you up with any dame you want; with his commission and the price of the room, it may come to as little as ten dollars for a night. The room itself will be about eight square feet, and there will be one bamboo bed with greasy unwashed sheets; you will have to climb dark, two-foot-wide stone stairs, smell urine from the lavatories on each landing, and finally find yourself with a woman who has been drinking raw local spirit in an attempt to envelop herself in painless oblivion.

If you tell her, as I once did, that you have merely come to talk, that you really don't want to "do the business," she will look at you as if you were some absurd malefactor from another planet, and call her pimp to boot you out.

In Calcutta, it will be another story in Sonargachi, a place where the ripe old tradition of men never spending the night with their wives is still decrepitly maintained. The landed gentry in the city would always keep a dozen or so concubines in this area some hundred years ago, in whose company they would retire after having consumed dinner in their palatial establishments—it was thought to be the mark of a sissy if you stayed home and slept with your wife at night, other than for the purposes of procreation, which was strictly an annual affair. Today, Sonargachi is a pale and hideous ghost of its former glittering self, where women lean out of windows and solicit custom for the price of a Pepsi.

Then there are the "Cages" in Bombay, where ladies with raging voices and grasping hands scream for fare in market competition. There is never a hint of sorrow in their words, only the sad, unspeakable hysteria of desperation, a mere attempt to survive.

Prostitution in urban India is not peripheral to the business of middle-class living, as it is in the West. It is at the still center of the turning world, an exact representational model of the cultural and moral perversions and hypocrisies that permeate the whole of society. You will not find many Indians discussing the subject, and some will tell you that it is the fevered product of sensation-seeking escritorial minds. But if you insist on taking them on a round of these lubricious spots in any city, as I have done, they will refuse to accompany you on the specious grounds that these areas are not "respectable," that although they have no personal objections themselves to the idea of empirical observation, they do still have to think of family and friends. It is a circular battle from which there is no escape. If you want to find out more about these places, or genuinely feel that perhaps your own eyes might have misled you, there is no way you are likely to be assisted by local knowledge.

These dark dives remind me of the original ghettos of Venice, with their low doors leading to black cavernous rooms, the stench of stale love, the acrid smell of urine and night soil on stiff, injured sheets that have witnessed recurrent coital joustings.

Extending this malign curve to a point of grotesque horror, here we have Captain Colaabavala, an investigative journalist, telling us in his booklet, *Sex Slaves of India* (1981), how abducted children might fare in the hands of the syndicate:

> Every person has his own way of beginning the morning. Some with eggs and toast. Some with tea and *roti* [flat unleavened bread], and some . . . rich Indians prefer a virgin.

He goes on to make the point that this is a fairly widespread practice, that children are systematically kidnapped from poor backgrounds to satisfy the cravings of wealthy patrons in the cities of India. I do not know if Captain Colaabavala is sensationalizing or if he is telling the truth. What I do know is that in 1983, some eleven thousand cases of abduction were officially reported in the whole country (the real figure must be twice as high), of which only thirty-three children were recovered. The others remain "an open file." It is also true that villagers often sell their children to touts from cities for a comfortable price, which enables them to buy seed corn for the coming season.

Again, it is a universally accepted belief that having intercourse with a virgin is a cure for syphilis and other sexual ailments. There is yet another superstition that lays down that impotence may be cured by rubbing a flaccid penis over a dry vagina just before sunrise, provided the child is under ten and soundly asleep.

On my last visit to India in 1984, I was invited to a lavish party in Bombay where most of the celebrities in town were due to make an appearance. Champagne and whiskey flowed, and I wheedled my way into the company of the woman editor of the glossy magazine that was hosting the party.

She was in her early thirties, slim (unlike many another Indian woman), articulate, and thoroughly Westernized, at least on first glance. She wore a sari, which clung silkenly to her lithe figure and made her look deliciously desirable to any male with an eye for such fare. Over dinner with me the next day, she indulged in the luxury of confiding to a stranger—a bird of passage myself, I was not part of the Bombay gossip circuit, and so posed no threat to her social life.

Once upon a time she had worked as a model, she had been abroad, had been married for seven years, and had a child of four from her ex-husband. Now she was the editor of this magazine, which was the talk of the town, if not of the whole country.

Ever since her marriage, which had been arranged by her parents, she had known that she would have to do *something*. But she had not figured out what that something would be.

Three years previously she had met a European (in India) who had opened up the *real* universe for this woman. Before that, even after four years of marriage (during which she had been entirely faithful), she did not know that kissing in each other's mouths was a normal method of foreplay before copulation. She had heard and read about orgasm but had never personally known what it was. Similarly, fellatio and cunnilingus were words in books, about which she would talk knowledgeably at cocktail parties without the faintest idea that they might occur in one's personal life. One child, and four years after her monogamous and faithful marriage, she discovered a different world.

This woman, like many others, had assumed that, much as one

discusses "the time machine," these phenomena existed in a plasma of unreality, an imagined universe into which one had no right of real access. They were not meant for "touching."

When I asked whether it was entirely honest of her to publish a magazine that purported to be "with it" and "give you all the gen," and yet be so ignorant about the basics, the woman answered: "I am like a hundred thousand women in India. We pretend to know, yet we don't. That's what makes me successful. I touch a chord!"

We then come to the last and final act in the human drama—death and its attendant rituals. Unlike the Chinese, Indians do not, in general, regard death as an occasion for celebration, although there is the inevitable *puja,* and a feast to go with it. Death is not treated as a finality, either.

Hindus believe that death is one of many ceaseless stops in the journey of the human soul from birth to a final merging with the Brahman, the timeless universal being, after which the travails of earthly life come to an end. This does not happen as a matter of course, but has to be paid for by virtuous acts and holy rites during each mortal span. The converse, for those who have sinned riotously, is to be born in an inferior state in the next life—a Brahmin, the highest caste, may be born again as an untouchable; someone lower down who has violated religious precepts might come back to earth as an animal (there are gradations among these, too!), and so on.

The other religious communities, such as the Muslims and Christians, do not subscribe to these notions, in theory. But once again, such is the absorptive power of Hinduism that you will frequently find an Indian Muslim using words and concepts such as *"Karma"* and "reincarnation" without any conscious awareness of having crossed a sectarian and religious divide.

Generally, a person whose death is imminent will be taken out of the house and laid out on a bamboo bed with coir matting under the open sky, thus allowing the soul a freer access to the heavenly spheres. At the very instant of death, when the life force has departed from the mortal body, there will be a tremendous crescendo of sound, usually made by women, which will announce that the final curtain has just come down.

In the case of a woman whose husband is still alive, the body will be washed in holy water and purified in religious rites ministered by a priest, and then vermilion powder will be sprinkled liberally on the center parting on her head, her feet will be painted crimson, and a glowing red dot will be placed in the middle of her forehead. All this indicates that she is a lucky woman to have escaped widowhood. Men are similarly washed and cleansed, but there are no paintings or decorative rituals that attend male demise. Nor are widows given such gaudy treatment.

Because of the heat, bodies are cremated almost instantly after death. A slow procession issues from the house, and heads for the crematorium, which is on the banks of a river—in Calcutta it is the Hooghly, a tributary of the Holy Ganges. The bamboo bed will be carried by some six to eight pallbearers, who are usually sons, cousins, and close relations, all the way to the burning *ghat* (riverbank), sometimes a distance of several miles. All the carriers will be unshod, they will be wearing special clothes that have been sanctified by the priest and will be thrown away after the ceremony.

During the procession, a man will shout, *"Bala Hari!"* (declare the name of Hari—an incarnation of Vishnu), and the rest of the pallbearers will reply in full-throated gusto, *"Hari Bol!"* This will continue throughout the journey, announcing to passersby that a death has taken place.

On arriving at the crematorium, further rites will be performed, a great hole dug in the ground, the body washed in the nearby holy river, and placed in that hole. Over it, a huge mound of wood will be piled. The quality and quantity of the wood will be selected according to the status of the deceased. Mahatma Gandhi was cremated in three-hundred weight (avoirdupois) of sandalwood. Poorer folk have to make do with cheaper varieties, in vastly smaller quantities.

Over this mound, gallons of *ghee* (clarified butter) will be poured, and the fire will be lighted, usually by the eldest son, exactly at the mouth of the dead body. The cremation will be supervised by a group of men called the *chandals,* who belong to the lowest strata of society, where even their shadows are held to be inauspicious. They will stir the charred remains with long iron rods, remove burned-out ash, and pile on fresh wood, and finally smash the skull and other recalcitrant bits of the skeleton to facilitate the burning process.

These *chandals* live in the immediate vicinity of the burning *ghat*, are ostracized by society even today, and do not have any access to the rest of the human world. In general, they cannot and do not marry outside their pariah community, and their status is lower even than the lean and hungry cows who loiter on the city streets, scavenging for food. Like the lepers in the Bible, once upon a time the *chandals* used to have to shout and ring bells to announce their arrival in a village, so that the rest of healthy society could move out of their way, and so remain uncontaminated.

Because of constant exposure to such intense heat, their skins are usually a shiny black. As they never wear shoes or any other kind of apparel, except a scant loincloth tied round their waists, they look like weird spectral figures, glistening with sweat and weaving about in the dark against the backdrop of a raging conflagration.

The body might take as long as six hours to burn. At the end, the ashes and little knots of kidney and liver will be scooped out from the ground and consecrated into the holy river.

The pallbearers will watch the whole proceedings to the bitter end and then return home, chanting those holy words, *Bala Hari, Hari Bol,* all the way back.

For a week, the entire household will be under *ashauj* (unclean, inauspicious). The sons and immediate younger male relatives of the deceased will not shave or pare their nails. They will eat only one unsalted meal a day, wear only a single *dhoti* without underpants or vests, and sleep on the bare floor.

At the end of that week, all these penitents will troop off to the holy river, have a barber shave off all the hair on their heads as well as everything on their chests and backs down to the navel. They will then dunk themselves three times under the chocolate-colored water to wash away their sins, and wend their way back home, for the great *sraddha* (consecration) ceremony.

A massive *puja* will be organized, at which Brahmins will be fed, gifts distributed to the priest, holy *mantras* chanted all day long, and a feast held for friends, relatives, well-wishers, et al. The purpose of this is to release the soul of the dead person from the bondage of earthly tribulation—the *puja* will be a symbolic prayer to

God to receive the dear departed into His heavenly arms.

There are several variations to this main structure of the ceremony. Many orthodox Hindus believe that if they die in Benares, the holiest of Hindu cities, they will attain instant *mokhsha* (release from the endless cycle of birth and rebirth), and so make the trek to the city on the eve of their possible demise. Yet others believe that performing the consecration ceremony in the Vishwanath temple in Benares has the same effect.

Of course, not all Hindus are cremated in this way, nor do they always go through the whole intricate procedure. But the number of people who use the electric crematorium or who do away with religious ritual is still a very small fraction of the whole community—no more than 5 percent at the most.

Muslims and Christians bury their dead according to customs that are similar to the practices in the rest of the world. The other sub-Hindu sects such as the Buddhists and Jains (sub-Hindu, because both these religions originally emanated from Hinduism, which we shall discuss in a moment) burn their dead, with minor variations on the same theme.

Only one other community in India, the Parsis, dispose of their dead in an altogether different style. The body is carried to the top of a lean, tall building, by attendants who are similarly ostracized as the *chandals,* and left on the roof for vultures to tear away the flesh and leave the skeleton to rot under the burning tropical sun. The building is called the *"Tower of Silence,"* and no non-Parsi is allowed inside the compound in which the building is located. There is also a fiercely enforced code of secrecy that forbids a believer to reveal the nature of the rituals to an outsider. This is a minority community in India, originally migrants from Persia (contemporary Iran), and they are followers of the prophet Zoroaster or Zarathustra.

Enlightened members of the Parsi community do not like talking about the strange method that their religion prescribes in dealing with the dead, but it is a custom that has lasted in India for well over two hundred years, and is likely to continue for a long time to come.

4

Desserts in the Barren Kingdom

Indian civilization is an implosion. It bursts inward. Art, architecture, music, dance, literature, and a million other things that the Westerner puts into neatly sealed, separate compartments, exist in one seamless whole in Indian culture. Religion, a subtle feeling for the transcendant, provides the all-enhancing glue that brings all these disparate departments together in a kind of vigorous, even violent, eulogy to the flaming aspirations of the human spirit, as they have never been displayed anywhere else in the world.

The fantastic frescoes in the Ajanta caves, the intricate dances of South India, the music of a "million mouths," the stupendous statues of Shiva and Buddha, the luminous love enshrined in the Taj Mahal, the sharp swordlike glory of the silver Himalayan peaks—they all sing a soft hymnful tune to the total unity of ancient Indian culture, which in contemporary visible reality is as dirty and diverse as what the commuters see daily on a Manhattan subway.

Robert Oppenheimer, in his defensive testimony to the House Un-American Activities Committee during the McCarthy era, quoted the *Gita* in support of going ahead with his personal decision to develop the atom bomb at Los Alamos: " 'Thou shalt see the radiance of a thousand suns!' That fascinated me, the sheer spectacle of such a magnificent conflagration," said Oppenheimer, losing both his case and his audience. Few in the House knew that the *Gita* is a Sanskrit text in which Krishna (one of the holy Hindu trinity) advises Arjuna (the principal combatant on the battlefield) how to overcome his qualms in the face of an evil enemy!

The Indus valley civilization, remnants of which were excavated at Mohenjo-Daro and Harappa (now in Pakistan), at the turn of the century, dates back about five thousand years. They left behind the oldest remaining relics of the human attempt to build a non-nomadic social structure. You see drainage, a central complex where the business of government was conducted, a whole host of complex housing branching out from the the central orb, and a splendid sense of town planning at a time when the British were still up in the trees.

Something happened between those ancient times and the point at which we begin to find historical records (another two thousand years). Indian civilization collapsed—how and why it did so is still a matter of hot dispute among scholars.

We shall not delve into these arcane matters, except to state that in India there was always an inner urge toward absorption, synthesis. This was and has been a principal driving force in the Indian philosophical approach. Every incursion from the outside was a challenge, and each time it was met with that ferocious capacity to take in, like seminal seeds in an enveloping womb. Foreigners came and raped, the sperm climbed up the labyrinthine canal and mated, but the progeny was Mother India's alone. A process of rejuvenation was set in motion, new blooms sprang out of the same tree, but the solid bark and the roots of that sturdy old oak remained exactly where they had been before.

Sanskrit is the oldest language known to Man, older by far than Greek or Latin. Scholars date its origin to about 2500 B.C. Since no written records exist, it is conjecture and speculation among erudite contestants.

The Vedas (from the root word *to know*) were composed by the earliest Aryans in India. *Aryan* derives from the Sanskrit word *Arya,* which means "noble," and originally it had no racial significance at all, just as *unarya* meant "ignoble," referring to nomadic tribes and forest dwellers.

Intriguingly, *swastika* is a Sanskrit word, a shorthand term for "holy benediction," although both Webster's and the *OED*, in almost identical phrases, say it is a symbol that brings good luck. There is a story, probably apocryphal, about how Adolf Hitler planned to kidnap a whole "pure Aryan" tribe from the foothills of the Himalayas so they could come and stud German women and produce a pure, blue-eyed, superior Aryan race!

Once again, no dates are available. The Vedas are a jumble of many things: hymns, prayers, rituals for sacrifice, magic, magnificent nature poetry. There is no idolatry in them, no temple for the gods. The early Vedic Aryans were so full of a zest for life that they paid little attention to the soul.

The *Rig Veda,* a whole string of invocations concluding in the Upanishads with that cryptic "That thou art!" *("Tat tam asi")* implying the paradoxical concepts of nondualism and deity, is the very oldest book that humanity possesses. It embodies the most ancient extant version of human quest in the face of death, and the ceaseless mortal search for meaning. Since it was an entirely oral tradition, no one is quite sure when they were set down in any kind of written text. But scholars are agreed from internal evidence that they vastly predate any equivalent endeavor in any other part of the world.

Orthodox Hindus believe that the Vedas are *revealed* scriptures. As an agnostic myself, I prefer to see them as aspiring probes into the mystery of human existence. In the earliest Vedas, there is not even a whisper of God. Invocations are made to a timeless universal being with no form.

As we climb down the ladder in time, we begin to get personalized representations of divinity. But that occurs rather late in the day, almost contemporaneously with the beginning of the Christian era.

When we get to the Upanishads, we are well into rationalist, empirical philosophy, about eight hundred years before Christ was born. What distinguishes Hinduism from all other religions is the singular fact that there was such a diversity of approach under one massive umbrella. There was ritual, a battle between idol worship and abstract loyalty of the kind that occurred between Aaron, with his golden calf, and Moses, with his tablets from the top of Mount Sinai. But there was abstruse metaphysical debate as well.

In the Upanishads, there are six distinctly different schools of philosophy, and any one of them might suit the modern temperament. There is no belief on earth, including atheism, that cannot be accommodated under the all-embracing canopy of Hindu doctrine. Which is why, once a Hindu, always a Hindu. There is nothing you can do or say or believe in, which will make you an unacceptable member of the fold. Entirely nonproselytizing, Indian culture is wholly hygroscopic; it absorbs everything. While nothing is rejected, you are also invited to the prospect of an omniverous swallow: like Jonah in the belly of the whale.

It might puzzle a Western audience to read about religion in a chapter on art and culture. But as I have said before, these things are intimately interrelated in India. And I have a problem here: Where do I place a religious epic like the *Mahabharata,* the most monumental record about socio-cultural-literary development that exists on this earth? It is generally thought to have been written by one man, the *rishi* (holy sage) Vyasa, but since it runs to some forty volumes at one thousand pages apiece, it is exceedingly doubtful that it was the work of one man alone. We simply do not have the records! We do know, however, that it predates Sophocles, Homer, Dante, Chaucer, and the authorized version of the Bible. I doubt very much if anyone has actually read the whole of the *Mahabharata* right through. I certainly have not. It is the most comprehensive document of human life, as it is lived on this planet, that I know. It tells the story of a fratricidal war, psychosexual intrigue, ego-combat (long before Freud!), and a myriad other things besides. The *Mahabharata* is an epic that cannot be pigeonholed into literature, history, or religion. It belongs to *culture* in the very widest sense, and because of its massive humanity, no one race can claim to own its legacy. The book belongs to the world, and it is simply an accident of history and geography that it originated in India.

Tucked way in the middle of the *Mahabharata* is a little lecture by Krishna (the incarnate version of the creator of the universe), to the general on the battlefield, Arjuna, who is exceedingly reluctant to fight his own kith and kin. This lecture, running into some seven hundred verses, is called the *Bhagavad Gita,* which is a vastly more sophisticated and philosophical version of Machiavelli's *Prince.* It advises the protagonist to think about right and wrong, to ask which is the greater evil: to allow wickedness to prevail, or to do something about staunching the flood of wrongdoing. More than this, the *Gita* is a dialectic discussion about ethical issues.

The *Ramayana* is an altogether different story. We are gently intruding into the Christian era here, getting into historical time. The theory is that this great epic was written by another *rishi*, Valmiki, an erstwhile brigand and plunderer, who then performed penance for several hundred years, during which time he was covered by an enormous anthill, emerging later as a saint.

It is an intriguing tale, if for no other reason than that it is the life history of Rama and Sita before they were actually born. We have here all the formative determinism of later Hindu belief: that the course of human existence is exactly predictable, that righteousness consists in paying due homage to your past life, that there is little you can do to alter the ordinations of fate.

The *Ramayana* is an excellent fiction, marvelous in its conception; the polarized distribution of good and evil, at appropriate points, is a fabulous representation of undying reality. Comparisons with the good guys against the bad guys come thickly to mind—especially in the contemporary configurations of the political map in England and America!

We then dive into the drama. The earliest beginnings of Hindu drama can be traced back to ancient Vedic hymns, which were both histrionic and thespian in character. Sanskrit drama, however, can be fairly precisely dated to about the third century B.C. The first significant playwright of whom we know wrote in the fourth century after Christ. His name was Kalidasa, and his play, *Shakuntala,* translated into English by Sir William Jones in 1789, created an absolute sensation in Europe at the time. One of his longer poems, "Meghdut" (The Cloud Messenger), makes Keats and Shelley look like amateurs in the art of poesy.

How does one make a transition from poetry to mathematics—other than assume that the two are one and the same thing? The simple efflorescent beauty of poetical enterprise was always so closely linked in India with the mundane calculations that involved *real* life, that in those antique days there did not appear to be a distinction.

During Napoleon's time, the French philosopher Laplace wrote,

It is India that gave us the ingenious method of expressing all numbers by ten symbols, each symbol receiving a value of position, as well as an absolute value. This was a profound and important idea, which appears so simple to us now, that we ignore its true merit. But its very simplicity, the great ease which it has leant to all our computations, puts it in the first rank of useful inventions; we shall appreciate the grandeur of this achievement when we remember that it escaped the genius of Archimedes and Apollonius, two of the greatest men produced by antiquity.

The zero, or *shunya,* in Sanskrit, was used in about 200 B.C. Here is Professor Lancelot Hogben, in his *Mathematics for the Million,* talking about the zero: "The importance of the creation of the zero can never be exaggerated. This giving to airy nothing, not merely a local habitation and a name, a picture, a symbol, but helpful power, is the characteristic of the Hindu race from whence it sprang. It is like coining the *Nirvana* into dynamos. No single mathematical concept has been more potent for the general on-go of intelligence and power."

The same professor goes on to ask, "Is it not equally strange that algebra, that cornerstone of modern mathematics, also originated in India, at about the same time that positional numeration did?"

Is there a connection between mathematics and poetry? I do not know. But in India there appears to have been an umbilical tie between the two apparently disparate disciplines. In the West, too, we can observe interconnecting threads. Lewis Carroll, of *Alice's Adventures in Wonderland,* was a profound mathematician, and Einstein was no mean player on the violin.

We cannot leave mathematics in India without mentioning Srinivasa Ramanujan, who had no formal education, but was invited to be the guest of a Cambridge (England) college, and went on to be elected a Fellow of the Royal Society. Before he came to England, he worked as a clerk in the Madras Port Trust. He died at the age of thirty-three from tuberculosis, and Sir Julian Huxley said at his funeral that "he was the greatest mathematician this century has produced," an opinion with which Einstein concurred. Ra-

manujan revolutionized the philosophy of mathematics. And today, computer science and digital research owe a great deal to his
original insights.

It is difficult in the West to make the transition from numbers
to poetry. But India functions in other ways. The Oriental name
most widely known in the Occidental hemisphere used to be that
of Rabindranath Tagore. Not many people read him nowadays,
largely because pop culture and authentic expressions of the human psyche are always at a wide divergence.

Tagore's poetry stinks—in translation!

Beautiful is thy wristlet, decked with stars and cun-
ningly wrought in myriad-coloured jewels. But more beautiful to me thy sword, with its curve of lightening, like the
out-spread wings of the divine bird of Vishnu, perfectly
poised in the angry light of the sunset.

Rendered into English by the guru himself, this is from *Gitanjali,* the volume of poems that won him the Nobel Prize in literature in 1913. In the original the metaphors are not mixed, the
rhythms are gripping, and the tone elegaic and haunting. Even allowing for the inevitable loss of music in a prose translation of
rhymed verse, the creaky archaisms are unnecessary graftings: They
are absent in the original Bengali poem.

The English reader has not yet been presented with any of Tagore's works that offer even a glimpse of his literary stature. For
this the poet himself is largely responsible. At the turn of the century, Tagore was the first Indian to make a significant impact on
the Western world. He did this by building up an image of "sage
and seer" (white beard and long flowing robes included), with that
didactic rhetoric that fitted in well with the times. His PR network
was extensive and efficient. He traveled widely, met Freud, Einstein, and Shaw, and corresponded with Tolstoy at great length.
W. B. Yeats fell for his "'mysticism," and inducted him into the
Nobelity.

From then on, Tagore poured out volumes of translations, always with a view to enchancing that pontifical stance: The small
but highly influential Western literary audience endured his lon-

gueurs, his piety, the tortuous language, all in the name of "harking to the voice of wisdom from the East." Three quarters of a century later, the very success of that early campaign has boomeranged into a benign indifference: Tagore is now embalmed in his own image.

The pity is that the image is so wholly incongruent with the real man. In personal life, far from being a pontiff, he was an outrageous renegade who often slipped out from his palace home in Calcutta and caroused with the low. In England, when he was sixteen, the daughter of his governess "devoured" him; he wrote a play (made into the film *Charulata* by Satyajit Ray) in which he more than hints at illicit sexual connections with his sister-in-law, who later killed herself. His first volume of love poems, which he pseudonymously signed "SunGod" (*Bhanusingha*—a clever pun on his own name—Rabi [the first half of his name Rabindranath]— meaning Sun; Tagore meaning God), provoked cries of "obscene" from literary pundits in Bengal at the time. Only after his acclamation in the West, when he was well into middle age, did he gain widespread recognition in his hometown. And it was then that the new image, which Bengalis so sanctimoniously revere, began to be fostered.

In the literary and artistic spheres, the disparity between the Bengali and English Tagores is even more startling. Far from being lumbering and archaic, Tagore's Bengali is fresh and modern. He was the first to use spoken Bengali in prose and poetry. He *created* a language and an idiom, wrote thousands of songs and poems, hundreds of short stories, and a good many novels. He scripted, choreographed, and composed music for dance dramas, wrote philosophical essays, established the first ever progressive coeducational college in India; his paintings hang in the Louvre!

Of course, there are immense difficulties in translating Tagore. The obvious hurdle is the absence of a shared mythology. *Maya* is *not illusion,* Vishnu is not merely *creator, mon* is not *consciousness.* Each of these words reverberates in a way that is incommunicable in English. This hurdle is surmountable only in exact transliteration, with pedantic footnotes; or alternately, by knowing both the cultures so intimately that the translator is able to ferret out an exact analogous transcription in the other language.

Then there is the texture and euphony in the two languages.

Bengali is soft and sensuous and lends itself easily to incantative diction; there are certain words and phrases that simply will not go into English. This problem becomes especially acute with Tagore's devotional songs and love poems. A line that sounds gooey in English could well have started life as vibrant and spontaneous in Bengali.

In some obscure way, Tagore lives. Perhaps he awaits a translator to show the world the vigor of Indian culture.

Other figures in the literary firmament include Bankimchandra Chatterjee, the first true Indian novelist, who wrote in Bengali and died in 1894. Then there was Sarat Chandra Chatterjee (no relation) who introduced risqué subject matter into his novels and broke away from the Victorian constraints that so shackled the Indian elite. Prem Chand is another considerable figure, who wrote both in Hindi and Urdu, and some of his works are available in English translation.

Although two other writers belong to the new nations of Pakistan and Bangladesh, they were writing at a time when India was undivided. Mahomed Iqbal is generally regarded as the father of Pakistani literature, and wrote in Urdu. Kaji Najrul Islam wrote in Bengali, and is considered the patron poet of Bangladesh.

The three Indian languages that have any kind of rich literature worth international comparison are Bengali, Marathi, and Tamil. The national language, Hindi, has hardly produced anything that deserves serious consideration, although many Indians will dispute this vehemently.

Internationally, a few writers have achieved world attention by writing in English. Among them, R. K. Narayan must get special mention, with his large string of books based in a fictional Malgudi, modeled after the village in South India in which he was born and has spent all his life. As he was once nominated for the Nobel Prize and has been compared to Chekov, it is fair to say that he commands an esoteric audience among literary cognoscenti in England and America, but I personally find his work miniaturist and facile, like the stories of Somerset Maugham.

Dom Moraes is a poet with a unique lyrical voice, and who writes only in English. He was the first young man to win the prestigious Hawthornden Prize, while he was still at Oxford, fourteen years after W. H. Auden got it (there were no intervening winners). Moraes now lives in India, and his journalistic work has appeared in such places as *The New York Times* and *The Observer* (London).

The only writer with the unmistakable stamp of genius, who burst into international prominence with *Midnight's Children* (1981), is Salman Rushdie. His novel is an intriguing panoramic survey of Indian history over the past eighty-odd years. What raises it to the level of a masterpiece is the incredible energy and versatility of his style, which derives as much from Laurence Sterne and Günter Grass, as his mammoth imagination finds its locale in Bombay, Pakistan, Bangladesh, and New Delhi. Rushdie was born in Bombay, and now lives in London with his English wife and small son.

No contemporary Indian painter has made as much of an international impact as Salman Rushdie has in the field of literature. In the first half of this century, however, two Indian artists (both now dead) did create a mild flutter among art lovers across the world. The first was Jamini Roy, a painter from Bengal whose line drawings, water colors, and figurative oils are exquisite, at least to my eye. The second was Amrita Shergil from the Punjab in North India, a woman who embodied fantasy in her physical presence, with whom Malcolm Muggeridge had a torrid affair, and whose paintings have a haunting melancholy as deep and ambivalent as the smile on the face of the *Mona Lisa*.

Drawing in closer to modern times, among those who are still alive there is M. F. Hussain, who started life as a street painter on the walls of tall buildings, and whose magnificent gray beard and shoulder-length shock of silver hair make him look like the archetypal guru that he is not.

His paintings sell for fabulous prices in India, as well as in Germany, Japan, and Sweden. He is certainly the most well-known artist from India at the moment. During the Emergency he painted gigantic portraits of Mrs. Gandhi, projecting her as the goddess Durga incarnate. There were those who wickedly whispered about Hussain's sudden conversion to eclecticism. As a Muslim, he was theoretically supposed to oppose idolatry in any form.

Not particularly articulate, Mr. Hussain has an endearingly personal style of approach. When I met him in a five-star hotel in

New Delhi, he hugged me close, and declaimed, as much to his entourage as to me, "You are a beautiful person! How beautiful you are! We should all try to be beautiful!" Hussain was pushing seventy at the time, I was an aggressive thirty-nine.

Then there is Raza, who lives in Paris with his lovely French wife, and whose paintings I cannot describe because when I visited his studio, they dazzled me as much for their variety as their superb craftsmanship. They are large, in oil, both figurative and abstract, and a couple of them hang in the Museum of Modern Art in New York.

Francis Souza is a Goan who first made a small international name while he was painting as a neighbor of mine in Hampstead, England. He now lives in Manhattan, and at sixty is somewhat forgotten, but his original works have a vigor and violence about them which, I suspect, will earn him a footnote, at least, in the annals of art. His oils, the old ones, are intensely and superbly Indian.

But no, India has not produced a Pollock, or a de Kooning, or a Bacon in the past fifty years. Connoisseurs might have heard of a few others whom I have not mentioned, but their works are imitative, there is nothing uniquely *Indian* about them, and their competence does not raise them to the level of serious discussion in international terms.

Swinging back, however, to a couple of hundred years before Christ, the only ancient *paintings* that remain are the frescoes in the Ajanta caves in central India. We shall talk about the fabulous sculptures in these caves in a moment, but the murals on the walls and on the ceilings are of a kind that cannot compare with anything else in the world, including the Sistine chapel in Rome.

All these paintings were done on lime plaster, and the colors were made from local herbal dyes. Two particular ingredients were not available in India, lapis lazuli and another variety, which came from Persia and Africa respectively. In the frescoes, we look at court scenes, intricate hairdos, carriages, and female adornments, among other things. This indicates that there must have been interaction with Greece and Egypt at the time (200 B.C.).

There is a flamboyant radiance in the men and women whose faces are immortalized in these frescoes. It is significant, too, that they show such an intimate knowledge of animal physiognomy.

There is one particular painting, halfway up the wall in cave number ten, on which one elephant's head sits in the middle of four other elephants' bodies.

Whichever way you stare at it, it looks as if the head belongs to the same body you are gazing at. It is difficult to describe. If you can imagine the *Mona Lisa* at the center, with four different women's bodies sprouting out from her face toward the four corners of a rectangle, and while looking at each one, you find that the face belongs to every one of the women separately and individually, then that is the effect you get from this particular painting in Ajanta.

It is *not* advisable to believe the guides who tell you incredible tales about how one such painting was done at this precise moment when Queen such and such was having a bath, and another when the king was angry with his courtiers and so ordered them to fight with fury. If you ask these very chatty, apparently erudite guides where they got their facts from, they will tell you without a quiver in their voices, "We Indians know these things." The reason they are still worth the three dollars or so they might charge you is that you are not likely to hear such fantastic stories ever again in your life.

Jawaharlal Nehru had this to say about these ancient murals, in his book *The Discovery of India* (1946):

> Ajanta takes one back into some distant dream-like and yet very real world. These frescoes were painted by Buddhist monks. Keep away from women, do not even look at them, for they are dangerous, had said their Master long ago. And yet we have here women in plenty, beautiful women, princesses, singers, dancers, seated and standing, beautifying themselves, or in procession. The women of Ajanta have become famous. How well those painter-monks must have known the world and the moving drama of life, how lovingly they must have painted it, just as they have painted the Bodhisattva [the serene visage of the Buddha] in his calm and other-worldly majesty.

If these paintings were done by monks in the second century B.C., life outside must have been lived like this for some considerable time before. Since they are the oldest pictorial representations in India, we might legitimately speculate about the longevity of civilized culture in the country.

After these majestic works in the brush, no further two-dimensional artistic representations of reality exist in India for roughly another seventeen hundred years. We have great monuments built by the Moguls (more about them later), but absolutely no heritage of painting. Caution here(!), since some minor artwork does survive. But, in general, no comprehensive survey of an era or even an epoch is visible today. One European critic's bewildered response was: "Nature's ravages and Man's vandalism."

Whatever the reason, we cannot conclude that a group of people who produced the Taj Mahal and built the Red Fort in Delhi did not make paintings of equal grandeur. We just do not have them anymore!

What we do still possess are beautiful miniatures of noble princes and grand ladies in oil and watercolor in the palaces of Rajasthan, which have withstood both Muslim and British onslaughts. These princely rulers managed to preserve some of the glories of the Indian legacy over the past 350 years, including magnificent oil portraits of their opponents.

Of course, there is another category of "Indian" painting that must be of interest to the transatlantic audience—the imported variety. In Bengal, where the British finally arrived, there is a magnificent portrait of a girl who has a perenially mysterious look on her face. There was also a great influx of French and Portuguese predators, who were a bit more cultured than the Anglo-Saxons, and they left behind some very impressive Catholic (Marian) murals and canvases in such places as Chandernagore, Pondicherry, and Cochin.

Portrait painting was quite the vogue in mid-nineteenth-century India. I would suspect that rich patrons traveled to Europe to have their portraits done by the "grand masters," and brought them back home with them. Or the lesser fry (the painters, I mean) were imported like slaves, bribed to live in opulent grandeur, and asked to paint a picture of the "master"—with food and local expenses paid for while their canvases went for free!

This, however, is conjecture.

But a considerable number of magnificent European oil-on-canvas portraits do exist in the old cities of India. I have seen at least two Joshua Reynoldses in lavish Calcutta households, where they did not even care to catalog their books and antique furniture.

We then come to the dance. One must first explain that Indian dance has nothing whatsoever to do with the tap dancing of Gene Kelly or the pelvic gyrations of Elvis Presley. The concept is purely balletic, in whichever school it may appear. It is entirely derived from imagery and symbolism from ancient religious mythology, like the intense but always ambiguous sexual connection between Radha and Krishna.

Although most "respectable" Indians will dispute this, Indian dance is largely the product of hand, face, and body movements, which were perfected by the *devadasis* (the maidservants of God in Hindu temples), who were in fact consecrated concubines to the high priests. There is an extensive stone-carved dance floor in Konarak, which is acknowledged to have been the platform on which these "God-maidens" performed.

There are two principal classical dance forms in India: the *Bharat Natyam,* which embraces a multitude of disciplines, and the *Kathakali,* from South India. Then there are the tribal (folk) dances such as the *Manipuri* and the *Odissi.*

The single most important feature that distinguishes Indian dance from all Western ballet is the hand movements and facial gestures of the performer. And, ultimately, the overwhelming religious infusion in the choreography. Even in comparatively "primitive," so-called secular dances, such as the *Manipuri,* you have finger tableaux that are strikingly reminiscent of statues of gods and goddesses.

A single Indian dance can last for hours. I have never witnessed the strange sideways swiveling of the neck, without moving the shoulder at all, on any Western stage. The pliant, unbroken plastic movements of the rest of the body are also unique, as far as I know.

For a Western audience, watching an Indian dance is like going to Wagner's *Ring* in Bayreuth without knowing the libretto. You might enjoy the music in parts, you might get a hint of the incestuous conflict, but at the end of those strenuous ten hours, you will be baffled and exhausted, and perhaps wish that you had stayed at home.

Smaller fry have tried without much success, but the two principal figures who have brought Indian dance to the Western world are Uday Shankar and Ram Gopal. The first died in penury not so long ago, and the second is a sad activist in one of those weird cults that originated on the West Coast of America.

Although I relish Beethoven's *Pastoral* and Bach's violin concertos, I am no music buff. And in order to understand and appreciate Indian music, you would have to be very committed indeed. The difference is quite simple, even stark. Western classical music is about harmony, while Indian music is exclusively about melody.

Bonnie Wade, from the University of California, has this to say in her book *Music in India*: "[Indian music] . . . encompasses a vast panoply of instruments, forms, performers, principles, and history in the religious, folk, tribal, 'hybrid' film, dance, and classical traditions."

Yes, but does that all-embracing definition tell us anything at all? Would Handel be excluded from such a category? Would Mozart?

I quote Ms. Wade to demonstrate how misleading scholastic verbalizing about music can be. All Indian music is unwritten, which is why it has an improvisational identity with jazz. A single note is strung out and embellished in a myriad ways. The instruments are really quite incidental; it depends who is playing what. The *tabla* (the stretched leather drum) might appear to be an accessory, but it can very easily take over from the sitar (the stringed instrument with a pumpkin bowl at the bottom, attached to a long narrow stem), just as in a jazz session the flute or the trumpet can outmaneuver the saxophone.

The *ragas* are a kind of inspirational music, each one keeping tune with the hour of the day, once again religious in origin, and in melodic resonance with time and timbre. A specific *raga* will have a particular note, a kind of signature tune, from which all variations and embellishments will follow.

Cognoscenti will recognize, at the very outset, which *raga* is being played, and then judge the performer on whether the improvisations have been up to the mark.

A proper concert of Indian classical music might start from about ten in the evening, and go on till well after dawn. There is the *aalaap*, an overture that by itself might go on for a couple of hours— a procedure in which the maestro and the listeners are getting acquainted with each other.

The player and the audience behave very much as a symbiotic entity. There is no prescribed duration for a session. Since nothing is written or prescribed, except that one given note for one *raga*, absolutely anything can happen. And it does!

Audiences sometimes applaud in a frenzy. At other times, like the last one I attended in Calcutta, over five thousand people may walk out of a huge canvas tent in hushed silence, as if they had been drugged—at 6:30 in the morning.

The oldest archaeological remains in India date back to about the third millennium before Christ. The two largest cities of Mohenjo-Daro and Harappa represent the acme of the Indus valley civilization, which must have lasted for about one thousand years. At these sites, we see houses built on a regular grid of streets, public wells and drainage, and a complex of official buildings. All surviving works of art, however, are miniature, except for five-foot-tall storage jars painted with emblematic designs.

There are also quantities of small terra-cottas, of stamp seals engraved in intaglio, and a few tiny bronzes and stone carvings. Most beautiful, perhaps, is a miniature bronze girl, with thin, sticklike limbs, who holds a bowl against her thigh. The seals must have belonged to individuals and been used to mark property and authenticate contracts; prism-shaped seals were records of such contracts. The scenes they illustrate include a large number of bulls, and there can be little doubt that there was a bull cult in the Indus valley, somewhat reminiscent of the earliest forms of the Mediterranean cult of Dionysus.

After the Indus valley, the finest examples of Indian art and architecture are to be found in the huge Buddhist *stupas* at Sanchi, built during the second and first centuries B.C. They are sacred burial monuments, not unlike the pyramids in Egypt, except that the *stupas* are semihemispherical in form, with a square enclosure at the top capped by a flagpole carrying a stone umbrella. Each *stupa* is accessible through a gate made of two stone pillars, with three ornately designed crossbars at the top.

At about the same time, the great Emperor Asoka built his famous many-pillared hall at Pataliputra (modern Patna) in eastern India. The British official who directed the excavation wrote in his report that this find was "in almost incredible state of preservation, the logs which formed it being as smooth and perfect as the day they were laid, more than two thousand years ago." He comments further on "the marvellous preservation of the ancient wood, whose edges were so perfect that the very lines of jointure were indistinguishable . . . . The whole was built with a precision and care that could not be excelled today. . . . In short, the construction was absolute perfection."

It is because of such excellence in sculpture and architecture in those antique times that an Indian has a little difficulty in being impressed with the comparatively modern buildings and monuments in Europe. History is quite literally strewn around everywhere in the country with a riotous profligacy. Even today, you will come across tombs and crumbling ruins of old forts in Delhi, wholly unattended and neglected, and at least four to five hundred years old. This kind of vivid and persistent presence of a rich and fabulous past works itself into the Indian mind in such subtle ways that the Westerner may be startled by an unexpected assertion or an apparently conceited outburst from his Indian host.

The architectural and sculptural history of India falls into three distinct periods. Of the primeval, Aryan, pre-Buddhist past, nothing remains except the two cities of the Indus valley. Then, from about the third century B.C. to the ninth century A.D., there is a profuse scattering of Buddhist sculpture and architecture, much of it in an excellent state of preservation. There follows a comparative lull, when a few Hindu and Jain artists were at work. After the Muslim incursion in about the fourteenth century, there follows the magnificent flowering of Mogul art and architecture, with the gorgeous and monumental Taj Mahal (seventeenth century) as its apotheosis.

There is a fourth period, too, in the form of British architecture, whose finest monument is the city of New Delhi itself, created by Sir Edwin Lutyens at the turn of the century. It is arguably the most beautifully designed and grandly conceived capital in the world. Radially set out, with fountains in the middle of every roundabout, the wide avenues branch out from the central hubs. The Presidential Palace (where the British viceroys used to live) is built out of red sandstone and is the most majestic building of its kind I have seen anywhere in the world, including Buckingham Palace and the Palais de l'Elysée.

To go back a little, however, there were Hindu contributions to art and sculpture, too, in the temples scattered all over the country—Benares, Bhubaneswar, and a whole host of them near Madras in South India. The most well known sculptural representation of Hindu art is the *Shiva Nataraga* (the Dance of Shiva) figure, about which Jacob Epstein wrote in his book *Let There Be Sculpture:*

> Shiva dances, creating the world and destroying it, his large rhythms conjure up vast aeons of time, and his movements have a relentless magical power of incantation. . . . [This figure] is the most tragic summing up of the death in love motive ever seen, and it epitomises, as no other work, the fatal element in human passion. Our European allegories are banal and pointless by comparison with these profound works, devoid of the trappings of symbolism, concentrating on the essential, the essentially plastic.

But the most monumental and breathtaking examples of art and sculpture are in the cave temples in central and western India. There are altogether some nine hundred of these rock shrines scattered across the country, the most famous of them all located at Ajanta, Ellora (central India), and Elephanta (off Bombay on the west coast).

The Ajanta caves are purely Buddhist in inception. There are twenty-nine of them in various states of preservation, and they were dug out of solid hillside rocks between the second century B.C. and the sixth century A.D. The craftsmanship is both intricate and stupendous. There is one gigantic statue of the Buddha that looks as if the face is smiling when seen from the left, in serene repose from the center, and contemplative from the right.

In a couple of caves, on the concave ceilings the stone rafters are such an exact imitation of wood that they look startlingly real, and almost feel as if they were supporting the massive structure, although in fact they serve no engineering purpose and are purely decorative. From this we may conclude that a vibrant contemporary civilization, reflected both in the frescoes and in the stone carvings, must have existed outside, though we have no record of it today.

These caves were carved from top to bottom and front to back, unlike modern methods of construction, which employ the reverse process.

The Ellora caves are younger, having been built between the sixth and ninth centuries A.D. The most impressive one in this complex is the *Kailasa* temple, excavated from one single granite rock, thus making it the biggest monolithic building in the world. It is a two-story structure, and from inscriptions we know that it took 150 years to construct. The temple is designed as a chariot being pulled by horses. It is 100 feet high, 175 feet long, and 115 feet wide. Remaining patches of color here and there indicate that the whole building must have been intricately painted once upon a time, though practically nothing survives. Stories from the epics are depicted in stone and there are long galleries where folktales are carved. At the center there is the massive *Shiva Linga* (phallus), and even today the temple is used as a place of active worship.

The other caves at Ellora show Buddhist and Jain influences, implying a degree of religious ecumenism among those ancient monks, although the newest ones, from the end of the last millennium, are exclusively Hindu.

It is this legacy in art, sculpture, literature, painting, music, dance, and drama that the modern Indian inherits from his past. And it is the impact of such history on the deeper layers of his subconscious that informs his responses to the complex and bewildering world of modern technology.

The difficulties in presenting Indian culture to the West were ambitiously confronted in an exhibition held in London in May 1982. At the time of writing, it has not been seen by an American audience, but it will be restaged in New York and six other principal cities in the United States during the Festival of India due in 1985–1986. I saw it in London and I wish to include my reflections here since, according to *The Sunday Times* (London), this was "probably the most comprehensive manifestation of Indian art ever assembled under one roof."

In the Image of Man was an immensely aspirational and ambitious venture. With five hundred pieces of painting, sculpture, and artifacts, the Arts Council of Great Britain and the organizers of the Festival of India attempted to convey to the British viewing public "the Indian perception of the Universe," over a period of two thousand years.

Whether this objective was achieved or indeed if it is ever achievable in any one place at any time, may be open to speculation. What was not in doubt was that the artifacts at the Hayward Gallery (in London) gave a dazzling display of a complex and a highly plastic civilization whose fundamental premises were dauntingly at odds with those of its likely spectators.

Mounted on three floors, with a learned and lavishly illustrated catalog (which was a feast in itself) and an audio guide (called "the listening post") with a crisp commentary, the exhibition should not have been missed by anyone with the slightest predilection for "culture."

It was grand in conception, pleasing in design, and informative in execution. Both the student and the scholar were able to learn from it, and even the casual visitor with any aesthetic impulse should have been intrigued.

As an Indian I was certainly awed by what I saw, heard, and read in and about the exhibition. On my second visit, however, I began to get a curious sense of alienation, which I shall attempt to define.

That the organizers were aware of a fundamental dilemma right at the outset in trying to present "the Indian perception of the Universe" was demonstrated by the fact that the exhibition was not arranged chronologically. Instead, it was divided into nine sequential sections with titles such as "The Natural World" (1), "Man in the Cosmos" (3), "Four Goals in Life" (4), the "Mythology of Vishnu" (8), and so forth.

This is not to argue that an alternative system would have been preferable, but to point out that in any hypothetical exhibition of "the British or American perception of the Universe," chronological presentation of cultural and historical evolution would be the natural and only choice.

The fact that Indian civilization does not automatically lend itself to chronological treatment is mirrored not only by its nonlinear conception of evolutionary development but by a complete lack of historicity in every aspect of its culture. Thus the notion of "progress," which is so central to post-Renaissance Occidental civilization, is alien to the Indian psyche, which conceives of Man's *Karma* as a spiral, and only capable of "release" from cyclic births and recurring cremations by the absorption into a supra-natural and all-pervading reality.

To grasp a wholly alien conception of life or the universe requires not only an effort in linguistic and cultural translation. It may demand the understanding and acceptance of totally different sets of modes and parameters. And to put five hundred pieces of painting and sculpture (however exquisite and *ostensibly* representative each individual exhibit may be) under one roof may be proclaiming an attitude and a perception that is precisely antithetic to the ethos of the culture those exhibits seek to portray.

The very idea of an *exhibition* is a totally Western and un-Indian one, not only because it smacks of twentieth-century technology, Madison Avenue, and the lecture circuit. An exhibition, any exhibition, anywhere in the world, that tries to depict the totality of Indian culture is bound to be a partial fraud, because each exhibit snatched from its natural environment becomes a "tinkling cymbal," drained of the euphony and potency of its associated myths.

This is not analogous to hacking out *The Last Judgment* from the Sistine Chapel and suspending it from the ceiling of the Met in New York, where the glint of Michelangelo's genius would still be visible. The only parallel I can think of is the circle at Stonehenge. If any one of those stones was carted away and put in a museum, it would be nothing more than a huge boulder, but where it stands today . . .

This is not to adopt a purist or pedantic stance. It is to emphasize that the attempt at rendering the ethos of Indian culture within an Occidental framework may negate essential elements of the very thing that is being projected. For example, the notion of putting a painting or a piece of sculpture within a historical context is wholly alien to Indian thinking. Facts, dates, even truth (of the legal and Western variety) are of little or no significance in the "universe" that the exhibition sought to portray.

The repeated dissolution and reaffirmation of form, the melting away of images and their relocation in a different guise, which so baffles the Western mind, in the manifold manifestation of deities, is a normal, humdrum idea for the average Indian.

Yet, paradoxically, the display of a stone phallus within a glass case (as it was in the exhibition) would be wholly incomprehensible to the same person, who would find nothing remarkable in a god assuming several forms simultaneously and commuting large distances in time and space.

These were hurdles that the exhibition did not even attempt to cross. The word *religious* is always implicitly used as a contrapuntal foil to *secular* in Western discourse. In India, a similar use of the word would be tediously tautological, since absolutely nothing is *not* "religious." Yet again, to describe the "amorous adventures" of Krishna, as both the audio guide and the catalog did, is to put a Western inflection where none exists in the original context.

The Lord Krishna is *expected* to flirt with and seduce the *gopis* (milkmaids); if he were to do anything else in their company, *that* would be unnatural. When he goes about his natural business, he is not being "amorous" in the sense that the Occidental mind envisions it, with forbidden fruits and naughty deeds. He is just being himself.

The organizers appeared to have adopted a deliberately coy attitude in the sexual sphere, as there was only one exhibit (Celestial Marriage) that showed a woman holding a man's penis. Though, admittedly, it is difficult to imagine what alternatives could be devised to show the power and pervasiveness of the *lingam* and *yoni* (the penis and the vagina) cults in India.

When I recollect scenes of numerous marriageable virgins, anointing clay phallic figures under instruction from priests during *Shiv Puja*, it is only with the hindsight of Western "perception" that I realize that the girls were being trained to handle a male phallus with proper expertise and thus qualifying themselves as desirable brides.

Yet there were no sniggers among the observers where the *pujas* were performed either at the temple or in private houses. And it is wholly unlikely that either the instructors or their pupils considered the ceremonies to be lewd or lascivious. One has only to think of the possible headlines in *The National Enquirer,* if similar rituals were conducted in a Catholic convent or a prestigious girls' school in the United States, to discern the gulf between the two societies.

There was a significant and interesting contrast between the various entries in the scholarly catalog edited by George Mitchell and the much slimmer guide written by L. A. Narain (keeper of the National Museum, New Delhi)—the same literature will be issued in America.

The catalog attempts to put Indian ideas within the intellectual frames available to Western Man, while Mr. Narain frequently slips into statements and explanations that may appear self-evident to the Indian mind but be totally perplexing to the Occidental.

As a final comment, I found four key words *(atman, maya, dharma,* and *Manas)* had been inadequately translated in the glossary at the back of the catalogue. The inaccuracy of the translations is not of the same order as the difficulty in finding an exact English equivalent of *de trop* or *poltergeist.* The problem is the lack of conceptual equivalents between the two different "perceptions" about the universe, which is inherently insoluble.

Just as a piece of music or an experiment under lysergic acid diethylamide (LSD) is never totally communicable in words in any language, the Indian "perception of the Universe" does not lend itself to historic or analytic representation. It is primarily an experience for which there is no cultural or linguistic equivalent in the Western world. When it comes to the United States, *In the Image of Man* may, however, make a valiant attempt to point the way.

5

Land of the Magic Carpet

*T*he Western traveler to India is faced with an acute dilemma at the very outset. For even though the most ill-informed tourist will have heard of the Taj Mahal, most of the other items on the agenda are likely to read like a menu in a foreign language. The erotic sculptures in the temples of Khajuraho will figure on the itinerary, but will make little sense when placed beside contemporary Indian mores that the visitor encounters almost on first landing.

The Westerner will have heard and read about the poverty and chaos of Calcutta, but neither the brochures nor the tourism ministry will urge him to visit the city. The holy city of Benares will be given a mention, but once again the pictures of temples and bathers on the banks of the Ganges will not incite the spark of enthusiasm that makes one say, "I must visit the pyramids and the Parthenon before I die!" The palaces of Rajasthan will come up for airing, but they will not seem to represent the key to the riddle of India. Temples, in both the North and the South, will be extolled at length, but they will, after a while, seem to merge into each other, leaving a vague sense of sculpture and deity and holiness in too rich an abundance. The idyllic lakes in Jammu and Kashmir will be lavishly described in the literature, but the Westerner might well feel that they sound a little too similar to those in Switzerland, England, or Canada.

The source of this dilemma lies both in India itself and in Western perceptions of the country. On the countless occasions that I have been told by an American or a Britisher, "Oh, I would love to visit India!" I have never ever received a cogent answer to my question "Why?" After the initial shot at the Taj Mahal, and perhaps even Khajuraho, the would-be tourist fumbles around in his mental baggage, trying to come up with something that resembles a specific *raison d'être* for wanting to make a journey across oceans and centuries. Yet the desire is very real, and millions of Americans and Europeans put their craving into practice every year.

The reason for this ambiguous response is embedded in the very idea of India in the Western mind. In a sense, there is no single answer to my query. Words like "magic" and "mystery" float up in conversation, but the origin of this attraction lies far deeper than in snake charmers and *sadhus*. It is a complex and composite awareness of a civilization that is at once different and enigmatic, the polar opposite of the kind of societies that exist in the West.

No other country, not even China or any other Oriental nation, evokes this kind of feeling in Occidental consciousness. Because India is both more and less accessible as a tourist venue, the Western visitor is liable to be charmed and incited by India as a symbol of that other life where beggars roam the city streets with the same proliferating impertinence as rickety cows and mangy dogs, where holy men meditate on beds of nails, and satellites are shot into space and atom bombs explode.

The symbol of India is the central source of attraction for the Western visitor. That it is incapable of precise definition and differs from person to person does not reduce its potency. Rather, by enhancing the ambiguity, it enables every individual tourist to formulate a unique India of his own, partially overlapping his preconceptions, but largely outstripping even the most fantastic ideas he may have had before he set foot in the country.

For the American, living in the opulent grandeur of a five-star hotel in Bombay or Delhi, the plaintive cry "But I want to see the *real* India!" is a desperate appeal to his host to explain the enigma of the country in a condensed form, to help him make some sense out of paradoxes and contradictions that assault him, even within days of his first encounter with "the mystic East."

Yet if the visitor is told that there is no such thing as the *real* India, that the country exists largely in the mind, that there is no solid nucleus from which everything else flows, he is likely to be disappointed or frustrated and feel that the key to some secret source is being withheld.

How can the Indian, who does not know the answer himself, explain that his country is many things, that it does not consist simply in the mountains and temples and lakes and mosques and tombs, but lies hidden in a multilayered awareness of subjugation and absorption, in the give-and-take of religion and culture, in passivity and arrogance, in the myriad different tales of gods and goddesses he has heard on his mother's lap?

Indian reality is multifaceted. Like those toy kaleidoscopes, if you turn India a notch, the same jumble of broken glass will produce a totally different picture through the prism of your consciousness. If you walk around the back streets of the big cities, smell the odor of cow dung in village huts, gaze in wonder at the Taj Mahal by moonlight, journey in fabulous comfort from Delhi to Calcutta by train, ride in a *shikara* (something like the gondolas in Venice) on the crystal clear waters of the Nagin Lake in Kashmir, by and by a picture of India will emerge in your mind's eye— unique, ravishingly seductive, and utterly different from the portrait that anyone else might have of the country. But it will be yours to keep forever.

Several key features that distinguish India from the rest of the world will assault the visitor almost instantly as he drives out of the airport. The kind of poverty he is likely to see will be incomparable with anything else that he may have witnessed or read about. Even his wildest fears and fantasies will be swamped by what lies before him with the raw vehemence of reality. If he is a little patient and allows the experience to filter through, however, he will soon notice, perhaps in horror, but more to his amazement, that though the people are poor beyond the most wretched states of degradation imaginable in the West, there is a passive serenity on those faces that does not conform to Occidental notions of what such destitution should incite.

Beggars will be near-nude and splattered with ugly sores. They will scavenge in garbage cans and pursue the Western tourist with ferocious persistence, but seldom will a rough word be uttered; there will never be any violence if the pleas for gifts and money are ultimately rejected. Even the little girl carrying a tiny skeletal infant in her arms will walk away with dignified composure once she knows that this particular quarry is not going to deliver.

In the South, where the people are as poor as in the rest of India, this inherent sense of self-respect is carried to extremes. A *cycle-rickshaw wallah* (a man pedaling a rickshaw bicycle) might be bathed in sweat in temperatures over 100°F, yet he will smile and express his thanks for the equivalent of four dollars after having cycled for more than twenty miles.

The poor in India will not make you feel guilty about their poverty. They will accept their condition as part of a larger cosmic pattern dictated by the ordinations of fate, over which neither you nor any other mortal has any control. And very soon, you will cease to feel the shock and horror that you first experienced on setting foot in the country. When you return to your Western home, and friends ask about the appalling poverty in India, you will be surprised to hear yourself say, "Oh yes, it is there all right. But there is so much else besides!"

The next hurdle for the visitor will be the incredible avalanche of humanity he will encounter at every step of his stay in the country. The "population explosion" will not be an abstract feature of his experience. If he goes to a railway station in any of the principal cities and attempts to catch a long-distance train, he should allow himself plenty of time. It will be next to impossible to move more than inches at a time, bodies will be packed shoulder to shoulder on the platform long before the train docks, the sweat and heat will add to the feeling of being in a tub of molten wax that is being poured into a molding.

Crowds will gather on street corners at the smallest sign of any kind of drama. Crossing a road will become a major enterprise in negotiating one's way through a throng of human flesh. Markets will be places where even the herding of cattle on a Texas ranch will look gentle and mild-mannered by comparison.

Of course, the visitor might well insulate himself, as many do, by religiously keeping within the schedule laid out by his tour operator, whisked from one airport to another by plane, delivered to his luxury hotel by limousine, shown the sights in one spot and driven to the next point on the itinerary in an air-conditioned coach.

If he does this, he will not miss seeing the "real" India, because what he will experience will be a species of reality, too, but he might well deprive himself of observing an aspect of the country that does not exist anywhere else in the world. Later, he might well have to ask himself, "Why did I go there in the first place?" (Other than to paste a few more photographs on his already overloaded album!) It is not a question to which I should wish to help him find an answer.

The other most startling quality about the Indian landscape is its extreme diversity, both in human and geographical terms, overlaid by the synthesizing power of its cultural heritage and civilization. If one hops from one city to another by plane, it is impossible to get a true idea of the stupendous vastness of the country, and its radically divergent terrain. In order to experience the sensation of awe, it is necessary to travel long distances by car, as I did, or take a train, get down on a platform at two in the morning, and watch a multitude, sleeping in huddled groups with bundles of household belongings under their slumbering heads, and the solitary stationkeeper, carrying a gas lamp in one hand and a green flag, to wave the train away, in the other.

Men and women talk and behave utterly differently in different parts of the country. They look different, speak different languages, dress differently, but they all react to strangers with the same unfailing courtesy everywhere. An American woman will be able to roam about anywhere in the country without fear of being mugged or molested, even in the poorest quarters of any town— something that cannot be said about most Arab or Latin European countries.

India is accessible, more than any other Oriental country in this respect, precisely because of an innate hospitality that characterizes the whole populace. Also, most people speak a smattering of English, which they do not in China or Japan. Even in remote villages, to which the average Western visitor will never go, you will always find half a dozen people—teachers, doctors, the headman— who will make themselves understood, if in the most rudimentary terms, invite you in for a cup of tea and a plate of sweets, if you happen to be a foreigner and white-skinned in the bargain.

173

The diversity is emphasized by geographical contrasts. If you go up to Darjeeling, some 6,500 feet above sea level, and watch the sunrise from Tiger Hill, you will look in awe at those glistening Himalayan peaks stretching out to infinity, capped by Mount Everest. At that precise moment, when you might allow a tiny shiver to roll down your spine, you would be hard pressed to imagine that down South at that very same instant, the thermometer was hovering around the 100°F mark, the humidity was 95 percent, and the torrential rain would soak you to the skin within a minute if you ventured out in the open.

Chaos and inefficiency will dog every footstep. The Western visitor, on his first foray into India, will be dismayed to find that if he misses an internal flight, he loses his ticket, and there is no automatic option on the next carrier. Even more unsettling might be the discovery that if he has paid for a ticket in advance, it does *not* mean that he is entitled to a seat on the aircraft. He must then seek a "reservation," which might take even longer than the original period of the two or more hours he has already spent *buying* his ticket.

The government-owned Indian Airlines are the only people who fly within India. They have some four hundred aircraft, which service more than seventy airports. Often, as I have experienced, flights are delayed or even canceled, with passengers waiting patiently for hours. Then one suddenly discovers that the man at the terminal building has to take a bicycle to the control tower to find out about the latest developments in arrival and departure times, because there is no car, and the telephones are not working.

The exasperation is born not only out of the inherent fact of inefficiency, but also because all the accouterments appear to be present at first glance. They simply do not work.

Indian Airlines does, however, have a twenty-one-day excursion fare, which enables you to travel to any number of places in India within that period, provided you proceed from one point to the next, without returning, except at the end of the journey. Since there is no option, it is worth considering for any tourist, as the savings in financial terms can be quite considerable.

Air India, the international carrier, used to have a very good reputation, when not so many Indians actually used their own airline. Today, because of cutthroat competition, Air India would

Women rowing family in canal, Kashmir

Houseboat on Nagin Lake, Srinagar

Woman in black veil on street, Srinagar

Ghat scene in Benares

Sasthi Brata

Camel pulling wagon

Beggar woman craving alms, Rajasthan

Sasthi Brata

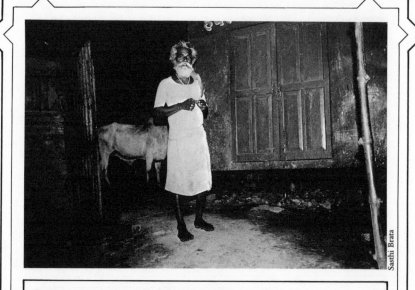

Sasthi Brata

Old man with cow

Public bathing

Sasthi Brata

Marble corridor in Mogul mausoleum, Agra

Sasthi Brata

Holy man outside temple

Sasthi Brata

Sasthi Brata

Erotic sculpture, Khajuraho

Women with firewood

Sasthi Brata

Sasthi Brata

**House where Indira Gandhi was born
and married**

Host and hostess at Sona Marg village

Sasthi Brata

Master craftsman at work on appliqué, Orissa

Silver filigree model of Lord Krishna's chariot

Courtesy Orissa State Government

Tribal girls

Beauty contest in Bhubaneswar, Orissa

Sasthi Brata

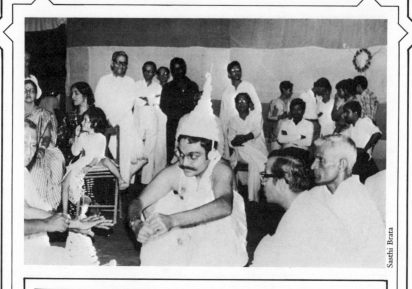

Nephew's marriage ceremony

The bride

Sasthi Brata

The Taj Mahal

Full moon on the Ganga, Benares

Sasthi Brata

Lake Palace Hotel, Udaipur

Lounge in Lake Palace Hotel, Udaipur

rather fill its planes with people who have paid bucket-shop prices, and pack the total load, than preserve some of those old traditions that once made the airline justly famous for its hospitality, comfort, and cuisine. It was Air India that coined the phrase *magic carpet,* using the mustachioed maharajah as its logo. Although the institution has been very kind to me personally, I should not mislead my readers.

Within India, train travel is the best buy. And there are special maharajah-style coaches that will provide the luxury of a lifetime for a comparative pittance. You can also buy a ticket in dollars, which will give you unlimited travel for ninety days (there is no restriction about which places you can go and come from) in first-class comfort. If it is summer, and you might need air conditioning, a little extra lucre will have to be shelled out. Once again, reservation of seats or berths is absolutely essential. Simply buying a ticket is not enough.

Hotels in India are an altogether different matter. One might have a gripe or two about a particular establishment, or wax eloquent about the virtues of another, but in general they are absolutely the best value that money can muster in the whole world.

For the price you pay for a decent meal for two in Manhattan, or for a crummy little room at a Holiday Inn in any principal city in the Western hemisphere, you will get the most fabulous suites and service in any of the four main hotel chains in India. There will be a swimming pool, twenty-four-hour room service, sauna, beauty parlors, and health clubs fitted with the best equipment open ten hours of the day, and a round-the-clock coffee shop that will be more elegant than any comparable institution in the Western world.

Service will be personalized to the point of a bowl of fruit from the manager in your room as you arrive, and an inscription of your name in gold-embossed letters on your personal stationery (provided you have booked in advance, of course). There will be no extra charge for valet service; come the time to pack, you will just have to ring for the bellboy and at least a couple of attendants will come instantly to your door. Laundry will be delivered the same day, at such ridiculously low prices that it will make you wonder about how much you could have saved in a lifetime on cleaning your shirts alone. In every corridor of a big hotel, there will be a servant on order by day or night. Your liberal conscience might object, but in a moment of accidental crisis, you will be grateful for such a facility. Sheets will be changed every day, twice in one, if you insist, again at no extra charge.

The restaurants will provide an extensive choice of cuisine, from French, Italian, and Greek, leading up to authentic Indian food. The lobbies will be so lavish that you will feel you are living in a palace. With everything else in total chaos, with beggars pestering you in the streets outside, once you enter your hotel, you will be cocooned in an altogether different world. The Telex operator will be at your service for twenty-four hours. On the phone, you will be able to call New York, Tokyo, or London at the press of a button.

In case you were worried about the price, all this would cost you, per day, in November 1984, just about eighty dollars a night, give or take a few percentage points either way. If you were part of a group, it would be less than half that figure. Not that these are the only available prices. You can book into a hotel at a quarter of these five-star tariffs, in some cases for as little as two dollars a night. But the water will not be "safe," the bathrooms will not be European-style, the bedsheets may appear less than appealing. According to your purse, and the extent of your fastidious concern for hygiene and health, you will have a choice, and a very large one at that, and the tourist bureau in any town will be happy to inform you about it.

I feel a special attraction to a few hotels in India among the hundred or so in which I have stayed. They belong, principally, to four separate groups, whose names I should mention before I go on to describe the individual establishments.

The government-owned agency, Indian Tourist Development Corporation, has the largest number of hotels in the country. It is also, comparatively, the cheapest among the five-star efforts. Then there is the Oberoi chain, which is the most expensive and also the most successful, having spread its wings far beyond the Indian shores—Jimmy Carter and the late Anwar el-Sadat of Egypt met at Meena House, Oberoi, overlooking the pyramids on the banks of the Nile.

The Taj Group, named after the famous mausoleum in Agra,

owns the most elegant hotel in the whole of Asia—the Taj in Bombay. And at the end of the queue, there is the Welcomgroup, which is gently proliferating into the hotel business, owned as it is by the India Tobacco Company.

The most famous and indeed the most exquisitely grand hotel in India is the Taj, in Bombay. It was built just after King George V arrived in India in 1905, not as king-emperor, but as the Prince of Wales, and it incorporates both majestic medieval European styles as well as Mogul minarets. The Taj is unique in its tasteful decorations. Unlike the American system, each room is individually furnished and adorned. There is a tradition in the hotel, a certain exclusivity, which discreetly forbids access to those who are merely moneyed.

The Lake Palace Hotel in Udaipur (northern India) is also managed by the Taj Group. This is the most deliciously romantic establishment in the whole of India, as it is set in the middle of a lake, and used to be the summer palace of the maharana who owned this whole kingdom once upon a time. The desert breeze blows over the artificial waters of the lake, and cools the verandahs. Each room is nearly a suite, and living in one is like swimming in fantasy about the time when some grand royal seduction took place on these very premises.

The Rambagh Palace (hotel) in Jaipur deserves a passing mention, if for no other reason than the fact that Prince Philip played polo on its grounds with the late maharajah who owned it, and his surviving widow, Gayatri Devi, once reputed to be the most beautiful woman in the world, got on very well with Jack Kennedy when he was president of the United States. It is a resplendent building, with long sweeps of green lawn, exquisite Rajasthani architecture, and beautiful interior design.

Talking of palaces, I should mention that the Maharana of Udaipur has recently opened up a part of his extensive establishment for those with taste and substance. There are no single rooms for hire, but there are suites that start at $450 a night. I have not lived in any of these luxurious establishments, but I was given a conducted tour of the premises by His Royal Highness Himself.

Each apartment, or bevy of rooms, is a delight on its own: There are a large living room, bedroom, dressing room, ladies' boudoir, and a small lounge, all furnished with those magnificent antiques that His Majesty inherited from his forefathers, over three-hundred-odd years ago. Some of the toilets are coated with twenty-four-carat gold. The common living area is furnished entirely with hand-cut Belgian glass, all the way from tabletops, legs, dressers, and all other accouterments that might have gone with royal living once upon a time.

There are not too many palace hotels in the world that offer such flamboyant luxury at so modest a price. Of course very, very few Indians ever live in these "apartments." His Majesty leaves them empty for most of the year so as not to violate the ambience for those who would know how to appreciate such grandeur.

Farther up north in Delhi, there is only one hotel that cries out to be mentioned in the roll call, if not for anything else, then simply because it is the grandest-looking hotel in the whole of India. It looks like a palace, the sweeping drive up to it is majestic, the massive building combines elements of both Hindu and Muslim architecture in its design, and it is called the Ashok, in Chanakyapuri, New Delhi. Built in red sandstone, it was constructed on an imperial command from Jawaharlal Nehru in about eighteen months. The rooms inside are elegant and individual, and it is the flagship of the Indian Tourist Development Corporation. Headed by Chairman Lieutenant General A. M. Setna, the Ashok *attempts* to set standards for the rest of the country, without always succeeding.

The Grand Hotel in Calcutta is always the grand, since it is my hometown. Compared with the others I have described on my list, it is not particularly distinguished. But it does happen to be the most expensive hotel in Asia, sitting as it does at the cultural nerve center of the Asian subcontinent.

Shifting a few hundred miles northwest, there is the Mogul Sheraton at Agra, which is worth a visit even if you don't spend the night, simply because of the spectacular chandelier in its central lobby, which is something like twenty feet in diameter and weighs one and a half tons, all in hand-cut glass made by local craftsmen. There are magnificent suites in the Mogul style, too (named after Tansen, Akbar's most famous courtier musician), designed like the reception rooms of the ancient emperors.

And finally, in the South, there is only one hotel worth attention—the Windsor Manor in Bangalore. When I think of this particular establishment, my old sneaking love for British archeticture resurrects itself, for the building is an astonishing imitation of the regency style, with suites named after famous Britons such as the Duke of Wellington, Lord Wellesley, and others.

Even the furniture is an exact replica of those far-off times; the library contains leatherbound volumes, bearing the names of authors like Macaulay and Gibbon and embossed in gold on the spine. In short, this whole magnificent building is a faithful facsimile of an English past, and to see it in the middle of puritan, Hindu India is at first a severe shock, then an enormous relief. Even the service, food, and interiors are in sync.

Since we are talking here about the tourist, I have to ask myself: "What does the visitor actually want to *see* in India?" For even as I write, in front of me there is a *condensed* list of four hundred sights that are totally exquisite, most of which I visited for the first time (though I had read of them before) while gathering material for this book. I wonder—would a Western visitor really want to go and look at *all* of them? Depends on why and how the visitor was going to India, I suppose. But basically my dilemma is insoluble.

"It is possible to learn more about India," said Mahatma Gandhi, "by talking to a real Indian woman than by reading a roomful of books!" But that aphoristic statement begs a question—who wants to *learn* about India? Perhaps one would simply like to be informed.

Chatting to a few students on a university campus might illuminate India more profoundly than a thousand lectures and a million film shows. Who knows? It is impossible to tell.

Cliché though it sounds, my personal list would start with the Taj Mahal. It is possibly the most stunning and beautiful building that was ever built on this planet. At the age of twelve, when first taken there, I remember telling my brother, "It is very cool inside here!" (The temperature outside was 105°F, and the white marble had produced a remarkable cooling effect inside.) I was wholly unimpressed, largely because I was very upset by all those hundreds of vagrants in their torn clothes who lay all over the marble floors, as if they were dead (at that time entrance was free, there was a refugee problem, and people went in there simply to sleep).

Since then I have visited the Taj at least twenty times. On each successive occasion it has brought me something that was wholly unexpected. The last time, I climbed up the narrow stone turret, just across from the Taj itself, because a deaf-mute fellow I had picked up on the road told me, in signs, that that was where I could get the best view. While we were both trying to walk up those constricted stairs, several local do-gooders warned us that there were snakes up there, real poisonous snakes. This made me even more determined. When I got up to the top of the turret, as I gazed in wonder at that white marble monument to everlasting love, I understood exactly what my mute friend was trying to tell me. Up there, snakes there were not, but a cold, deserted terrace it was. I later discovered that there was a superstition that said that anyone who went up there died within a year. As I write these words, I am still alive.

The Taj has to be looked at from different angles at different times of night and day. The view from the turret was an angular one, silhouetting the minarets against an azure sky, with the dome raping the covering canopy. Yet again, try it from the Red Fort across the river Jumna, for example. Use a pair of binoculars, if you must. Try again, looking through the keyhole, as it were, through those massive wooden gates. And try, do try, to see it by moonlight.

Shah Jehan constructed the building in the mid-seventeenth century. It took eighteen years to build, and was dedicated to the emperor's dead wife, Mumtaz Mahal, in 1648.

The inlaid stones are the work of craftsmen who did not do it for mere money. And the architectural design is of a kind that compares with nothing else in the world. The marble is incandescently magnificent.

Shah Jehan also built parts of the Red Fort in Agra, which any Western visitor will see as a matter of course. But he will not know that the same emperor began building a *black* Taj across the river for his own entombment, so he could look at his darling wife, eye to eye, for the rest of eternity.

When Aurangzeb, his son, imprisoned the old man in the Red Fort, the one request that the new emperor granted his father was to be able to see his beloved Taj. On a wall in the Fort across the river, at a singular angle, a pillar was erected and a multifaceted diamond inserted into a hole, so that it could act as a reflecting telescope for the old man's failing eyesight. That hole in the pillar is still there. The massive diamond was removed by the British. But the spectacle of the splendid Taj can still be seen today from across the river, through the latticed window of that very cell where that magnificent man was held captive by his own son, and where he finally died.

Today, there are craftsmen who claim to be descendants of the same masons and artisans who built the Taj Mahal. There is a special herbal glue, they say, whose composition is not known to anyone other than the eldest sons of those who worked at the original Taj, inlaying the precious stones that are embedded in its majestic body even now, nearly 350 years later.

Before I leave, I must pay a tiny homage to one other monument to Indian civilization—the holy city of Benares, perhaps the oldest continuously living city in the world, at an age reckoned to be a little under three thousand years.

But I shall quote. Here is what an American woman, Diana L. Eck, an associate professor at Harvard University, has to say about the place in her book *Banaras: City of Light:* "It was an awesome city—captivating, challenging and endlessly fascinating . . . [with] its complex mythological imagination, its prodigious display of divine images, its elaborate ritual traditions, and its total understanding of the relation between life and death."

This is the place where Hindus go to die. It is a city of burning and learning, where metaphor and reality interweave to form the tapestry of living history.

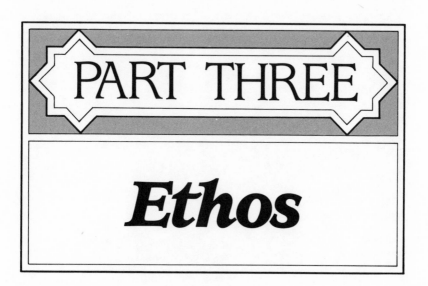

PART THREE

Ethos

Deities and Devotees

Caste Typing

6

Deities and Devotees

*E*xcept for Taoism and Confucianism, largely confined to China, there is no religion in the world, including Judaism and Christianity, which does not have a local connection with India. There are mosques and synagogues, with a sizable number of adherents from each faith, Buddhist shrines, Sikh *gurdwaras*, Jain and Parsi places of worship, Christian churches and cathedrals, and a myriad Hindu temples, all of which testify once again to the religious and cultural diversity of India.

All these religions established their roots in the country many hundreds of years ago, and none of them constitutes an esoteric cult practiced by a handful of followers. There is a Hebrew synagogue in Cochin (South India) that is nearly four hundred years old; the Bene-Israel claim to have arrived on the west coast of India before the birth of Christ.

Persecuted in Iran (in what was then Persia), the Parsis, followers of the prophet Zoroaster (or Zarathustra), sought refuge in India as long ago as the seventh century. Buddhism, Jainism, and Sikhism all originated in India, though there are fewer Buddhists in India today than there are in China, Japan, and the Southeast Asian countries. Islam came to India in about the twelfth century, and Hinduism was conceived on the Indo-Gangetic plains way back in the second millennium before Christ, and commands a following of about six hundred million people in the country today.

Just as the British coined the name "India" to denote the land-mass bounded by the Himalayas in the North and the oceans of the South, the word "Hindu" is of Greco-Persian origin, referring to the people who lived beyond the Indus River on the Asian sub-continent. At the time of the Greek incursion, since most of the population followed a particular faith, in due course "Hinduism" came to be used synonymously with the religion practiced in the land.

The most significant difference between Hinduism and any other religion is that there is no single body of doctrine that a Hindu is expected to aver. Nor is there one particular scripture to which he must pledge his allegiance. Although there are many holy texts, the nearest thing to the Bible that Hinduism possesses is the *Bhagavad Gita,* yet the paradox is that it is perfectly permissible to be a de-vout Hindu without believing a single line in the sacred book.

In a sense, Hinduism is not a *religion,* as the term is under-stood in the West. But since there is no other expression for de-scribing the massive array of ancient texts, rituals, customs, social behavior, medical, hygienic, and dietary exhortations, animal sac-rifice, dictations on ethics and morality, mystical poetry and hymns to nature, abstruse metaphysical debate, the vast pantheon of gods and goddesses, phallic and vaginal symbols, and the ugly institu-tion of caste, any writer on the subject is obliged to call it a reli-gion, and must attempt to devise analogues that might make the phenomenon comprehensible to the Western mind.

Hinduism is hygroscopic. It has, like India itself, absorbed everything, rejecting no intrusion. Ceaselessly, rape has been con-secrated. In post-Buddhist times, you will find distinctly Buddhist ideas incorporated into the Upanishads (we shall talk about these scriptures in a moment). Much later, in the nineteenth century, the Brahmo Samaj (an offshoot of Hinduism) simply swallowed the Christian method of prayer and worship and proceeded to declare itself the *true* inheritor of the Aryan Vedic traditions of Hinduism. This process of invasion and subsequent assimilation has gone on for well-nigh five thousand years. So that the enormous holdall that is called Hinduism, both by foreigners and by indigenous believers, is in many ways riddled with enormous contradictions.

But in spite of these many conflicting and contradictory ingestions, Hinduism managed to remain a unified whole. The secret of the *religion,* if you can call it that, is that it tells you to take what you want out of it, and not bother about the rest.

Hinduism does not dictate. It is the only nonprosyletizing religion in the world. It not only does not seek to convert, it advises members of other faiths to hold fast to their own creeds, because as the *Gita* says, "In true belief, there is salvation." No one can *become* a Hindu, even if he or she wanted to. The Hare Krishna followers in London and New York camouflage this by shaving their heads, wearing saffron robes, and beating drums. They can be, and indeed are, the devotees of the Lord Krishna, but Hindu they are not, and never can be.

Conversely, a Hindu can lose his caste, and all manner of evil things can befall him, but cease to be a Hindu he cannot, because any belief he embraces will be encompassed in one or other tenets his own religion offers him. Christ will be a reincarnation of Krishna, Buddha will reappear as Vishnu, and Mohammed the prophet will be an *avatar,* an incarnation several generations down. Nothing will be rejected. The tentacles of Hinduism are so elastic and infinite that there is no belief you can profess that will make you an infidel.

This is where *sadhus* and gurus come in. The exportable variety of Hinduism, represented by Maharishi Mahesh Yogi (of Mia Farrow and Beatles fame in the sixties) and a score of others, are resented by most Indians who have even the tiniest knowledge of Hinduism in all its multifaceted eclecticism. They fiercely argue that these quacks and charlatans go to the West, prey on a gullible public (immersed in psychosis of one sort or another), extract gallons of liquid lucre, and then manage to drive around in Rolls-Royces and live in châteaux in France.

Educated Indians contend that these fraudulent gurus do a lot of damage to the concept of Hinduism, behaving as if it were a free-for-all. Anyone can do what they want, vent and release their frustrations, punch a man in the face, have one or many cathartic copulatory sessions, and be all the holier for that, because Hinduism allows everything.

I understand the chauvinistic and aggressive contempt that Indian intellectuals and journalists feel about this phenomenon, which is thankfully on the wane. And I must confess I experience a certain uneasy sensation when open quackery is sold in the Western marketplace as genuine Eastern wisdom.

But there *are* points to be made here, on both sides of the fence. These men, the Indian gurus, *do* have something that most people do not have. The awesome fact is that even a novitiate in Yoga acquires powers that transcend the comprehension of the average Western man in the street. Practicing Yoga (of whatever variety—we shall get to that in a while) certainly increases your concentration, enables you to do in one hour what you used to do in four, hugely vitalizes your sexual appetite and prowess, and makes you remember things that others have long forgotten.

But these are the initial stages of Yogic exercises, and the *rishis* were very insistent in telling us not to be ensnared at this level, because at a superficial glance, you will have acquired enormous powers. But the goal is higher!

My speculation is this. The exported variety of gurus reached this particular stage of Yogic development. And since it made them so much more powerful than other men, they exploited it. I have met some of them myself, and every single one had such a devastating, rapierlike power in his eyes, and an extraordinary hypnotic timbre in his voice—which could not have been learned at any drama school—that I was finally convinced that more than mere showmanship was involved here.

What happens, however, is that the more the power is exploited (for material gains) the weaker it becomes. How else explain the initial phenomenal success of these semiliterate bums from the unproductive hinterlands of India in the most competitive market in the Western Hemisphere? How else explain their subsequent relative failure?

After all, gestalt has been a going concern over the past thirty-odd years or more, and group therapy (which some of these gurus recommend and charge the sky for) is not an entirely novel device. These Indians, who have made a fortune in the West by selling their psychic wares, were traitors to their own system of beliefs, maybe, but were perhaps more than authentic to the audience that heard them.

When I was last in India (1984), I asked an old teacher of mine how he thought I should respond to these charlatans in the Occident. Smiling, with an amused and accusing look, he replied, "Why worry? They'll burn themselves out in the end! And if they make a few pennies before they go, will you be jealous?"

Hinduism is represented and misrepresented with casual abandon. But no one dares to claim what the authentic article is, because absolutely no one knows! Every argument for can be counteracted with a reasoned rebuttal. Yet the whole body of beliefs, superstitions, ritual, and commitment remains in some amazing manner a composite unified entity. And it is this dialectic, between internal diversity and external unity, that perplexes the Western observer.

The Occidental will see these *sadhus,* naked or near-naked, on the banks of the Ganges in Benares or Allahabad or on the foothills of the Himalayas, with yard-long matted hair, four-inch fingernails, splattered with ashes, and sporting long red marks on their foreheads, sitting in postures that will appear indecent, wholly unconcerned about what is going on around them. They might well be sleeping peacefully on a bed of nails, even, and a prod with a stick might elicit a small smiling response, but the prodder will be bound to feel ashamed that he had ever doubted the authenticity of the experience. This, too, will be Hinduism, but not the whole of it.

The Western onlooker will be tempted to ask questions, because the spectacle in front of him will be incomprehensible. He will be further intrigued to see that hundreds of men and women are passing by as if there were nothing extraordinary in the scene.

Translation will be useless. The man, sitting there cross-legged with his eyes shut, his penis and testicles dangling down, does not know English, and certainly does not wish to speak through an interpreter. The intermediary might be impatient because it might involve waiting four, five, or even six days, until the holy man might deign to open his mouth and sip a little water. The Westerner, if he gets himself into such a scrape, will find all of this weird and mystifying. But of course he may not go there in the first place; he might be content simply with listening to stories in his luxury hotel, in which case he will not be inconvenienced. But the raw reality of those intriguing and fascinating tales will remain, persistently.

When I was nine, my mother took me to a holy man on the slow slopes of the Himalayas in northern Bengal. The man was supposed to have been one hundred and ten years old, and blind. I may not have been very bright, but I reckoned that a blind man at that age could not teach me much (my mother had said, "The holy man is a *teacher*"). So I hung around with a kind of sophisticated boredom slouching around my nine-year-old shoulders. The blind man then dared to offer me a sweetmeat, extending his hand. I took it, as dutiful sons taken to holy men by their mothers are supposed to do.

"And why are you angry?" said he.

"I am not!" I shouted instantly to my mother. "Who is he talking about?"

There was a little silence.

"You, my son!" he replied.

I munched away at my sweetmeat, not knowing what to say. Then suddenly I had a brainwave.

"If he is so clever and holy," I half-whispered to my mother, "then why can't he make himself see?"

I had forgotten to add earlier that the man was naked and covered with white ash, which added to my sharp disgust.

"Of course I can, if I want to," the holy man said sweetly. "What would you like me to see?"

I looked into his eyes and they were the color of opal blue, but cloudy. The lids were open but they did not blink. I could not tell if he was pretending.

But getting into the spirit of the thing, I transferred the remaining bit of sweetmeat from my right hand to my left (young Brahmin boys are taught *never* to eat with their left hands, as that is the hand you use to wash your behind after evacuating), and held up the empty palm in which he had handed me the sweet. "OK," I said, "What have I got here?"

Smiling, the old man said, "Nothing."

"OK." I retorted, picking up a stone with my left hand and making an adequate noise in doing so, and then holding my empty right hand up in the air, "What have I got here now?"

"Nothing!" he said, and started laughing.

A little later this hundred-and-ten-year-old man got up and started to walk toward his little hut (the *sadhu* was naked, we were all in several woolens, the temperature was around 35°F), and as he stumbled on a stone ledge, even I, as a nine-year-old skeptic, knew that he was unable to see.

Just as he was about to disappear into his little hideaway, the naked old man shouted to my mother, "Your little son will be either a demon or a saint." Since my horoscope predicts the same thing, I reckon I should be wary.

The fact is *sadhus* do exist, and they are scattered in wide abundance all over India. They do not necessarily *represent* Hinduism, but the real ones certainly live at the peak of whatever it is the religion tries to achieve. They look and behave like quacks, and certainly no Westerner would be able to meet a genuine *sadhu* or emancipated holy man. The difficulty would consist not only in translation, but would lie also in the fundamental incommunicability of one way of looking at the universe as against another. The notion of psychotherapy would not be frowned upon, it would simply be laughed at.

At best, the refined Oriental finds Occidental company "charming and stimulating." At worst, he discovers that it is crude, because it lacks a fundamental religious base, and is therefore beyond redemption. It is Hinduism at its most fundamental and pervasive level that dictates these responses.

The hurdles in translating Oriental modes into Occidental terms have existed since the time of Alexander the Great. Nirad C. Chaudhuri, in his book *Hinduism,* describes the confrontation with characteristic wit and imagery:

> The Greeks were meeting men who claimed to be philosophers (Gymnosophists or naked philosophers—*sadhus*), a type very well known to them, and who yet struck them as being very strange in their behaviour.
>
> [They had] an over-bearing sense of superiority, a gravity which was not consistent with their appearance, total absence of humour or malice in their exhibition of unconventionality, and a self-confidence which would not even

condescend to air any contempt for worldliness.

They employed both speech and silence with equal effect as instruments of self-assertion: they poured out rigmarole which gave an impression of profundity, and at the same time affected a taciturnity which had the same effect. Above all they could sink into unconsciousness and yet seem to have attained to the highest state of consciousness. The basic aim of Hindu mystical life, which is to convert all inward experience into physical states perceptible to the senses, was so far realised by them as to intimidate most rational minds. The Hindu Sadhus were pythons of the psychic world, whose slumbrous coils contained, and at the same time hid, the force of a battering ram in the head.

Like the WASP's consciousness of effortless superiority, most Hindus, especially Brahmins from the highest caste, who have any direct knowledge and experience of their religion inherit a whisper of this legacy. The late Indira Gandhi did, as does her son Rajiv, in however mutated and Westernized a manner, and so perhaps do I, alas, in the most glancing touch from that old Brahmin psyche that my ancestors bequeathed.

The Ganga (or the Ganges, as the British renamed it), is the most sacred river of the Hindus. It winds its lazy liquid ways over 1,560 miles of undulating terrain, changing color as it goes along, from chocolate brown, to hazy blue, to an absolutely incandescent green, and back again.

People are cremated on its banks, legends build up, family myths unfold. As religious custom forbids the cremation of children and *sadhus,* their bodies are floated down the ever-flowing waters of Mother Ganga. Being rowed in a boat on the holy river, you will frequently see corpses, face up, sliding down the surface of the brown, rippling fluid, aspiring in death to reach that final salvation of being buried at sea, the Ganga's ultimate destination, in the blue-green mass of liquid called the Bay of Bengal.

The river weaves its sinuous path through three of the holiest cities in India—Hardwar (North India), Benares (modern name, Varanasi, farther south), and Allahabad (central India). In its angry wrath, it demolishes villages in full flood; at its quiescent best, it becomes a demure little stream, gently picking its way through harmless, green paddy fields. In winter, up in the foothills of the Himalayas, it freezes into a bluish-white ribbon of gently trickling water under the ice.

But the Ganga remains the everlasting Ganga. No other river in the world commands the religious and revered devotion of more than six hundred million people, whether they be orthodox believers or secularly hygienic. Not the Nile or the Amazon, or the Danube, the Rhine, the Yangtze Kiang, the Mississippi, or the Thames have elicited such loving and evocative prose as the Ganga. Even as professedly atheistic a man as Jawaharlal Nehru lapsed into lyricism about the Ganga in his last will and testament:

> My desire to have a handful of my ashes thrown into the Ganga at Allahabad has no religious significance, so far as I am concerned. I have no religious sentiment in the matter. I have been attached to the Ganga and the Jumna rivers [the other holy river] . . . ever since my childhood and, as I have grown older, this attachment has also grown. I have watched their varying moods as the seasons changed, and have often thought of the history and myth and tradition and song and story that have become attached to them through the long ages and become part of their flowing waters. The Ganga, especially, is the river of India, beloved of her people, round which are intertwined her racial memories, her hopes and fears, her songs of triumph, her victories and her defeats. She has been a symbol of India's age-long culture and civilization, ever-changing, ever-flowing, and yet ever the same Ganga. She reminds me of the snow-covered peaks and deep valleys of the Himalayas, which I have loved so much, and of the rich and vast plains below, where my life and work have been cast.

Millions of people drink the waters of the Ganga, as they believe it leads to salvation. Millions more bathe in it, hoping that their sins will be washed away. Yet, potentially, it is the most infested and infectious river in the world. Professor Eric Newley of McGill University (Canada) plaintively poses in a book on the Ganga a query that scientists have been unable to answer:

A peculiar fact which has never been satisfactorily explained is the quick death, in three or five hours, of the cholera vibro in the waters of the Ganges. When one remembers sewage . . . numerous corpses, often cholera casualties, and by the bathing of thousands of natives, it seems remarkable that the belief of Hindus, that the water of this river is pure and cannot be defiled and that they can safely drink it and bathe in it, should be confirmed by modern bacteriological research.

Like the Greeks, who set up their gods on the heights of Mount Olympus, the Hindus put them up on the Himalayas, slightly higher in stature. Like the Greek gods, Hindu deities are said to have frolicked with mortals, often making carnal and emotional contact. Ganga, the sacred river, was supposed to have been sent down from heaven in order to rescue the souls of thousands of people who had been engaged in loose living (do we get a whiff of Sodom and Gomorrah?) down here on earth. Several different tales merge at this point. But the central thread of the story remains. Ganga was sent down to redeem the world:

> Ganga was angry at being brought down from Heaven, and Shiva (the Governor of the World), to save the earth from the shock of her fall, caught the river on his brow, and checked its course with his matted locks.

It is from this legend that the sanctity of the Ganga derives, why it is assumed that no one knows where it springs from and where it ends. Hinduism has many tenets, and the sacred Ganga is centrally one of them.

The holiest of Hindu cities, Benares, sits on the banks of the Ganga, and manages to attract both Western visitors and Indian pilgrims in equal and abundant measure. It is an ancient site, perhaps the only one in the world with an uninterrupted living history going back three thousand years. The *sadhus,* the *pandas* (tour guides, basically), the holy deaths, the gold temples, the menacing monkeys, the crumbling ruins of huge ungainly palaces on the riverbank, the stench, the indescribable aroma of human misery, the fatal frenzied acceptance of inescapable destiny—they all combine to make Benares a fascinating, beguiling, and depressing city, a dropped comma in the longueured paragraphs and chapters that make up the life of the Ganga. Over a hundred years ago, Mark Twain remarked about this hideously dirty and sacred city:

> "Benaras is older than history, older than tradition, older even than legend, and looks twice as old as all of them put together."

Much later, Diana L. Eck, in her book *Banaras: City of Light,* has this to say about the place:

> If we could imagine the silent Acropolis and the Agora of Athens still alive with the intellectual, cultural, and ritual traditions of classical Greece, we might glimpse the remarkable tenacity of the life of *Kashi* [modern name, Varanasi, usually used nomenclature, Benares]. Today Peking, Athens and Jerusalem are moved by a different ethos from that which moved them in ancient times, but *Kashi* is not.

Despite its perplexing diversity, Hinduism may be roughly divided into two distinct sections. That which is accessible to the mass of the population—the rituals, the worship of clay idols, the *pujas,* the annual *melas* (religious fairs) on the banks of the Ganga, which are quite literally attended by millions of devotees, the priestly ceremonies associated with birth, marriage, and death—this is the most visible part of the *religion* that the Western observer is likely to encounter. Woven within it will be overtures to the great epics of Hindu mythology, the *Mahabharata,* the *Ramayana,* and the seminal lecture by Krishna in the *Bhagavad Gita.*

The other part consists of metaphysical discussions, intense intellectual speculations about the nature of reality, the origin of the universe, and other such arcane matters, embodied in the Vedas and the Upanishads. Except for outré inquirers such as Aldous Huxley and Christopher Isherwood in the Western world and assiduous scholars like Max Müller, this is a territory of Hinduism that is largely unexplored by the Occidental visitor, not only because it is not on visual display, but also because it is not amenable to casual inspection.

There are pedants who assert that *real* Hinduism has nothing to do with the former, but consists entirely of the latter. This is an elitist view to which I do not subscribe, because the vast majority of Hindus who profess the faith have very little awareness, let alone any intimate knowledge, of these sacred founts of knowledge.

Significantly, however, the flight to the East from the West that occurred in the sixties had a great deal to do with the kind of descriptions of *reality* that one finds in the later Upanishads, and bear a startling congruence with the type of experience induced by the hallucinogenic drugs, such as lysergic acid diethylamide (LSD), dimethyltryptamine (DMT) and mescaline. The feeling of oneness with an all-pervading supranatural reality that engulfs one when under the influence of these drugs is nowhere better described than in the Vedas and Upanishads. Because hallucinogenic experience is essentially nonverbalizable, the young men and women who took the drugs found the ancient Hindu scriptures to be the nearest written accounts of their mental, emotional, and psychic states, which were so wildly divorced from the mundane realities of their immediately recognizable Western world. They sought refuge in a species of Hinduism, with *sadhus* and gurus, which appeared to offer them some external paradigm with which they could compare the enormous upheavals going on inside their heads.

The Sanskrit translation of the Western idea of *philosophy* is *Darshana,* which means seeing, and it is this insistence that all inward experience can and must be converted to physically perceptible states that distinguishes Indian philosophical endeavor from its counterpart in the Occidental world.

The Vedas are a huge range of poems, originating in a verbal tradition, of which only a hundred thousand verses have survived. Orthodox Hindus believe them to be revealed. There is no one single author, since they span a period of over two millennia. There is no personal signature to these invocations, nor are they mutually consistent in what each of them asserts about the nature of universal reality.

There are four Vedas in all—the *Rig,* the *Sama,* the *Yajur,* and the *Atharva,* theoretically in chronological progression, though there are scholars who deny this. Here is a snippet of one of the most famous and earliest Vedas (the *Rig*), which gives a flavor of the kind of thing I have been talking about:

He, the first origin of this creation,
whether he formed it all or did not form it,
Whose eye controls this world in highest heaven,
he verily knows it, or perhaps he knows not.

The absence of Semitic certainty, which we find in Judaism, Christianity, and Islam, is perhaps the most delightful and invigorating element in these antique poems, at least to me.

The Upanishads are known as the *Vedanta,* or the end of the Vedas. We are now well into Aryan times, about a thousand years before Christ. The Upanishads are reverential about the Vedas, but slyly impertinent as well. A great deal of the flowery language has vanished, and a hard intellectual core has taken its place. The debates are vastly more rigorous, cerebration has replaced wonder and awe. One hundred and eight Upanishads have been preserved, and only fourteen are of major importance.

One whole Upanishad, the *Mandukya,* is devoted to the word *OHM,* which is held to be the phonetic and visual equivalent of the timeless universal reality, the Brahman. It is intoned from the bottom of the stomach, and when you hear it uttered by a real holy man who knows his Sanskrit, it causes goose pimples on the back of your neck. It has no equivalent in any European language, not even in the Latin *amen,* which comes nearest.

The other word, often mistranslated, *maya,* (rendered as illusion), is a germane concept in Hinduism, meaning the veil that is cast between mortal man and his access to supranatural reality, which he has to consciously pierce in order to arrive at the state of unison with the Brahman. The word illusion, whether in the Berkeleyan or optical sense, simply does not do it justice.

Unlike Occidental ideas of time, the Hindu concept is cyclical, not linear. The universe goes through four different periods, and comes back again to the first. These are the *Yugas* or aeons of time— the *Satya* (the truthful), the *Treta,* the *Dvapara,* and the *Kali* (the black or untruthful one).

Progressively, virtue disappears and is replaced by evil. At the end of each cycle, there is a great *Pralaya,* or flooding, after which the golden age reappears. Brahma, the great creator, breathes in and out, comprising the span of each cycle. It is significant that contemporary cosmological theory is increasingly inclined to accept the idea of a pulsating, expanding and contracting universe, as against previous ideas of the Big Bang, and so forth. Currently, we are supposed to be nearing the end of Kaliyuga, or the evil cycle. It cannot be entirely coincidental that most other religions that assert the notion of a "Second Coming" have some equivalent theological scenario.

Hindus also divide their span of life into four distinct stages. The *Brahmacharya,* the *Grihastha, Vanaprastha,* and finally, the *Sanyasa.* The first is one of celibacy and learning at the feet of a master, the second is when you marry and bring up a family, the third is a stage where you go into semiretirement and gradually detach yourself from earthly concerns. Finally, you renounce the world altogether to contemplate your imminent demise and probable merging with the universal reality.

These were basic Aryan concepts, and the rigidly analytical ways in which they were formulated reflect themselves in another institution called *caste,* about which we shall talk in a moment.

Hinduism also prescribes four goals in life: *dharma, Artha, kama,* and *moksha.* The first instructs you to follow the path of "right conduct," virtue and do-gooding, if you like, but a good deal more than that. It encompasses the ideas of ecological preservation, of doing right by your neighbor, of worshiping your own god, and so on. The second specifically instructs you to acquire wealth and become prosperous, a far cry from Christian renunciation. The third prods you into using sex and sensual enjoyment for the full flowering of your soul, hence the *Kama Sutra,* all within the accepted format of religious sanction. And the fourth and final one, to attempt that final unity with timeless reality. Intriguingly, nothing that earthly man may want is left out; the goals are not set so high up that they cannot be reached by the average man or woman. Once again, a distinctive feature of a religion that is no religion at all.

The means by which these goals may be attained are called *Yogas,* meaning "yoking" yourself to a discipline, and once again they are four in kind: *Jnana, Bhakti, Karma,* and *Raja.* They range from intellection, to devotion to sensual and sexual exercises, to total sublimation. This omniverous facility of embracing everything, leaving nothing out, mystifies the foreigner, especially when he has to consider that this is no psychotherapeutic lesson, but a *religion* talking. But Hinduism really is a massive instruction manual for living in this world, in all its variegated resplendence, and the reason we have to call it a religion is that no other body of beliefs has embraced the secular and the divine with such fierce and eclectic intensity.

By about the sixth century B.C., Hinduism had become corrupt, flabby, and living off its own fat. Siddhartha Gautama was born, so the legend goes, in 563 B.C. He grew up in a luxurious royal home, protected from the evil sights of the mortal world. On accidentally discovering that there was much suffering around him, he left his father's palace and his beautiful wife, and began meditating. He attained "enlightenment" at the age of thirty-five in Bodh Gaya in central India, and became known as the *Buddha.*

Buddhism commands a following of about thirty-five million Indians today. It originated basically as a reaction to the esoteric turn Hinduism was taking. It began as a materialistic ethic that suggested an eightfold path for avoiding the miseries of this earthly life. There was, in its origin, no idea of a godhead, and no idol-worship. *Nirvana,* which is a mildly plagiarized version of the Hindu *moksha,* was a prescription for attaining a state of bliss uncontaminated by earthly considerations. Buddhism believes in *Karma,* but does not accept the existence of the human soul, or the Brahminic *Atman.*

There are two main categories of Buddhism, at least in India—*Mahayana* and *Hinayana.* The former sect believe that enlightenment for oneself is useless; one should try to get everyone else to attain Buddhahood. The other sect is called "the lesser vehicle," which means that followers of this creed believe that attaining or trying to achieve Nirvana for oneself is a perfectly worthy exercise. Zen Buddhism, about which I know next to nothing, has absolutely no following in India.

The remarkable thing about Buddhism is that it originated in India, and through the efforts of a particularly bloodthirsty Hindu ruler, Asoka (who renounced his conquistadorial ambitions *after* he had vanquished most of his foes), the religion was taken as far afield as China and Japan, not to mention the Southeast Asian countries. The impress of Buddhism in Indian architecture is extensive and profound, and lasts a span of some fifteen hundred years, between the third century B.C. and about the eleventh century after Christ.

Literally, millions of Buddhist pilgrims flock to Bodh Gaya, the place where the Buddha attained enlightenment, from all over the Asian continent, and it is the most awesome spectacle to see them, as I did, on the Buddha's birthday, kissing the ground and prostrating themselves from the point of their arrival in India to their final destination at the holy shrine. They lie facedown on the road, with spread-eagled arms, and slide along, lip to toe, lip to toe, like human earthworms, all the way for more than five miles. But Buddhism does not have a strong hold on India, and Zen certainly has no original roots in the place that gave the religion its name.

Jainism is another of the indigenous religions in India, and has a following of some four million believers. Like Buddhism, it started as a revolt against orthodox Brahminic Hinduism, and was led by Mahavira who, like the Buddha, was a member of the second rung down the caste hierarchy.

Once again, it is materialistic, accepting no godhead, no spiritual destiny other than the emancipation of the individual human soul. Ideas from pre-Aryan Hindu beliefs are incorporated, but historically, one suspects, a great deal of ritualistic Hinduism was being violently spewed out. Significantly, Mahavira and Buddha were contemporaries, but while Buddhism caught on, at least for a time, Jainism never did. But the Jain contribution to medieval Indian architecture, especially in those cave temples, cannot be overemphasized.

Jains believe in twenty-four *Tirthankaras,* roughly the equivalent of prophets in the Old Testament. There are several totally divergent legends about the founder of the religion, but there are two principal sects, the earth-clad, who actually wear clothes, and the sky-clad, who do not.

Jains are strict vegetarians and do not believe in killing any kind of life. There are orthodox Jains who actually go around wearing mufflers over their mouths in case they inhale a live object whose life they might inadvertently extinguish. The actual number of Jain followers is quite disproportionate to the power this community wields in India. Since they are so closely knit, their financial clout is enormous. Some people have been heard to whisper that there is no such thing as a poor Jain—a charge that has been made about another community in the Western hemisphere, and intriguingly, the emblem of the Jain religion is the swastika.

Till the recent bloody massacres following the assassination of Indira Gandhi, Sikhs did not regard themselves as non-Hindus. The inception of this other great religion in India was a two-pronged attack on the flabbier aspects of idol-worshiping Hinduism, caste barriers, and the barbarities of the Muslim onslaught from the northwest.

Sikhism fundamentally accepts most of the tenets in the Hindu Aryan tradition, but aspires to go further back into the Vedic sources, where monotheism was the declared norm. Even in contemporary India, the eldest son in a family living in the Punjab was quite frequently inducted into the Sikh faith without coercion.

Why these recent gory events occurred will be discussed in another place, but here we have to say that Sikhism and Hinduism are not as far apart as say, Judaism and the Greek Orthodox Church.

The religion was founded by Guru Nanak (1469–1539), basically as a shield against the Muslim invaders (Babar), and to wield a fierce ax against the Brahminic caste system, which was then threatening to reduce a large part of the population to the position of serfs.

One of the fundamental tenets of Sikhism, which is enshrined in the holy text, the *Granth* Sahib, is "all men are brothers and equal in the eyes of God." The early gurus in the faith paid their due homage at the holy Hindu places, and apart from not worshiping deities in clay, adhered to all other aspects of the Hindu religion.

The martial element in the religion crept in about two hundred years later, at the end of the seventeenth century, when once again the Muslims were beginning to use their imperial and ruthless military might. Guru Gobind Singh, in direct lineage from the founder, asked for five men to offer their heads as a sign of faith. When the five followers duly appeared, the order was called *khalsa* or pure, hence the contemporary demand by extremist Sikhs for a new nation called *Khalistan*. It was this guru who also decreed that every Sikh is called a *Singh,* meaning "lion," and every Sikh would have a distinctive badge, which would make him stand apart from everyone else, caste distinctions would vanish, and Muslims would know very clearly where they stood against *this* brand of Hindus.

From this point on, every Sikh would accept the five Ks—*kesh,* long unshorn hair (wrapped in a turban), *kara,* iron bracelet, *kachha* (long drawers), *kangha,* comb, and *kirpan,* small sword—even today, the government of India legally allows a Sikh to carry a *kirpan,* because it is demanded by his religion, though it is forbidden to any other community.

There are some twelve million Sikhs in the world, though not all of them live in India, and a quarter of the Indian army is composed of this martial tribe. The frictions that resulted in the recent grotesque tragedy are not religious in origin, and will be discussed in another chapter. It is enough to say here that Sikhism originated as a partial rebellion against Hinduism, but much more potently against the Muslim barbarities of mass rape and coerced conversion of the local Hindu population.

Its militaristic stance is more recent than the conception of its founder, Guru Nanak. Sikhs worship in temples called *gurdwaras,* and on June 6, 1984, the late Mrs. Gandhi sent the Indian army into the Golden Temple at Amritsar, the holiest of holy shrines for Sikhs, to rout out so-called holy men, who had dug themselves into a military forification with carbines, hand grenades, and automatic machine guns, in case just such an assault took place. It did. And both parties lost. Religion was used, as it has so often been in India, to mask political rivalries and economic tensions.

Zoroastrianism, practiced by the Parsis of India, could claim to be the smallest recognized religion in the world, but it has persisted in India for well over thirteen hundred years. Parsis fled Persia in the seventh century, so the legend goes, and there are something like 130,000 alive today, most of whom live in India.

They worship the Fire God and are followers of the prophet Zoroaster (or Zarathustra), on whom Nietzsche devoted a whole book. Their principal scripture is called the Zend-Avesta, and despite their numerical inferiority, the Parsis exercise an inordinate influence in the financial and industrial life of India. In general, they tend to marry within their own community, look after their own kith and kin, and have the most strange and macabre way of disposing of their dead.

* * *

We are left with the three nonindigenous religions, which did not originate in India, but which nevertheless have a strong connection with the country. Of these, Judaism must be the most intriguing to the Western visitor.

Facts here are notoriously unreliable, but Jews in India claim to have arrived in the country somewhere between two to three hundred years before Christ. The only synagogue I have visited that is even remotely ancient (in Cochin, South India), was donated to the Hebraic race by the then maharajah, and is about four hundred years old. There is no rabbi in the place, the tiles on the floor are two hundred years old, a gift from China, and the congregation consists of twelve people, although the temple is supported by the state.

There are three main categories of Indian Jewry—the Bene-Israel, the Cochinis, and the Baghdadis, all following the Sephardic tradition. For a community as tightly knit as the Jews, I have heard widely different figures as to how many there are in India. A Jewish friend of mine tells me that there are at least 45,000 Jews living in India at the moment, while a book called *Religions of India,* which devotes a whole chapter to Judaism, puts the figure at 7,000. It is impossible to tell.

What must be interesting to the visitor is the number of philanthropic institutions that Indian Jewry has created, with names like Sassoon and David floating around in preponderance. And the astounding fact is that no other country in the world, including Britain and the United States, can boast that anti-Semitism has never existed within its boundaries.

I went to an English-type boarding school in India, and only became aware that I had had a whole hive of Jewish classmates, *after* I arrived in London, and was told about such things as noses and names, some eight years later. The only difference between the Jewish boys and the rest of us, that I can recall, was that instead of going to chapel on Sundays, they went into another hall, where little old men with strange caps on their heads came to teach them Hebrew.

Islam did not originate in India, but arrived in the country at about the end of the twelfth century with the Muslim invader,

Mahmud of Ghazni. The contribution of Islam to Indian art and architecture and history is not relevant in a chapter on religion.

The two sects in the Islamic community, the Sunnis and Shi'ites, exist in India, too, but the Sunnis predominate. Between the fifteenth and eighteenth centuries, Islam had the most profound impact on India, and the reverberations of that collision still echo down the corridors of time.

A great number of conversions took place about four hundred years ago, not always under coercion, but because the lowliest Hindu peasants had become sick and tired of being downtrodden under the caste system. One, but not the principal, reason for the partition of India, was this caste/class barrier between the upper caste/class Hindus and the remaining vast majority of lower-class Muslims: an obvious inequity and division, which the British exploited with relish and devious cunning. Macaulay advised the governor-general, in a phrase that has gone down in history books, to—"divide and rule."

But we are not concerned here with the political resonances of Islam in India, but rather with the religion itself, which is much like what it is anywhere else in the world. And it should be recorded that apart from one short period under Aurangzeb, the last Great Mogul Emperor, the impact of Islam on India was benign and to the great advantage of the country in every sphere.

Today, Muslims comprise about eighty million of the total population, though Islamic centers of learning, such as Aligarh University (in central India), have witnessed a few disruptions in recent times. Also, Urdu, the language of Islam, has fallen into relative decline.

Not much can be said about Christianity in India except to repeat the old myth that Saint Thomas, one of Christ's disciples, was supposed to have landed in India in about the seventh year after the death of Jesus. The earliest Christian incursion into India was almost certainly by the Portuguese in about the sixteenth century. As far as I have been able to discover, the oldest existing Christian church in India is in Calcutta—St. John's, built in the first decade of the eighteenth century, and the one in which Warren Hastings was married. But I have roamed around in Christian graveyards, not far from my own home in Calcutta, where tombstones carried marks indicating that they were there in the middle of the 1600s.

In the past two hundred years, Christianity has played a much more potent role than mere religion could aspire to do, but that again is another story. A large number of conversions took place, once again, because of the exploitation of caste, fear of being caught in the Hindu-Muslim crossfire, and so on. There are twenty million Christians in India today—amazingly, a larger number of adherents to the faith than exist in the whole of Ireland, though not all Indian followers of Christ owe their allegiance to the Holy Father in Rome.

India has received all religions with a mixture of grace and passivity. No religion that has ever come into the country has wholly gone away again.

7

Caste Typing

When Orwell wrote *Down and Out in Paris and London* and *The Road to Wigan Pier,* none of the reviewers in the posh London journals doubted for a moment that here was the voice of an old Etonian talking. Eric Blair (his original name) was taken seriously precisely because no one from his class in England had deigned to write about the plight of the underprivileged for nearly a century.

Dickens managed to rise from his proletarian fastness by the sheer force of his descriptive and voluminous prose, despite the fact that he was not born with a silver spoon in his mouth. English society did not take kindly to "little upstarts" telling them about how "the other half" lived. In England, where the Mitford variety of Anglo-Saxon culture originated, it has always been easier to descend from top down than ascend from bottom up. Radicals were born and bred in the upper echelons of society, and watered-down versions of revolutionaries had firm congenital connections with the top crust of British society.

There *were* exceptions, of course! Aneurin Bevan, a miner's son, did challenge the great Churchill in Parliament, on the rolling vowels of his rhetoric. Occasionally, eccentric personalities have been the sauce with which the meat of British life has been digested.

But the rest of the world would not have heard about caste in India, if the British had not encountered an institution that was vastly more intricate and cussedly persistent than class, so close yet so far from their own rather wretched formations of hierarchical systems of power manipulation. In American terms, I am tempted to think of the apocryphal lines from that poem: ". . . the Lowells talk only to Cabots/And the Cabots talk only to God"!

The reader will have noticed that I am trying to introduce the subject of caste in India by an indirect route. It is an institution that has been much maligned, greatly misunderstood. But it also happens to be the most disgusting and evil thing that persists in modern India. By total accident, I am in a better position to talk about it than many another commentator. There are writers on India, with some acknowledged status in the Western world, who have claimed to be Brahmins. In the course of this chapter I shall try to show why it is not possible to assert Brahmin lineage when you are not, how your name alone will reveal your caste genealogy, how the Western audience has been fiercely deceived by pomposity and efficient public-relations exercises. It will not be my intention to name names and attack individuals, but to show that caste is such a powerful phenomenon, that even those who have achieved remarkable success in various spheres still wish to acquire the mantle of high-caste status in order to appear to the Western world as the authentic speakers for that particular culture.

As a Brahmin myself, I really could not care a damn. Here I shall try to explain why, if one is a Brahmin, it does not matter, but if one is not, it probably makes a great deal of difference. There is an internationally known author who at this very moment is going around claiming to be a Brahmin, though he is not. His writing is superb, his style is mellifluent, to me it is wholly irrelevant where he comes from and in which caste he was born. But to him it is obviously a matter of some significant concern. I have neither the heart nor the desire to name the man, since I admire his writing enormously. But I cite him as an example of how potent and insidious caste can be.

Personally, I did my very best to detach myself from the Brahmin tag. My full name is Sasthi*brata* Chakravarti; the last, the family name, firmly indicates my lineage, meaning a "suzerain of the realm." At the age of twenty, I lopped it off, split my first name in two, so that no one would know what family I came from, and into which caste I had been born. There is absolutely no one in the whole of India who is called *Brata,* since it is not a name. I thus managed to make myself a holographic nonperson. I doubt though, if psychologically I would have had the same kind of confidence, if I were not already subconsciously allowing myself an incipient superiority because of my caste. As I said, it is easier to be a radical from top down than from bottom up.

When the British arrived on the scene, they muddied the waters. They encountered an institution that appeared to be so like their own on the surface, but on further inspection, turned out to be so very different. Caste was imbued with all the nastier aspects of British class, but had a great deal more to it than simple social gradations. The contemporary version of caste in India is an intriguing amalgam of what it used to be some three hundred years ago and what the Anglo-Saxon injection has molded into being. Which does not mean that it is any better, nor any worse for that matter, but emphatically different. Rural and urban India react to caste in such utterly disparate and divergent ways that to make generalizations about the phenomenon lands one in the risky field of talking pompous nonsense.

Caste began as an attempt to consolidate an agricultural community into regulated positions. It was trying to structure a nomadic tribe into the habits of settled life. Vocational apartheid was encouraged, but not at first enforced. We are talking about the first Aryan incursions into India, roughly 1,500 years before Christ.

Reflections of this transformation occur in the Upanishads, but nowhere in the early scriptures do we hear about the rigid impositions of caste. If this sounds contradictory, let me explain that the notion of caste distinctions was endemic in the Vedanta, but not expected to be enforced. The literature is wholly imbued with shamelessly elitist notions. But it was expected to be practiced voluntarily.

In contemporary times, Jawaharlal Nehru implied in his writing, and was accepted as such by the Western world, that he a was "blue-blooded aristocrat."

Absolutely nothing could be further from the truth. Nehru was indeed a Brahmin, and by that very fact, he could not possibly have been an *aristocrat,* as the term is defined in my *OED.* Brahmins were never supposed to own property. The much neater analogy would be with the American Kennedys, where Patrick was a bartender, Joseph was a film mogul (multimillionaire) and Jack subsequently became president.

Aristocracy, however, does not consist of mere wealth, or even political power. In his own autobiography, and in the authorized versions of his life, Jawaharlal boasts about the fact that his father arrived in Allahabad in the late nineteenth century and began his legal career, earning five rupees a month (in exact terms today, it would be fifty cents, but multiply that figure by a factor of one hundred, for precise contemporary comparison, and even then you get a miserly five dollars). This was the same man who told his son, Jawaharlal, that he (the father) could earn in one day what his son might make in a year. It was at this point that Nehru, as a failed barrister, took to politics in India.

However admirable this may be for an individual (I am referring to Papa Nehru), this is *not* the stuff out of which aristocrats are made. Just as the Kennedys served as a national symbol, and words were misused to describe their status, so did the Nehrus. Aristocrats they were not, and never could be! In a land with such strong, living past history, the Nehru-Gandhi dynasty has acquired all the ambient appurtenances of regality. But they still cannot talk as equals with the Maharana of Udaipur (whom I met, and who insists that he is directly descended from the Sun God), because they did not own or rule a vast area of land for over three hundred years.

Indira Gandhi played on this theme of aristocratic heredity, and most Indians and all Westerners fell for it. But it was false. Brahmins were supposed to be scholars, wholly unconcerned with material possessions and worldly power, rather like Jewish rabbis, and their connection with terrestrial life was always expected to be tenuous at best.

This is where we arrive at mutation, how an original concept begins to change into something that it was not initially designed to be, but retains the vestigial semblance of a cast and a mold whose vigorous figurations persist beyond the point of legitimacy.

I must be careful here, since I am talking about a subject of anxious personal concern. About a century or so ago, when I was a little boy, not higher than about three foot four, I had ventured into our large kitchen. The servants were eating. I sat down on the floor, talking with them, because I always enjoyed speaking with the menials more than with my own family. Within minutes, my mouth began to salivate, and the old woman, who had been my constant companion since I was about two, offered me a piece of tiny fish. I took it, and began to chew the juicy flesh with greedy pleasure. My mother then arrived on the scene. I shall never forget her face. She commanded me to come away. I was ordered, under direct supervision, to wash my mouth. Holy Ganges water was then brought in for gargling purposes. The priest was called to perform adequate *pujas* and offer penance for the fact that I had eaten with the lower castes. This whole business lasted two days. At that time I did not know what caste was, but my mother told me that I should never ever tell anybody that I had actually eaten with the lower-caste servants. It is not entirely impossible that she might have been apprehensive about losing caste, not only for myself, but for the entire family, if word got around about this awesome lapse. The servants were severely penalized but not sacked, because they had been with us for so long, but never again was I allowed free access to those regions of the house in which I most enjoyed being.

Before I actually describe caste, let me say where it differs from *class*. Although there are various points at which caste in contemporary India is no different from Western class, there are also fundamental differences between the two institutions. Just as there are wide variations between class in England and the professed nonexistence of the same phenomenon in the United States today, so caste in India just now is different from what it used to be even fifty or a hundred years ago.

Simply because caste isn't what it used to be does not mean that it does not exist, nor that its evil influences do not affect the body politic. For an Indian like myself, it is extremely difficult to steer the middle course that might give a true picture of what caste is about in today's India, without leaning too far one way or the other, about how good it once used to be, and how hideously misrepresented it is today.

At the beginning of the eighteenth century, trade began to marry into the aristocracy in England. It was, by many parties, not least by royalty itself, regarded with horror. A very similar thing happened with caste in India, except that it occurred about four hundred years ago. In the previous chapter, we have described how Buddhism and Jainism originated with Hindu leaders who were not Brahmins.

Originally, the theory of caste was formulated in rigorously analytical Aryan terms for efficient social functioning—or so at least we are told. (You will note my tone of skepticism, because I am here repeating what I have read.) It started off as being a purely regulatory structure. The four main castes were: *Brahmins*-the scholars, intellectuals, those who passed on the wisdom of the tribe to the next generation. Then there were *Kshatriyas*—the warriors, the defenders of the realm, the kings and fighters, and so forth. It was quite clear that they were inferior to the scholarly caste, just as the prophets in the Old Testament were superior to their kings. Then there were the *Vaisyas*—the merchants, traders, bankers, basically the kind of people we would call businessmen today. They kept the wheels of society turning. Finally, last on the scale, were the *Sudras,* who were agricultural workers, people who did all the basic workmanlike things that fed and clothed a nation.

These, then, were the four principal castes. Yet, notice, we have not yet heard of another community of people who are essential to any civilized society: the men who empty your lavatories, mend your shoes, cremate your dead, and so forth. They were called *ajanya,* unpeople. If their shadow crossed your path, you were expected to take off your clothes and throw them away. If they touched you, even by accident, you were required by religion to take a bath in the holy river before you could be accepted by society at large. These were the *untouchables.*

How the caste system originated is a matter of total conjecture. There are millions of theories, each one as speculative and unsupported by facts as the others. However, all the theorists do converge at the point where they declare that the darker the skin, the lower the caste. This is an issue that may interest a Western audience, but it is infinitely tedious for an Indian one. Caste has existed in India for over two thousand years. There are no written records of anything that happened at that time. We know that divisions along caste barriers is an irksome physical reality. No one really knows how it all came about. Or how the choice was made about who should do what!

The constitutional euphemism for *untouchables* is "scheduled castes," and there are four tiers among this group of people, considered to be the lowest of the low. In ascending order, from the bottom up, there are the *doms,* attendants at crematoriums; then the *mochis,* workers in leather (an occupation that means living with a very nasty stench all day long); the *bhangis,* sweepers and lavatory cleaners; and finally the *dhobis,* laundrymen, who are considered clean enough to be allowed mild contact with proper-caste Hindus.

But even within the four main castes, there are gradations and hierarchies. Among the Brahmins there are four tiers of subcastes, as there are among the *Kshatriyas,* too. The *Vaisyas* have subcastes according to the professions practiced by the family, and it is the same with the *Sudras.*

The subdivisions of caste within caste are so ramificatory that no average Indian can possibly know the whole complex structure. In a book called *Systems of Indian Caste and Marriage* by P. M. Chakravorty, the author asserts, "It is estimated that in present day India, there are not less than three to four *thousand* castes, spread over the whole country [emphasis mine]."

He goes on to list a mere four hundred, pleading lack of space. Personally, I learned a great deal from the book that I did not know before. I was not aware, for example, that there is whole subcaste called *Kathak,* who began as storytellers in northern India, and that *Bauris* were specially deputed members of society who carried brides and bridegrooms in palanquins to and from weddings, and that *Devars* are a caste of musicians of Dravidian origin in South India, who live mainly by begging.

In a predominantly agricultural, preindustrial society, it probably made a lot of sense to have these enclaves, and thus ensure that crafts were preserved and passed on from father to son, generation to generation. When caste barriers were not rigidly enforced, and the odd individual was allowed a free transit from one to the other according to his own independent will (as in class within contemporary Western society), it is arguable that society functioned more efficiently and less inequitously under caste than it would have under any other system at the time.

But when the fluid regulatory mechanisms began to set into a rigid mold, when penalties were extracted for violation of barriers, when the higher castes began to exploit those lower down the ladder, it was then that evil and inequity raised their ugly, fearsome heads.

In contemporary India, however, it is not as if vocational transitions from one caste to another do not take place. As a civil and sanitary engineer, my father (from the top Brahmin caste) made a fortune during World War II by providing American GIs with ice-cream machines and lavatories (an occupation originally reserved exclusively for untouchables) in Burma, because no British firm would dare risk sending their workmen to the front lines while the Japanese were on the offensive. A friend of mine who is a *chamar* (an untouchable belonging to the leather-working subgroup) makes his living as a very eminent journalist in Delhi.

Where this apparent flexibility breaks down is in village life, in politics, and in the institution of marriage. While urban India allows you to switch from your original caste vocation to any other, it does not take kindly, even today, to the marriage between an untouchable and a Brahmin, except at the very top, anglicized and affluent crust of society.

In village India, the barriers are much more rigid and enforced much lower down the ladder in social intercourse, such as dining together, using the same shops, or having tea in the same shanty hutment. In politics, it helps to be a Brahmin in most places, as Nehru and Indira Gandhi knew full well during their meteoric passage across the ever-enduring sky of Indian politics.

The threat of *losing* caste (the Hindu equivalent of Catholic excommunication) comes from several kinds of activities. You can lose caste by eating beef or pork or by dining with a member of a lower caste. Orthodox Brahmins are supposed to be strict vegetarians, expected to abstain from eating fish, fowl, and even eggs. My mother, who was a very rigorous observer of rituals, ate meat only when the goat had been sacrificed (head cut off with a massive steel cudgel at the feet of the gory clay idol) at the Kali temple in Calcutta and duly consecrated by priestly incantations. But most Brahmins today, certainly in urban India, do not adhere to such rigid regulations, though beef is still anathema to the vast majority of Hindus of all castes.

You can also lose caste if a member of the family marries into a lower order. In order to preserve tribal purity, often a Brahmin son (who has chosen to marry a Vaisya girl) is disinherited and banished from the joint family home, because his continued presence would contaminate the rest of the household, and make it especially hard to find suitable husbands for the unmarried women in the house.

When a particularly headstrong young man from an affluent and mildly orthodox Brahmin family decides to marry a woman of his choice from a lower caste, the phenomenon is called *intercaste* marriage, and is spoken of with awe and admiration, indicating that something quite radical has occurred. His family, of course, don't talk about it at all.

The implications are in fact much more mundane and vulgar than the superficial assertions of ideology would lead you to imagine. By choosing to do what he has done, the eligible young bachelor has forfeited his right to a dowry, because no father of a lower-caste girl is going to fork out money for a daughter who has already hooked a good upper-caste catch. The boy loses out on the money stakes, his family lose out because it is a stigma on the purity of the family line, the children of such a marriage will obviously have a tougher time finding husbands and wives than if they were "pure" (unless of course they manage to climb so far up the socioeconomic ladder that these distinctions don't matter anymore).

Just as a "love marriage" (meaning a wedding between a man and a woman that has not been arranged by their parents) is regarded, even now, as a fairly daring and novel thing in most middle-class homes, an intercaste marriage is both vilified by establishmentarians and gaped at with admiration and wonder by those who profess liberal opinions but dare not take the practical risks of indulging in such heretical activities.

The term *half-caste* does not, however, mean what it apparently signifies. That more than pejorative expression does *not* refer to the offspring of two Indians from different castes. It was coined specifically by the British to categorize the issues of those carnal connections (often outside the institution of holy matrimony) between white British males and Indian females. The progeny were called *Anglo-Indians* or *half-castes,* and there was many a wicked tongue that whispered in London clubland that Rudyard Kipling was an Anglo-Indian, in the worst possible progeniturial sense of the phrase.

The nasty thing about the fate of Anglo-Indians was that they were totally outside caste and were not accepted either by Indian society or by the *pukka* (pure) British. They were suspended in no-man's-land, their identities in limbo. After independence in 1947, a majority of these half-castes migrated to England, where they were treated with far greater kindness than they would have been in India.

Even today, if I were to marry a white woman of European or American origin, and produce children by her, those kids would have a rough ride in India, unless I were very rich or very famous. Rajiv Gandhi married an Italian girl, and his political fortunes were reckoned to be distinctly downgraded because of his marital connection with a foreigner. If he were not the scion of a noble family, his kids would not have had an easy passage in Indian social life.

The other odious aspect of caste is reflected in the attitude toward *intercommunal* marriages. If a Brahmin lad from Bengal were to marry a Brahmin lass from Madras (South India), the wedding would be disapproved by both families, even though religious dogma would offer no objection. Even today, Kashmiri Brahmins (the Nehru-Gandhi line, for example) mostly marry amongst themselves, because they consider themselves purer than other Brahmins in India. This notion of racial purity (not a particularly Aryan concept, since it is significantly eulogized in that very non-Aryan book called the Old Testament), has been used by exceedingly unsavory characters throughout history. It still persists in modern India.

A great deal of pious nonsense has been spoken and written about caste, sometimes with the best of motives. And most Indians, faced with a barrage of vitriolic onslaught, have sought refuge in trying to defend this wretched institution by attempting to point out its relative benefits. But I have not read one single defense of caste written by someone who came from the bottom end of the ladder. Here again is Jawaharlal Nehru, trying his desperate liberal best to defend an indefensible institution at the bar of Western opinion:

The idea of ceremonial purity has been extraordinarily strong among the Hindus. This has led to one good consequence and many bad ones. The good one is bodily cleanliness. A daily bath has always been a feature of a Hindu's life, including most of the depressed classes. It was from India that this habit spread to England and elsewhere. *[Really?]* The average Hindu, even the poorest peasant, takes some pride in his shining pots and pans. This sense of cleanliness is not scientific and the man who bathes twice a day will unhesitatingly drink water which is unclean and full of germs . . .

But even while he is eulogizing cleanliness, purity, and so forth, Nehru finds it hard to justify an institution that had become grotesquely exploitative. Note this passage, only six pages farther in his *Discovery of India:*

> The conception and practice of caste embodied the aristocratic ideal and was obviously opposed to democratic conceptions. It had a strong sense of *noblesse oblige,* provided people kept to their hereditary status and did not challenge the established order. India's success and achievements were on the whole confined to the upper classes; those lower down in the scale had very few chances and their opportunities were strictly limited. These upper classes were not small limited groups but large in numbers and there was also a diffusion of power, authority and influence. Hence they carried on successfully for a very long period. But the ultimate weakness and failing of the caste system and the Indian social structure were that they degraded a mass of human beings and gave them no opportunities to get out of that condition—educationally, culturally, or economically. That degradation brought deterioration all along the line including in its scope even the upper classes. It led to the petrifaction which became a dominant feature of India's economy and life.

And here is the thundering and unequivocal final verdict from the same pen:

> In the context of society today, the caste system and much that goes with it are wholly incompatible, reaction-

ary, restrictive, and barriers to progress. There can be no equality of status and opportunity within its framework, nor can there be political democracy and much less economic democracy. Between these two conceptions conflict is inherent and only one of them can survive.

Some people argue that the caste system in all its cussed resilience *has* survived, even after thirty-eight years of independence, while democracy, so dear to Nehru's heart, has not and will not meld into India's essential ethos, whatever apologists might claim. We shall have to wait and see.

To me, however, the case is proven. A vast number of people were ruthlessly exploited by a system that said that some men were inferior, and religion was used to stamp its fiat on this evil proposition. No amount of ratiocinative verbiage can justify such wicked inequity.

Originally, these categories were not meant to be rigid. But by and by, they became very firm indeed. The people at the top, especially the Brahmins, exploited the vast majority at the base of the pyramid with ruthless cruelty. Superstition came into play, dues were extracted, as they have been in any institutionalized religion anywhere in the world, and the poor suffered. Caste became immutable, you could not change from one into another; if your father was a cobbler, you would have to remain one for the rest of eternity, to the third and fourth generations.

Mahatma Gandhi tried to do something about this in the late twenties and early thirties. He redesignated the untouchables as the *Harijans*, or the "children of Hari," Lord Krishna, that is. It did very little to improve their lot. But it provided a massive political platform for the Grand Soul to launch himself as the savior of India. There are villages in the country today where the untouchables cannot draw water from a well, even in times of drought, because the caste people would stone them to death if they tried. Though the constitution of India absolutely forbids discrimination, and the Untouchability (Offences) Act of 1965 outlaws the enforcement of disabilities on "the ground of untouchability," these people are still denied access to the temples, restaurants, shops, and communal water supply.

Not many Indians whom the Westerner will meet will accept that caste is a horrid and persistent cancer in the body politic of the nation. He would rather return the Westerner's query with a question: "And how about your country? Don't you have any *class* divisions back there?" As if one man's homicide was justifiable grounds for another person's murder.

In India, caste slides into class with such sly imperceptibility that it is difficult, even for an indigenous observer, to perceive the points of transition. The fact that class is theoretically transferable, and that caste is immutable, is never given any serious thought, even by those ferocious minds who profess to be liberals.

Admittedly, urban India does not respond to caste in the same way that village India does. But it does occupy a place in the accepted ethos of the nation, almost as if it were a subconscious layer on which all other assessments of personality were made. It is much easier to witness this from the top—when one is at the receiving end of fulsome tributes and privileges that have nothing whatsoever to do with oneself—and instinctively discern that the old caste system is working overtime, in however subterraneous a manner.

Politics comes into it, too. It would to be too tedious to list the number of occasions when, in the past twenty or so years, caste has played a very crucial role in the choice of candidates in provincial legislatures, when the center (New Delhi) has played the caste card, when tensions were deliberately stoked between Brahmins and the other castes in order to get a particular party into power. But these things have happened, and no doubt they shall continue to do so.

One of the most potent features of the Indian politico-social landscape is the fact that over one hundred million people in the country belong to what is euphemistically called the *scheduled castes,* a term derived from the immaculate Indian constitution, whose founding fathers recognized that there was a problem here, without knowing quite how to deal with it.

The reason why there were massive conversions to Islam about four hundred years ago was that the untouchables and lower castes were so ruthlessly exploited that they reckoned (rightly) that they would be better off under a new religious regime that did not acknowledge, in theory at least, the divisions along hereditary caste barriers.

The irony, of course, was that those who converted either to Islam or later to Christianity (about two hundred years ago) preserved their old caste identities in their heads, and even though they might have been untouchables in their earlier faith, on conversion to Islam or Christianity, they continued to regard themselves as superior or inferior according to the subgroup from which they had originated. Thus were the sins of the third and fourth generations perpetuated into infinity.

Even today, migrant laborers who came to Britain in the fifties are known to change their family names by deed poll, so that their sons and daughters may fetch a better price (by changing to a higher-caste name) in the marriage market back in India. Caste has such a firm grip on the Indian soul that it is difficult, if not impossible, to unshackle the population from its hideous clasp, even with oceans and decades and generations insulating the present from the past.

In more recent times, when Indira Gandhi was routed at the polls in 1977 and the Janata party came to power, the incumbent government fractured within twenty months. The then prime minister, Morarji Desai, resigned, and it was up to the president to call upon another man from the elected legislature to try and form a majority government. He overrode the only man, Jagjivan Ram, who would have easily commanded a majority in Parliament, in favor of Charan Singh, who did not even have the courage to put himself to the vote. Where caste comes into all this is simply what I heard at the time and what was vehemently underlined by the man himself. Jagjivan Ram, who could have commanded a majority vote in the lower (elected) house had he been given a chance, was from the untouchable caste, and the president was from a higher caste. Jagjivan Ram told me at the time, "Why are we so backward in India, you ask me? Well, I don't want to blow my own trumpet, but I *am* the leader of one hundred and ten million Harijans [untouchables], and that really does make me far too powerful to be prime minister. Apart from the fact that they would not want to *touch* me [he laughed]." I checked out his assessment, and even now, at a distance of nearly five years, there are many astute political analysts who agree that the man was denied the highest office in the land because he came from the lowest caste.

This does not mean that caste infects everyday activity everywhere in India. In urban centers, among the upper crust, it hardly plays a part. But even there, I have been the recipient of both fulsome praise and gratuitous insult simply because I am a Brahmin. It is rather difficult to describe this without falling into the trap of implying that the *whole* of urban life is dictated by caste considerations—which would be quite untrue. But to assert the opposite and say that it plays no part at all would be equally false. As a member of the top crust, you are grudgingly or otherwise accorded a status that is not made available to lesser mortals. Not entirely to your advantage, always, as a politician recently discovered when standing among a constituency that was composed, in the majority, of people from the lower castes.

In general, however, it helps to be a Brahmin, or a Kshatriya. The divisions in Indian society do remain, whatever Oxbridge Indians might assert. In urban centers, the rigidities are not as fierce, but nevertheless persist. In village India, they continue, in the main, to be as vicious as they ever used to be.

The signal distinction between caste and class, evil as both these institutions are in my mind, is that one is sanctioned by religion, and held to be immutable, while the other is a social regulatory mechanism, which, with power of will and intelligent machination, can be bent to suit the purposes of one's own independent destiny. The two things do merge, but it would be very difficult for an outsider to tell where the lines come together and where they diverge.

PART FOUR

Systems

Clockwork Lemon

Slaves and Masters

The Robot and the Plowshare

Debates and Dialecticians

Oyster World with Thorns in the Thigh

8

Clockwork Lemon

*W*hen John Kenneth Galbraith (the renowned economist and an erstwhile American ambassador to the country), remarked appositely and memorably that "India is a functioning anarchy," few people noted that *functioning* was the crucial word, not *anarchy*.

It is true that most things do not function. If you go to a post office and try to deliver a letter to the United Kingdom or the United States, it is highly probable that you might have to wait at least two hours before you could be sure that your epistle would get to its destination. And even then, there would be no guarantee. The governmental bureaucracy attempts to make things more, rather than less, difficult for a foreign traveler. Instead of being welcomed, except at the top end of the hotel establishments (five star et al.), you will be treated disdainfully.

In general, you will feel that whatever you have learned from your guidebook and your brochures was wholly useless. India does "function," but differently!

Indian ethos cannot be made to fit into preconceived patterns. The time scale is different, ideas of hospitality are radically incongruent. The Westerner will always find the social landscape rather indigestible, initially at least.

But the positive end of the scale consists in attempting to see how the country has functioned since it was unyoked from foreign rule. There have been eight general elections, each time observed under enormous scrutiny from the West, and at no time has there been an accusation of widespread corruption, or "rigging." The reason for the latter is not that it was not intended, but that in a country as vast as India, it is simply not physically possible to rig every ballot box. Which is not to say that individual instances of such malpractice did *not* occur; it is to declare that such things cannot happen over the whole country.

On the other hand, when the queen of England arrived in New Delhi not so long ago, security was so tight as to make the pope's bodyguards and Reagan's outfit look like amateurs. There were ninety-three heads of state, and none of them had any cause to worry.

But the paradox, as in all things Indian, is that a country that can mount such rigid security for foreign dignitaries could not protect the life of its own prime minister. Why did Mrs. Gandhi get killed? The answer is intimately connected with that old Indian ethos once again. She insisted, against the strongest advice from her advisers, on not dismissing the Sikhs. Mrs. Gahdhi asserted, rightly in my opinion, that if she discriminated (racially) against the people who protected her, she would have no authentic voice in projecting a secular and nonpartisan stance to the rest of the country. Of course she was right. And in the conviction of that belief, she lost her life.

There is no doubt that anarchy is what seems to prevail. The Westerner looks on with condescension and disbelief. But what is not immediately apparent is the enormous sophistication, the scientific progress, the simple fact that India belongs to one of an exclusive club of space people (rockets and satellite launching pads) in which her erstwhile conqueror, Britain, does not have an entré.

The nation has also functioned, albeit with a few hiccups, as a legitimate democracy, when no other nation in that region of the world has anything comparable to show. It has had communal troubles, it has had riots. In the immediate period after Mrs. Gandhi's assassination, there was massive carnage in New Delhi and some neighboring states. But given its enormous problems and its natural centrifugal tendencies, it must be surprising that the country has not fallen apart.

The status that India occupies in the international arena was created largely by Jawaharlal Nehru. But it cannot be said that Indira Gandhi diminished it. Admittedly, the prime minister was vastly more authoritarian than her father, but in retrospect, she achieved, I believe, as much for India as Nehru ever did.

In order to understand how modern India functions, it is vital to comprehend the genesis of the country. The incursion of the British was invited, rather than repulsed. At about the middle of the seventeenth century, Indians welcomed the foreign invaders, while initially (a hundred years earlier), they had not.

In the latter half of the nineteenth century, the British, by then the established rulers in the land, encouraged the education of the Indian elite in the intellectual norms that were then fashionable in England and Europe. Having sown those potentially rebellious seeds, they could not but reap the forthcoming harvest. Both Gandhi and Nehru were the direct inheritors of a tradition that had no Indian roots at all, but had everything to do with the liberal humanism derived from Kant, Locke, Adam Smith, and Hume.

When independence finally came in 1947, Mahatma Gandhi, who did not believe in democracy, vacated the scene. Nehru, his protégé, was a vacillating liberal who had looked up to Gandhi as a father figure, and simply did not know what to do when "Bapu" (Father Gandhi) died in 1948 from an assassin's bullet. It was as if a senior prefect in an English public school had suddenly become headmaster. The subsequent hodgepodge is what the country is suffering from.

What both Nehru and Mrs. Gandhi did, however, was to keep the country together. Nehru died in bed, succumbing to senility and other ailments. Indira Gandhi was riddled with machine-gun fire. But in stark contrast with what happened elsewhere in that vast continent of Asia, it is nothing short of miraculous that no coup took place, that the Indian military have stayed nonpolitical and well out of the picture, and that father and daughter, between them, managed to preserve the fabric of the nation.

Whatever other faults both these people possessed, they projected an impeccably secular and noncommunal persona. There was no other leader in the whole country who could claim the allegiance of the whole nation, at any one instant. Even when Mrs. Gandhi was being her most notorious, authoritarian self (which was frequent), she never failed to talk with the authentic voice of a national leader.

Over a period of thirty-seven years, Jawaharlal Nehru and Indira Gandhi managed to keep the country together. It goes against the grain of Western liberalism to accept that dynastic rule succeeds.

In the last (eighth) general election, more than 67 percent of the electorate voted, and Rajiv Gandhi returned to power with a larger percentage of the popular vote than that with which Margaret Thatcher currently rules Britain.

Which does not mean that everyone likes Rajiv, nor that he will have an easy ride. It is to make the contrast with China, Pakistan, Bangladesh, Afganistan, Burma, Bhutan, and even Nepal. They do not have the same system of democratic franchise. In India, at no point has a democratic verdict, expressed at the polls, been *violently* overturned. Of course, there have been two spectacular assassinations, but only two, and neither of them has resulted in the overthrow of a government.

India is a vast country. Larger than Europe, without its Russian part. The ethos that keeps it together is stronger than the Judeo-Christian adhesives that operate on the Continent. The country functions as an amalgam of the British and American systems. Its constitution is, according to the pundits who know these things, one of the marvels of demotic writing. It establishes the equality of Man in a ringing paragraph on the first page:

> *All citizens, irrespective of religion, race, caste, sex, and place of birth, shall enjoy equality before the law and no disability shall be imposed upon them in any respect.*

It further goes on to announce:

> *"Untouchability" is abolished and its practice in any form is forbidden.*

Those, then, were the golden rules laid down by the founding fathers of the new nation. Not all those rules were executed in practice, and many were flagrantly violated. The fact that these rules were sacredly enshrined in the most precious document that the country possesses acted on the conscience of its rulers. Even after she had abrogated the rights of the common man in 1975 by declaring an arbitrary Emergency, Indira Gandhi never failed to take heed of the Indian constitution. That she mangled it, drove amendments through Parliament, only went to show how powerful a simple piece of paper can be, if it asserts universal truths.

The constitution of India declares that the country is a democratic republic. Every adult above the age of eighteen has a vote irrespective of caste or religion. Governments are elected every five years, though the prime minister can call an election any time before that if he or she feels that the prevalent political climate demands such action.

The political apparatus is a fusion of the American and British systems. The president of the country is a constitutional figurehead, with no executive powers, and he is elected by an electoral college comprised of the two houses in the central Parliament and representatives from the state legislatures. The president is also the commander in chief of the armed forces.

The checks and balances imposed upon any drastic political action such as launching a war or declaring an Emergency are not dissimilar to those in the American process. But there are differences. The prime minister is *appointed* by the president, not directly elected by popular vote. He or she is usually (though not always) the leader of the party that has won the largest number of seats in the Lok Sabha (elected House). The president calls upon such a leader to form a government after an election, but such a preference is conditional upon being given a vote of confidence in the House immediately after the appointment. If the prime minister cannot garner a majority, despite the appointment by the president, then the incumbent has one of two options. He or she can either recommend a dissolution of the House and advise the president to call for fresh elections, or resign, and the president is then able to call on someone else who might be able to form a majority government.

The first of these options was taken up by Charan Singh in 1979, and there were many constitutional pundits who ruminated at the time that if Jagjivan Ram had been invited to form a government, he would have easily commanded a majority in the House, and Mrs. Gandhi might never have got back to power. These are the ifs and buts of history, over which there is no final verdict.

The president of India cannot do anything (except under special circumstances, such as when the integrity of the nation is threatened, or when the prime minister becomes insane), without the "advice" of the prime minister. The prime minister, in turn, cannot issue any executive command without such action being ratified in Parliament and expressly approved by the cabinet and countersigned by the president. And the actions of both the president and the prime minister may be challenged by any member of the public in the Supreme Court of India, which is theoretically outside political and electoral control.

That is the theory.

In practice, however, if president and prime minister are in collusion, and there is a rubber-stamping majority that approves every piece of prime-ministerial legislation in Parliament, then just about anything can happen. If, furthermore, the judicial checks and balances are rendered ineffective by parliamentary fiat, then the common man has no recourse, and the state becomes, in effect, a version of Kafka's nightmare world or a prototype of the Soviet Union.

This is what happened during Mrs. Gandhi's Emergency in 1975. Fortunately, correctives did not have to be imposed from outside, and there was no internal rebellion. Conscience worked. The daughter of Jawaharlal Nehru could not forget her obligations to the constitution of India, and she desperately needed to demonstrate her legitimacy. So she called an election, hoping she would win, as all dictators do. But the system and the electorate proved more resilient than the passing whims of a tyrannical woman. Indira Gandhi was routed at the polls, and democracy won!

There are two houses of Parliament—the *Lok Sabha* (People's House) and the *Rajya Sabha* (Kingly House), Lower and Upper, according the the British model. The Lower House is a political body directly elected by the voters (in the last elections there were twelve principal parties represented in the Lower House, including two species of Communists), while the Upper House has appointed members and representatives from various professions, some of whom are elected by respective bodies, while a small number are directly appointed by the president. There is preferential discrimination here, embodied in the constitution, where a certain number have to be nominated from the disadvantaged minorities.

Each state has its own legislative assembly, again with a two-tiered chamber like the central Parliament. Once again, each state has its own chief minister, rather like the governors of the different states in the United States, except that the chief minister is not directly elected by the voters, but chosen by the majority party in the assembly.

It is a federal system within which defense, foreign affairs, communications, and certain other functions are the responsibility of the central government, while most local matters are handled by the respective state governments. Given the diversity of the country, it is obvious that the party that wins an election for central power need not be the same one that secures a majority in any one state legislature. This creates tensions, which Mrs. Gandhi exploited with ruthless skill in her capacity as prime minister. At the time of this writing, there are six states that are ruled by parties other than Mrs. Gandhi's Congress (I), which now governs the center under her son Rajiv. The prominent "dissident" state legislative assembly is the one in West Bengal, which is run by a China-inclined Marxist party. But politics are a volatile business in India, and defections and floor-crossings (whereby members change allegiances midstream), make it impossible to paint a stable picture.

India is currently the union of twenty-two states and nine territories ruled directly from New Delhi. State governors, who have no executive powers, are appointed by the president, but chief ministers are elected. The central government funds state projects, which on the basis of applications submitted by the individual states, have to be approved in Parliament. The internal stability of a state, such as the police force, are within the jurisdiction of the state's chief minister.

Also, India is professedly and determinedly secular, unlike any other nation in the region. Its constitution not only allows, but guarantees, freedom of worship to any religious denomination, but the nation itself does not avow any faith at all. You are not required to swear either on the *Gita* or the Bible in a court of law. You can simply "affirm."

One of the distinctions between the Indian system and its constitution from many nations of the West and almost all its neighbors, is this insistence on a universality, which will not preclude the participation of any member of the community in the great affairs of state. And though this theory has been frequently violated in practice, I believe that one of the signal adhesive elements that have kept the nation together in all its tortuous postindependent history is its theoretical commitment to this secular ideal.

Though Hinduism is the majority religion, minorities have always been capable of invoking the universal ideals to which the founding fathers dedicated themselves. It is not often accepted that though we might do wrong, the fact that we have an idea as to what is right might provide a moral corrective dictated by the deepest areas of one's soul.

In the recent disturbances that resulted in Mrs. Gandhi's assassination, there was one element that was not emphasized either in the international press or within India itself—that the problem was created by Mrs. Gandhi herself. That it was precisely because the secular universal ideals of the Indian constitution were initially laid aside that fanatics came to the fore, and a situation developed where nothing but drastic surgery could amputate the gangrene. But it need not have been like that; the confrontation could have been averted. By playing with communal rivalries, Mrs. Gandhi stoked the fires whose subsequent massive conflagration she could not contain.

I was in Chandigarh (some sixty miles away from the scene of the theater) at the time when Indira Gandhi sent in the army to storm the Golden Temple. I had checked into a tiny hotel owned by a turbaned Sikh (Sardarji). He was a retired major from the Indian army. We polished off a bottle of the finest Scotch whisky between us during a long night. In his late fifties, the man was in a loquacious and *recherché* mood.

"You know," he said, "I fought against Pakistan during the Kashmir war. I staked my life for this country. I have been a loyal citizen." Tears rolled down his face, admittedly encouraged by the Highland brew.

"And I don't like to be told that I am a traitor." He banged his fist on the table, the two glasses fell on the floor, he whistled to a minion to have the mess cleared away. I felt sad and unable to speak.

"That Bhrindanwale [the fanatic who was shot by the Indian army and who has now been installed as a martyr by the separatist movement] is a rogue and a murderer. But who built him up? Mrs. Gandhi did, for her own political purposes. Now she does not know how to bottle the genie, contain her own Frankenstein!"

We had another Scotch.

"Is that our fault? Tell me! After this incident, every Sikh will feel that he is not an Indian. She has divided us from the rest of the nation. I can tell you that there will be *trouble,* big trouble!" This was June 6, 1984.

"Does that mean," I queried, "that you and I, or people like us, will never be able to talk as friends again?"

The Sardarji burst into a hilarious laugh.

"You are not Indian," he declared. "You are not even Hindu! In a way you are nothing. I shall go on talking with you forever. You don't belong here. That may be your advantage, but it is also your sadness. You are a bit like a world man, but the world, my friend [he gave me a hug], is not ready to receive you. I shall remain a Sikh, and a loyal Sikh till the time I die!"

Next morning, I read in the papers that Khushwant Singh, a contributor to *The New York Times* and the most revered "liberal" journalist in India, had returned his Padma Bhusan (the highest honor that the government can bestow on literary figures) to the president of India, as a gesture of repugnance about what had happened the previous day at the Golden Temple. Mr. Khushwant Singh is a Sikh.

There are fissures within the system, some endemic, others imposed. There is a respectable body of opinion that argues that democracy is an unsuitable vehicle for India. It is a theory to which I have, personally, an ambiguous allegiance.

A country where 75 percent of the population is totally illterate, where the gross per capita income is less than two hundred dollars a year, where the radio and television networks are wholly state controlled, where feudalism still rules in most village areas (85 percent of the country), where communication between one part of the country and another (between the North and the South, for example) is still conducted in a foreign language (English), where male parental oligarchy is the effective norm within any house, where females are still held under the most enormous and fatal subjugation, it may be a little like *Alice in Wonderland* to talk about "democracy."

During the interregnum, when Mrs. Gandhi was not in power, I interviewed the then prime minister of India, for Independent Television News (London). The meeting was set up for 1:00 P.M. and Morarji Desai arrived in his immaculate Indian outfit exactly on the dot in the ornate cabinet room adjoining the parliamentary chamber in New Delhi. He held a piece of paper in his hand, and I could see it was a Telex message. The first words he spoke to me were: "I see you have written that 'Indians prefer the despot to the democrat.'" He smiled, put the paper down on the table (at eighty, still standing, while I was cowering like a dog), and said, "In that case, I don't think we have much to talk about."

Mr. Desai was quoting from an article I had written for *The Spectator* (a London weekly magazine with some prestige), which had appeared only the previous day in England. A Telex copy had been sent to him, and he was carrying it in his hand just before I was about to conduct this momentous conversation in front of the cameras.

I was naturally dumbfounded, not having expected such direct confrontation. I fumbled for words. The prime minister helped me out. He said, smiling once again, "But since we *are* a democracy, we allow everyone to have their own opinions."

He sat down, adjusted his spectacles, asked the sound fellow to fix the microphone on his jacket, and said, "Now, what is it you would like to ask me, young man?" I have remained friends with him ever since, though I disagree with almost everything he believes in.

India is a state-controlled economy. The government is the largest employer. The railways, coal, steel, telephones, telegraph, power supply, postal communications, broadcasting, both radio and television, and most major industries are state owned. The country is committed to state planning, and currently in the process of executing its sixth five-year plan.

Private enterprise does play a part, but a proportionately minor one. Once upon a time, Air India was privately owned, but now it is government controlled and has suffered obvious deterioration in efficiency. The interaction between private ownership of industry and the government is at best a mutually wary one. Jawaharlal Nehru was much more committed to full-blooded socialism than his successors have been. Though Indira Gandhi used the same vehement rhetoric as her father, she did veer away from rigid socialist doctrines in practice. Her son, the successor, will go farther along the same road, without making too much of a song and dance about it, because socialism in India, like capitalism in America, is a bit of a sacred cow, and no one dares to disacknowledge allegiance too openly.

Elsewhere, a system of extensive control on the economy provides a fine bed for seeds of corruption to flower. Exchange of currency is controlled; no Indian can take money out of the country without governmental permission. Even foreigners wishing to take their own money out of the country have to prove that they brought it in themselves in the first place.

India is one of the more credit-worthy borrowers from the International Monetary Fund. It is not generally regarded as a "breadbasket" case. In conversation with businessmen, I have been heartened to hear Canadian and German businessmen tell me how surprised they have been to hear the way Indians disparage themselves, when in the opinion of industrialists across the world the country is one of the best places for investment. The reason for this is that India has had a relatively stable political environment in comparison with her neighbors, and labor is exceedingly cheap. Also, the life-style that an Englishman or an American can afford in India, on a comparable salary, simply does not exist in his own homeland. But, once again, this will be described in another place.

The economy functions in a haphazard fashion: It is called *mixed*, in tune with fashionable jargon in the West. But basically it is a form of state capitalism, where inefficiency is rampant, where bureaucracy rules, where free-market competition is the exception, rather than the norm.

Fashionable fads do infect the psyche of the nation's urban youth, but they are barely 1 percent of the total population. Urgent convictions of possible spiritual renewal are not treated with skepticism as they are in the West, nor are prescriptions for instant solutions treated with the same gullibility. Suicides are exceedingly rare, divorce is a freak phenomenon. Judgments are seldom made.

The country functions anarchically at times, smoothly and efficiently at others. But the overall picture is of a lunar landscape, like a piece of matured cheese with great holes in the middle. What must intrigue the foreigner is the facility with which the country switches from primeval to modern and back again in every sphere of its life. As the ninth biggest industrial power in the world, and a member of the nuclear and space clubs, India still owes most of its agricultural output to the bullock cart and the iron plow. That is the conundrum!

9

Slaves and Masters

*W*hen Gayatri Devi, written up in *Vogue* magazine as one of the ten most beautiful women in the world, wafted down the spiral staircase at her palace in Jaipur (Rajasthan), barefoot and clad in a simple cotton sari, it struck home to me more forcibly than any number of books could ever have, as to what aristocracy is all about.

The blurb on the book *A Princess Remembers* by Santha Rama Rau (the well-known Indian novelist who occasionally writes for *The New Yorker*) and Gayatri Devi, had said: "She is the daughter of the Maharajah of Cooch Behar and the widow of the Maharajah of Jaipur. She was raised in a sumptuous palace staffed with 500 servants, and she shot her first panther when she was twelve. After she had won a seat in the Parliament of India, John F. Kennedy introduced her as 'the woman with the most staggering majority that anyone has ever earned in an election.' She is the Maharani of Jaipur, one of India's most glamorous and wealthy aristocrats."

But even this introduction had not prepared me for the kind of individual I was to meet in person. Far from being immediately intimidating and haughty, the lady came across as the most ordinary Indian housewife, in her late fifties (or could it have been her

247

early sixties?), anxious that her guest was comfortable and felt relaxed. She asked what I would like to drink and ordered tea for herself. Gayatri Devi sat down on the sofa, and indicated with a nod of her head that I was allowed to do so as well. (I had been gently but firmly instructed in advance that I should not sit in the presence of Her Royal Highness unless I had been specifically instructed to do so.)

As I fidgeted for words, the lady set me at ease. "You don't have to worry, I don't bite." Her eyes were brown and deep-set in bronze sockets, the face had a chiseled symmetry that might have pleased Rodin. With slightly pouting lips and an imperceptible air of arrogance, she made me feel as if there was nothing she could not do simply by flicking the fingers of her right hand. So I thought I would dive in at the deep end.

I asked, "Do you think that aristocrats have a place in contemporary Indian society?"

She raised her right eyebrow, looked at me deeply for a good thirty seconds, allowed a fleeting smile to drift across her lips, and replied, "Are you implying that *I* have no place in contemporary Indian society?"

To royalty you do not answer such direct questions, so I changed tack. "You speak Bengali?" I asked. (As I come from Bengal myself, I thought that a common language might provide some basis for mutual comprehension.)

"Of course I do!" she retorted, with the voice rising a gentle pitch or two. "You must know that I was brought up as a Bengali!" But the message was unmistakable. There was absolutely no question of speaking in the vernacular! English was the lingua franca under the Raj, and so it would remain under the current dispensation. Speaking in Bengali would indicate a degree of familiarity that Her Royal Highness had no intention of permitting.

I looked around the vast room, with autographed pictures of the Kennedys and the British queen with her consort, old and fading oil portraits of all those rajahs who had ruled Jaipur for nearly four hundred years, mementos of polo triumphs in which His late Royal Highness had excelled, the gilded and ornate furniture, massive glass chandeliers, hand-cut and imported at fabulous cost all the way from Europe in the late eighteenth century, Persian rugs and stuffed tigers hung up on the walls. I wondered how a woman who had been educated entirely in the Western mold could put up with the fact that her late husband already had several wives when he offered his hand in marriage to this most delectable creature (who had been madly in love with him ever since she was barely twelve)?

The princess said that there was no contradiction at all. Maharajahs were *expected* to have several wives. It would have been improper not to have more than one wife. But she also made it clear that she was his favorite one. Only *she* had been allowed to address him in the familiar *tu,* and call him *Jai,* an abbreviation of Jaipur.

I realized all over again that value systems cannot be transferred from one culture to another, that surface similarities of behavior do not necessarily indicate a congruence of moral and ethical approach, and that there was no way of asserting that one particular system was superior to another.

Among the kingly class in India, the really rich were spared the scourge of having to carry the burden of hypocrisy. While in the West today there would be secret mistresses tucked away all over the place, Indian maharajahs simply went ahead and married them all, set them up in palatial establishments, and proceeded to have the most torrid affairs with the latest acquisition in their harem. Since it was socially accepted, and as the older woman was never left out in the cold, everyone was happy.

The princess talked about her experience in prison during Mrs. Gandhi's Emergency, how she had had to clean her own lavatory (absolutely the most degrading thing that could be imposed upon royalty), how they had raided her house to find precious jewels, how Mrs. Gandhi's government had concocted a fictitious case about tax evasion and smuggling.

The feeling I got was that the lady was not even attempting to tell lies, nor trying to project a false image. She was just not aware that her own sense of being unjustly treated had no reflection in reality. That her complaint about "how poor we are" rang with a hollow note. When she said that no member of the old aristocracy had ever lost an election in democratic India (factually incorrect, incidentally, as the *Rajmata*—Queen Mother—of Gwalior stood against Mrs. Gandhi and was devastatingly defeated), and asked the rhetorical question as to why the poor peasants still voted with their feet in favor of the old regime, Gayatri Devi was implying that feudal loyalties still prevailed in contemporary India.

When poor people have been oppressed and ruled by autocratic kings who quite literally held the power of life and death over them, then the idea that such despotic regimes can be overthrown by the ballot box takes a little time to sink in. The old fear remains. There is as much an attraction for modern notions of autonomy and independence, as a superstitious dread that all this may be a transient phase, and that the ancient leather whip and the steel sword (once used to cut off hands and sever necks) would soon return again. So it was better to pay one's dues to the old regime and keep oneself in the good books, rather than venture into some unpredictable terrain from which the gains were likely to be nebulous.

As Churchill once remarked, "Democracy is a rotten system, but I don't know of any better." The Indian peasant, exploited as he has been for centuries, does not yet see it that way. Which does not mean he never will.

Most of the palaces in Jaipur have now been converted into luxury hotels. The present maharajah, still addressed as such by the people in his kingdom despite the fact the title was constitutionally withdrawn when the country achieved its independence, runs a small but very exclusive hotel himself, in which Queen Elizabeth and Prince Philip last stayed when they visited India. The old aristocracy are having to adjust to the brasher ways of contemporary quasicapitalist India. And more often than not, they are making a fairly successful job of it.

It is impossible to assess how much money these old maharajahs still possess. That they salted away a large part of their liquid fortunes into numbered Swiss accounts immediately after independence has never been in doubt.

Nicholas Kaldor, a British economist of international repute, calculated that but for all the money that was drained out of India within seven years of independence, there would have been no need for foreign aid at all.

Little has changed in rural India over the centuries. While empires have come and gone, while rulers have fought and squabbled in the various capitals of the country, the life of the peasant has remained static, culturally and economically.

The lack of revolutionary fervor among India's masses has often led the Western observer to conclude that Indians will put up with *anything*. But such judgments have been frequently and drastically proven wrong.

Passivity can often cloak an incipient insurgence that a different culture, an alternative perspective, might interpret as acquiescence. But it need not always be so. Like a leopard waiting in enormous patience to leap on its prey, the illiterate Indian, having been granted universal franchise (in 1947) after centuries of total deprivation, may appear slow to take advantage of his new legacy. But that does not necessarily mean that he is unaware of what he has inherited, and is selflessly and ignorantly willing to squander what he might now regard as his birthright.

When Mrs. Gandhi called an election in 1977, I was in the country to cover the event for *The Observer* (London). Since I had not been a great friend of the Gandhi regime, I was not allowed access to the highest coteries of the land at the time. So I spent my leisured hours roaming around the villages. After the *Janata* party won, I thought I would take my own personal sample of what had actually happened in the minds of the electorate—since Mrs. Gandhi had called the election on the certain assumption that she would win.

What I found both disturbed and heartened me. Villagers, the most ignorant and poorest of the lot, told me that all these pundits who had come from the cities had asked them how they would vote. They had unanimously replied that they would cast their ballot in favor of Mrs. Gandhi's party. When the time came, however, they kept their own counsel and voted for the opposition. A major electoral upset occurred, which none of the pundits had predicted in the papers. The peasants won!

When I asked them (the villagers) what they thought of the new regime, which was barely ten days old at the time, they were cautiously optimistic, and hoped that the campaign for mass sterilization (initiated during the 1975 Emergency regime) would not be repeated. But I remember one old, bearded man, hunched over his *hookah*, dragging on this clay pipe and raising his wizened head to say, "You tell them, my son, you tell them when you go back to the fancy capital [referring to New Delhi], that they had better watch out, and do what they have promised. Otherside, we shall throw them out, too, just as we did Nehru's daughter!"

His words require partial explanation. He was telling me that the peasants had done something unthinkable. They had gone against prescribed wisdom, had thrown out the aristocratic incumbent of the man (Nehru) who had been the idol of the masses. They had done this surreptitiously, without letting anyone know of their true intentions. This, he was implying, was his new awareness of the power of the individual vote. And he was asking me to convey the message to the gaudy metropolis that *if it can be done once, it can happen again.* Under that rustic visage and illiterate vocabulary, there was a shrewd political awareness of what it means to live under a democracy. Other journalists and political commentators had been sharply mistaken in equating a lowly status with a lack of inherent political wisdom.

The villager may be humble, he may put up with ceaseless exploitation, but he bides his time. And when the opportune moment arrives, he strikes back with conviction and ruthless vehemence. One then begins to wonder, "Who is the slave and who is the master?"

A colleague who was in college with me in Calcutta is currently a member of the West Bengal legislative assembly. His family has been ruling an estate the size of New Jersey for over two hundred years. My friend inherited the title when his father died in the early 1950s. Though the Indian constitution expressly forbids the use of *any* kingly nomenclature, his *prajahs* (serfs) still address him by the old name *Raja;* his "democratic" majority against his political opponent is unassailable.

I was once in a village where this "king" held sway. And I was totally flummoxed by the way in which the people kowtowed to a man who no longer had any legal power over them. My friend explained, "These are my subjects, you see," throwing me a wide grin. "They have not been to Oxford. They treat me as their lord and master, and they shall go on doing so till they die. Unto the third and fourth generations!"

"You don't really mean that?" I queried, in astonished wonder.

"You bet!" he barked back. "You lot, you think that by living in London or New York for a few minutes, you know everything! We have been here for centuries. How can you block that out?"

The villagers looked at him as if he were God incarnate. He had no need to assert his authority. I could see it in their eyes.

They touched his feet in such solemn reverence that it was impossible not to be moved. My friend smiled at each such supplication, waved his hand in benediction, and walked on, leaving behind a trail of people satisfied in the deepest atavistic corners of their souls.

Subdued, not knowing what to say, I walked apace with him for a good ten minutes. He put his hand on my shoulder, turned my head around and grinned. "Don't worry," he whispered, "your democratic day will come! But not in our lifetime, not certainly in yours!" This was in 1959. I was barely twenty at the time. My friend was not wrong in his general prognosis, but he was entirely awry about the time scale in which events would occur.

Twenty-five years later, I was in the backseat of a car driving up winding mountain roads in Kashmir, with sheer mile-long gorges on either side, and snowflaked hillsides ascending in the distance. It was the middle of an Indian summer. The temperature was below freezing, I had no gloves, and the polo-necked sweater I was wearing was wholly inadequate for the climate. Once again I had made the wrong assumptions.

At Sona Marg (a place where Europeans come to ski in the spring and tourists throng to in the summer) I was shivering in my summer clothes. My little guide smiled and said in Hindi, "I did tell you, *Sahib.*"

I nodded and acknowledged his superior local wisdom, and insisted we drive back down with all possible haste. "But, sir," he said, "you told me you wanted to see a village!"

"All right, if you insist," I barked back, "but I want you to hurry!"

We drove down the most spectacular terrain. Ribbons of silver liquid trickled over fantastic boulders. Foaming like horses, the narrow streams gushed, sprouting sprays of white fluff, bouncing here, and straying there. Gray slate slopes rose on either side. In the far far distance there were visible signs of green vegetation. Whether they were higher or lower was not apparent. I could not really tell what I was feeling. I knew, though, that my eye was taking in something that would never be erased. Streams parted and met again, white and green coalesced. Snowcapped mountaintops began to recede. Viaducts came and passed by us on the other side. Suddenly, we were back again on the flat plains of Hindostan. Or nearly.

"We have arrived," said my guide, as he nimbly parked the car on the edge of a little dirt track, no wider than eight feet.

We walked and walked for what seemed to me like ages, but it was a mere half mile, and I slipped and fell several times. By the time we arrived at "the village," I was thoroughly used to the stench of cow dung, and the slippery slush created by animal excreta.

The roads, if they could be called that, were barely three feet wide, sinuous, muddy, with large holes that one could not see since they were filled with brown slush, cakes of animal feces plastered on either side of walls that one had to grasp in order not to lose one's balance. Goats meandered down the path to meet us. I was beginning to feel distinctly edgy! "Don't worry, *Sahib*," said my guide, "it won't be long now."

We finally arrived at a little hut. There was a congregation to greet us—we had been announced! When I speak of a congregation, let me talk numbers. There could not have been less than a hundred people at the top of the mild hill we had just climbed. Naturally, I was awed.

There was a tray with an oil lamp that feted my arrival, held by a most demure damsel. I was instantly garlanded with marigolds. Several goats came and paid their respects, poking their horns into my trousers. A battery of screaming children shouted hosannahs. I knew I was meant to feel like a king.

I was then led up to the "sitting room," after I had, according to local custom, taken off my shoes at the outer edge of the house. Sitting down, feet flat on the floor, I waited for the next item on the ritual. And sure enough, it happened within minutes. A cup of steaming tea was brought in, gently imbued with butter (made from goat's milk), and sprinkled with salt. I took one sip, and knew I would get sick if I drank any more. But the cussedly staring eyes of the host, all of sixty-eight, with the geographical visage of a W. H. Auden, caused me to persevere. I did!

When I had finished, after about fifteen minutes, a tray of food was brought in before me for instant consumption. As I was speaking through a translator (my guide), I explained that I did not know Kashmiri custom or the language, and I did not wish to be rude, but I really did have to get back to the valley tonight, and would they please excuse me?

There was a great deal of flamboyant hand-waving, gesticulations, and eruptions in language that I could not comprehend at all. My guide explained. As it was already 4:50 P.M. and it would soon be dark, there was no question of our leaving tonight. These people would feel insulted if we left just now, because they dare not leave us in the hands of such inadequate contraptions as motor vehicles. Now, if we were *walking*, that would be a different matter!

Having been well and truly pincered, I gave in with grace. For the next two hours, I was offered several drags of the *hookah* (hub-ble-bubble) (stuffed with tobacco and injected with a generous dose of the local hashish brew), which I accepted in the spirit in which it was intended. Came eight o'clock, and it was time to eat.

We went downstairs into the living room, whose floor was made of mud, newly and liberally coated with liquid cow dung specifi-cally for my benefit. Two goats roamed in and out with the casual amiability of long-established friends. There were fourteen chick-ens (I counted them) who lived within the same room (that is), and a countless number of children and infants.

In the same fire against which the goats warmed their posteri-ors, and the chickens roosted, flat unleavened bread was being baked. This was not only the living room, it was the dining room as well, and, as I was soon to discover, it was the bedroom for most of the sixteen-member family who lived in this little house.

We ate the bread, a thick soup made of lentils, and a spiced curry cooked out of a freshly slaughtered chicken, which was only distributed to me and three other older male members of the fam-ily. None of the females ate with us, and since there was so little meat on the bird, I am quite sure that the rest of the household consumed a vegetarian meal.

When the time came to go to sleep, I was given the only real room there was in the house. I lay down on the floor, according to instructions from my guide, and dared not insist that I did not need a *whole* room when there were sixteen other people to con-sider. On my way down to have a pee at dawn (I slept with my clothes on), I noticed that in the living room there were neatly arrayed bodies on the floor, the men on thicker cushions, at one end of the room, the women on the other, while the two goats were cozily slumbering in the nethermost corner. The chickens were crowing outside, with free access to the somnolent fire, since the door had been left ajar.

In the morning, when the same tea was offered again, I declined both the brew and the accompanying breakfast, pleading a weak tummy. I thanked my hosts profusely, and wondered if I could be of any assistance. Yes, I could, the old man said, drawing on his *hookah,* perhaps I would like a Kashmiri rug, which his eldest daughter had just made. I said I would have a look. He brought out this exquisite carpet, hand-done, with six hundred stitches to the square inch, and asked whether I liked it. I said I most certainly did. How much would it set me back? Only ten thousand dollars, he replied.

He had told me the previous evening that the total family income was three hundred dollars a year, he cultivated four acres of land on which he grew his food, his sons aided tourists who wanted to "trek," and his daughters made a meager living weaving carpets.

Now, after all this ostentatious hospitality, he was asking ten thousand dollars for a rug which, down on the plains or even in New York, for that matter, would not cost half that sum. I could not understand the psychology!

Once we were in the car, my guide explained: "You should not have asked the price. He would have given it to you for free!" *Mea culpa, mea maxima culpa.*

While 85 percent of the population still live in the villages where illiteracy is sometimes as high as 75 percent, there is a growing exodus from rural areas into towns, often hundreds of miles away. This creates special tensions within village communities, where one family may have a son who sends back money from the city, while neighbors starve. The old harmony is disrupted, and the role of the village elder is gently but surely eroded.

Mahatma Gandhi believed that industrialization was no answer to the problems that plague the mass of India's poor, and that villagers should be taught to be self-sufficient in food, weave their own cloth from cotton, and eschew the glittering prizes that the twentieth century so temptingly offers. Such an idyllic and rural paradise did not appeal to those who inherited the reins of political power. Nor do I see how it could have done, for it meant resolutely refusing to accept the march of time. But one element of Gandhian thought still has a contemporary relevance—the role of the peasant in shaping the political destiny of the nation, as it did in driving out the British from India!

*　*　*

There is a certain iron consistency in the Indian ethos. The exploiter and the exploited still coexist, the slave and the master do in fact make up a social fabric that is different from czarist Russia. Who knows who has the last word? Does the Indian peasant, with his mute and incomprehending stare, always lose? Do his apparent superiors, the politicians and the technocrats, always win? If *democracy* really means anything at all, the answer should be obvious.

10

The Robot and the Plowshare

Unlike most other nations belonging to that cluster of countries now euphemistically known as the Third World, with the exception of China, India does straddle the preindustrial, agro-feudal world and the contemporary universe of the computer and the microchip with a fair degree of competent vitality. The signs of technological progress are not token symbols. The steady march toward an industrial economy has indeed covered real ground, as hardheaded businessmen from the West and skeptical accountants from the International Monetary Fund have freely admitted, with gulps of astonished admiration in their voices.

As the ninth largest industrial power in the world, India's headlong somersault from the base of a predominantly agricultural and rural economy to the conundrums of an urbanized and technological society has been achieved in the past thirty-odd years at some cost to the social fabric. Apart from the two superpowers, she lags behind France, Britain, and Germany in Europe; Canada in North America; and Japan and China in Asia. In the industrial league of nations, India enjoys a far higher prestige than the impression with which the tourist is likely to come away after a short visit to the country.

The reason for this is twofold, but interrelated. The visual im-

The Robot and the Plowshare

pact of urban deprivation and ubiquitous poverty is likely to be much greater than any number of lectures on the rise in the industrial production index (by 450 percent in thirty years), the total self-sufficiency in food (as a result of the so-called green revolution), and highfalutin chatter about India's space program at fashionable cocktail parties.

When the taxi you have just hired is over twenty years old, when you drive down dirty, winding streets, where open rubbish accumulates on pavements in huge mounds, and cows amble through city traffic, picking at bits of garbage here and excreting masses of dung there, it is a little difficult to imagine that this is a country that competes in world forums for the most advanced theoretical breakthroughs in nuclear physics, that it has its own rocket launching pad, that India's scientists and technicians are among the most sought-after personnel in the international market.

Urban poverty, which the visitor all too frequently confronts on first landing, is a direct consequence of the very success that lies hidden from view. It has been contended (correctly) that there were far fewer beggars under British rule than there are in independent India. Cities looked cleaner then than they do now. Malnutrition was not as rampant and did not so universally assault the eyes. Nor as frequent was the sight of wiry-boned roadside urchins, deformed by disease, creeping leglessly up the curb to grasp your ankle.

Under the British there was a healthy, optimistic air that silently proclaimed that here was a stable universe in which the rich would remain rich forever, the ruler would rule, and the poor, like children in Victorian England, should be neither seen nor heard. This philosophy was subtly but sternly enforced by the *dunda* (steel rod), the whip, and, under extreme conditions, the gun. When none of these instruments worked, the troublemakers were incarcerated in prison. Of course, that is one way of solving the problem of poverty, and removing eyesores from view. I think we call it "sweeping the dust under the carpet" nowadays.

In independent India, the massive drive toward industrialization, initiated by Nehru with such schemes as the Damodar Valley Corporation (modeled after the Tennessee Valley Authority), the Sindri fertilizer factory, the Chittaranjan Locomotive Works (where India began to produce her own engines, which, previously, had all been imported from Britain), began to create a sense of instant urban prosperity.

This news filtered back to the villages with a slow but sure basslike beating of the drums. A rural exodus to towns and cities began with a trickle but soon rose into an overwhelming tide. Since 1947 (the year of independence), the population of Calcutta has increased over *ten* times (exceeding twelve million today, in the greater Calcutta area), while the civic amenities have remained nearly static. The drainage system, installed over a hundred years ago by the British, remains much the same as it used to be, with a few patchwork modifications. Sewage is treated in the same old tanks with an additional ad hoc plant or two. Electricity (provided under the old Calcutta Electric Supply Corporation) has been supplemented by several other power stations, but the demand exceeds supply so sharply that the city does without any power for four to six hours a day all through the year, and the figure rises to unconscionable levels of fourteen to sixteen hours during the monsoons. Yet no one seems to mind very much. The very rich install their own generators, the middle classes suffer viciously and grumble under their breath (since it is no longer permissible to make the subject a conversation piece at a party), and the poor do without.

On the last occasion when I was in Calcutta, in May 1984, I had been invited to a dinner party by some long-standing friends. A couple of hours before the function was due to begin, I received a note, delivered by taxi, saying that I should report to a certain suite at the Grand Hotel, rather than to their house for dinner. I was a little perplexed about the message, since I was in a house where there was a telephone, and I could not see the reason why I should be summoned so imperiously to a hotel, when in fact it was to have been a family dinner all along.

When I arrived at the hotel, as I had been instructed, I realized, to my utter astonishment, how easily we make assumptions that do not tally with reality. The couple had tried to contact me on the phone for over two hours without success, since the whole of the neighborhood in which I was staying was "not operating." So they had sent a taxi with the message. They had also been forced to vacate their house, since the area in which they lived had been without power from the previous evening and it looked unlikely that electricity would be restored that night. Rather than take a chance with all their invited guests, they had moved into a hotel. I was both humbled and flattered. But I did wonder what happened to people who could neither afford a taxi nor move into a hotel, where the room itself (let alone the meal) would cost $80 a night, while the average middle-class salary is $160 a month.

Most cities in India (Calcutta is merely an extreme example of the same phenomena) are bursting like pregnant women breaking water before their time. Medical facilities simply cannot cope with even a tenth of what they have to face. I once took a woman with a fractured skull and a couple of broken ribs to the hospital (she had been thrown out of a speeding taxi), and after the most cursory attention, I was told to "remove" her, since there were thirty others waiting in the queue. As this was at three in the morning, and as I had some idea that a fractured skull does not mend as easily as a finger cut from a kitchen knife, I persisted with the house doctor. In outraged exasperation, he shouted, "You tell me what I should do! Turn all these people away, so that *your* patient may be attended properly?" I looked at the casualty victims waiting in the hall—broken limbs, gashed eyes, one man with a knife wound in his chest—and I knew I had no answer. They were all emergency cases, some thirty of them. There were only six beds, and two doctors on duty.

The city acts as a magnet for hopes and aspirations of villagers who have heard gaudy tales of milk and honey flowing on the streets, but who do not believe, when they arrive at the metropolis, that conditions are as unwholesome as they witness with their eyes. Both pride and an addiction to myth prevents their return to the comparative idyll of their rural existence.

For it is a salient and often unobserved fact that in rural India, although there is poverty, there is seldom any visible destitution. In any village, even among the lowliest, in their tiny thatched huts and mud floors you will always be offered tea, and if you stay a little longer, there will be food, inevitably vegetarian, cooked in front of you, and a cordial hospitality that will surprise the urban visitor. The rural person belongs to a community, and even with landlords exacting huge fees, there is always a patch of cultivatable land where the family of ten or twelve or sixteen will be able to grow enough staple diet to feed themselves throughout the year.

(Times of drought are another matter—that is when famine sets in.) You will very seldom see a real beggar in the villages of India. You might look at a holy mendicant, there might be little boys chasing you down a narrow, two-foot-wide mud alley for "money, money," but these children will be shouting and laughing as they hunt their quarry. There will be no sorrow on their faces, and even their scantily clothed bodies will look respectable in comparison to the scavengers who accost you on the streets of Bombay or Calcutta.

The reason is that though the villager earns a great deal less than his counterpart in the city, everyone in a village *works*. There is no such thing as unemployment. The average wage, if you divided the total family income by the numbers who are "employed," may come to less than ten dollars a month! But since every person works (including the four-year-old child who has just led you to the house of his grandfather), all members of the household will be fed.

If one particular family falls on hard times, neighbors will chip in to help with the cultivation, lend seed corn, and so forth. There is a kind of pride among the country's lowliest rural poor that is totally absent among the destitutes in urban India.

When this closely knit network is disrupted, when a family, or even a part of it, decides to migrate into a town or a city, the most important amenity that becomes immediately unavailable is food. For though villagers may be underfed and lack the adequate supplies of vitamins, no one actually starves (except in times of famine). In the city, it is a different story. There is no longer the communal hut to which one may repair for the night. So, shanty towns grow up on city pavements, ditches dug for new constructions or sewage pipes get converted into makeshift habitations. Beggary becomes an occupation.

All kinds of fancy things like steel, cement, commercial vehicles, jute, coal, oil, and other bases for industrial regeneration have risen in production by enormous leaps and bounds since the British left India. Tourism, too, has increased by a factor of some 400 percent. These are impressive statistics.

There are the legendary houses of the Tatas and the Birlas, which are reputed to control the whole of India's economy, and a great deal of its politics besides. But only a couple of years ago, it was revealed by an erstwhile Indian who has subsequently taken British citizenship, that almost all the money invested in these companies belonged to the government. That only ten families in India controlled 95 percent of the private-sector wealth. And that though these families were, in theory, only managers, and risked no private capital of their own, they lived in a vastly more regal style than any of their counterparts in the West would ever dream of doing.

The man who made these disclosures was of course a businessman himself, and he must have had his own ax to grind. But when I met him at his London office, Swraj Paul appeared to me the very epitome of the scrupulous entrepreneur that his enemies characterized him not to be. In any case, it did not seem to me that whether he was a saint or the devil incarnate was really the issue.

Was it true that a handful of people were using public funds to live in lavish profligacy, while the projected image was one of immense industrial efficiency being achieved at the expense of enormous personal financial risk?

The story turned out to be true to the letter. I am told by my colleagues in financial journalism that when businessmen get at each other's throats in public, they tend to get their facts right first.

The implications, however, totally outside the esoteric world of commerce, were enormous. What had apparently happened since independence was nothing short of scandalous. The government, while making all kinds of socialistic noises in public, had been quietly succoring a capitalism of the most inefficient and grafting kind.

Public money had been fed to private enterprise on the apparent understanding that competition and free-market laissez faire were to operate, while both government and borrower knew that in any particular sector, nothing of the kind would happen. The whole of the economy had been hived off by a few powerful families (who injected liquid cash into the coffers of the ruling political party, to wit, the Congress) into different segments, within which there would be neither private nor public competition.

I sought and obtained an interview with the head of the largest industrial organization in the country still owned by a private family, where no public funds had ever been received or invited, where the shares were not quoted on the stock exchange, where the enormous outfit was still run as if it were a small grocery store round the corner, run by brothers and relatives. The only difference was that this was the house of Godrej, a name as fabulous as Tata or Birla, established a bare eighty years ago, but vastly more renowned for its integrity and philanthropy.

Mr. Godrej was a sprightly and exceedingly handsome man in his early seventies. He had come into the office on a Sunday afternoon specifically for my benefit. As soon as I entered his room, he stood up and greeted me as if I were a long-lost friend: "How absolutely nice to meet you," he said, hugging me hard. "I do hope the dogs were not too ferocious!" (There were guard dogs at the gate.)

"Do sit down," Mr. Godrej announced, indicating a lavish leather sofa, "while I get you something to drink." He had heard of my predilection for the hard stuff, unlike the Maharani of Jaipur. We sipped malt whiskeys. When the social banter was over, within less than ten minutes, Mr. Godrej remarked with a steely joviality, "You Westerners seem to assume that we Indian industrialists are all philistines."

As I had noticed several volumes in French by Balzac and Zola on the bookshelf, I was going to make no such assumption.

Mr. Godrej led me by the hand to his roof garden. I noticed that he jumped two steps at a time, that he hopped about in glee as he showed me his private treasure (the only roof garden in Bombay), and that he knew an enormous amount about the architecture of the neighborhood, as he patiently explained the genesis of various different housing complexes that could be observed from the assured height of his garden niche.

When we came down, I asked him about Swraj Paul, and the so-called exposés. Mr. Godrej replied, "Of course, Paul was right! These people are literally living off other people's money. I don't much believe in *isms* myself, but what they are doing is neither socialism nor capitalism. It is simple, old-fashioned robbery."

Mr. Godrej, even with his gray-haired, wimpish, seventy-odd years, had a winning smile. "We run a little old family business here. I shall invite you to take back this little brochure we have prepared; it will tell you a lot more than I, in my old age, can hope to do."

Godrej started off as the inventor of a fire-proofing compound that is still used in India (and in many other parts of the world, too). The company then branched out into making safes, locks, filing and recording systems, typewriters, steel tubes, furniture, machine tools, architecture, interior design, forklift trucks, steel castings, oil-based chemicals, a soap composed of vegetable oils (as against the chemical variety), animal feeds, and oil cakes, and determinedly spread its wings to virtually conquer the entire Southeast Asian market.

That, then, was the success story *par excellence.*

This old man who was talking to me had a faintly waspish sense of humor. At the end of our two-hour-long meeting, he said almost casually, "You know, I am a dear friend of Prince Philip, we serve on the same committee for the Wildlife Fund!"

As someone remarked about Curzon's *style,* Indians are infatuated with the stuff. I certainly was, with the way Mr. Godrej projected himself. He would not tell me his first name, but he treated me as a friend, made me feel at home in his lavish office. When I subsequently discovered that his outfit made an annual turnover of a little less than a *billion* dollars, this did not make as much of an impact on me as the fact that the *owner* of the company had come out on a Sunday afternoon, merely to talk to an oddball writer.

In my own sneaky way, I tried to discover if there were hidden loopholes here, whether he had tried to inveigle me. But, alas, the slate was wholly clean. Mr. Godrej did not control anywhere as large an empire as either the Birlas or the Tatas. But whatever he did control, he owned entirely himself, or between himself and his family. There was no public funding, no floating of false shares. His was a clear and pristine example of capitalism at work—oligarchic, admittedly, wholly autocratic in the methods by which company policy was devised and administered. But somehow wholly beneficent, even to the extent of providing extensive gardens and large recreational facilities for workers.

The other not so contrasting experience was the one I had with Professor U. S. Rao at the Indian Space Research Centre in Bangalore, South India. I asked him if, in a country like India, with its abominably low gross national product and a terrifyingly low national average income, the idea of space research was not a luxury.

Professor Rao, educated at MIT and in Germany, replied: "Space research is a luxury only for those nations of the world which are already industrially developed. For developing countries, it is an absolute necessity. Not for the reasons which are spectacular and press-worthy, but for the simple reasons of communications and meteorology, which have become essential to our survival."

I queried whether sending rockets up into space would help either of these endeavors.

The professor answered: "We need these things for survival, and we cannot depend upon other nations to provide us with this kind of elementary technology. We are not trying to show off. If we need to communicate between one part of our nation to the other, and there is a flood, then we have no terrestrial methods to do so!"

India has launched several rockets, it has a liaison with the Soviet Union whereby it can use Russian rocket-launching facilities to spin its own satellites into space. The professor certainly convinced me that for determining where deforestation is happening, what kind of weather to expect (crucial in India), what amount of snow is likely to pour down from the Himalayas, how to communicate with a totally flooded area, satellites were indispensable. India is building its own space program on the firm assertion that in ten to twenty years' time, it will not be dependent on any other country. The robot will have finally come into his own.

What, then, of the plowshare? The handicraft industries will survive. I remember being taken to a little hideout in Agra where the man said that this was where the real artisans who built the Taj Mahal actually lived. The semiprecious stones were stuck into the marble by a special glue that has no modern equivalent. And it is absolutely true that the brass work in Rajasthan, silk in Murshidabad, clay ornaments in the southeastern sector, and marble work in the North will never be forgotten. Once these families perish, however, these particular crafts will die with them.

The old, nearly blind man, beating a piece of brass into a thin sheet, is doing what his father and grandfather before him have taught him to do. The British are supposed to have cut off the fingers of all those silk weavers in Murshidabad, because the fine fabric they spun out of their homemade spinning wheel was driving British textile importers out of business. Kashmiri carpets are still worth a great deal more in the Western markets than any kind of machine-manufactured artifact. Some crafts, such as embroidery and wood carving, simply cannot be learned at school. They have to be imbibed through a process of osmosis, from generation to generation.

There is no way that the old-fashioned smithy who lived in my father's house will ever be truly replaced. The things he made are now constructed out of aluminum, the handles for the lavatory chain are available at Woolworth's, and my ancient carpenter friend will find that his services are no longer required.

Yet there will be a longing for the things that were made by hand. I have a wooden chess set, carved in mainland China, where every piece is slightly different from the other. No two castles, either white or black, look alike, and some of the pawns lean like the Tower of Pisa. My friends who come to play always covet my set, when theirs look so much more elegantly finished, replete with the machine manufacturer's label.

For swift turnover and cheaper prices, machine production will never go away. Computers will, of course, come into their own, as they are already beginning to do, but so will other, richer variations of the old traditions. Cottage industries will be encouraged. Perhaps some of their authentic color will change, but something of old India *will* survive, as it has over centuries of depredation and ravishment. Indian identity is not rigid. It is susceptible to infinite variation. The humble plow can, and often does, stand up to the most mechanized contraption on earth.

11

Debates and Dialecticians

Politics in India are different from anywhere else in the world. Apart from the stark contrasts between profession and practice, the human faces behind the greasepaint in the political theater are at least as intriguing as the acts they perform in public.

When a former prime minister of the country (Charan Singh) asks a Western reporter (me—representing a British paper) at the end of a formal interview, with his civil-service adviser present, why "you journalists do not write about the fact that . . . [referring to a former foreign minister who was a bachelor and a political rival] sleeps with . . . [mentioning a particular married lady]"; when a chief minister of a state announces in public that between four and five in the morning, he likes to dress in women's clothes; and when all of this is smoothly taken in its stride by the public at large, then one gets a glimpse of the kind of drama that goes on in the political arena in India.

Of course, there are local commentators who denounce the Western press for picking up such incidents and trivializing the serious job of running the machinery of the country in the search for sensationalism. And to an extent they have a point. The counterargument is that if leaders display such quirks, their foibles cannot necessarily be separated from political actions. Morarji Desai's insistence upon totally avoiding the services of Western medicine resulted in the Australian Parliament having to pass special legislation to allow the man (when he was finance minister under Nehru) into the country without being vaccinated. When private life and public performance is seen to be wholly divorced, then journalistic curiosity may be condemned as prurient. But not when they merge, and are known to influence each other.

Charan Singh's query displayed an underlying assumption that a bachelor who fornicates with a married lady is unfit for public office. Others might contend that susceptibility to corruption and nepotism (allegations that had been made against his wife, if not directly about Mr. Singh himself) constitute far greater handicaps.

Desai's dietary and medical habits stemmed directly from his personality, which was literally as stubborn as a mule and as conceited as a peacock, not the least reason why the *Janata* government fell from power in 1979, and Mrs. Gandhi was voted massively back to power.

Such maverick politicians are not rare commodities in India (though urine drinking is an extreme example of the phenomenon); they are the staple diet on which the electorate feeds.

The present chief minister of Andhra Pradesh (south-central India), N. T. Ramarao, was an actor for thirty-five years before he joined politics in 1982, and was massively voted into power through his party, the Telegu Desam (Telegu is the state language and *desam* means nation). He is the most successful and popular regional leader in the country, whom Mrs. Gandhi tried to oust in 1984 while the politician was on a fund-raising visit to the States (there are a huge number of Telegu-speaking Indians who are residents of the United States). On his return to India, he was quickly reinstated despite political interference from New Delhi, because the popular upsurge was enormous.

When I asked for an interview, I was given a time by his personal assistant, 5:15 A.M. I was also told that the CM does not live in the official residence of the chief minister, but prefers to stay in his old palatial house, which he occupied during his thespian days.

N. T. R. wore saffron robes, sandals on his feet, and there were holy marks on his face made out of various kinds of herbal pastes. The man who had openly proclaimed his transvestite inclinations in public print not so long ago appeared to be as shrewd a political animal as any I had met. When I questioned him about his roles in film, he replied, "The masses like to worship, we are a very religious country." He was referring to the fact that he invariably played the role of Rama, the legendary god (hero of the epic *Ramayana*), who rescued the world from evil. The masses identified his celluloid role with the man in real life. When it came to the vote, they preferred to cast their lot with someone they had known as being holy on the screen. N. T. R. had campaigned on a platform to weed out corruption from public life. Who better suited than the matinee idol who had won such fantastic battles against the devils assailing his kingdom? Once again, it was that deification syndrome, the God-in-human-form complex that swept an aging actor into the driving seat of the state political engine.

There was another actor, M. G. Ramachandran, who won power in Tamil Nadu (formerly Madras) on a similar platform. And recently, yet another star has got into Parliament as the heartthrob of India's filmgoing masses. The significant feature of this connection between politics and the screen is that it deeply reflects a feature of the Indian ethos, quite dissimilar in kind to the electoral avalanche that recently returned Ronald Reagan to the White House. The distinction between celluloid fantasy and political reality is not only blurred in the public mind, the identification is quite openly fostered: The good guy on the screen is seen as someone who is more likely to be a good guy in real life. Someone who plays a god is certain to be more *godlike* than any other scrambler for the prize. Whether this is a facile and naïve equation is a matter of value judgment. What can be asserted with some authority is the fact that none of these actors have performed with any less efficiency than their predecessors, and their record in office has been far less tarred with accusations of corruption. As the British say, when a judge puts on a wig and gown, he *becomes* a different person, his outfit compels him to behave and respond in a way that raises him above the frailties of the man on the street. That, at least, is the theory. Who is to say that there is not some deep psychological truth embedded in the fable?

To cite another example from the opposite end of the spectrum, there is the case of Dr. Farooq Abdullah, Western-educated former chief minister of Jammu and Kashmir (in northwestern India). Abdullah succeeded his father, the great sheikh, the "Lion of

Kashmir," in 1982. Family squabbles ensured that Mrs. Gandhi was able to oust him from power and install his brother-in-law in 1984. But the dynastic element in the first succession (after the sheikh's death) was not the point at issue.

When I met Dr. Abdullah in May 1984, he was riding on the crest of a popular vote of confidence that appeared to make him impregnable to any kind of political machination from New Delhi. Outside his office on that summer morning, Dr. Abdullah came out with a statement (on tape) that I found astonishing by any standards. He had previously told me that Mrs. Gandhi had been sending emissaries from Delhi with suitcases full of rupee notes to buy off members in his state legislature, so that he would lose his majority in the assembly and thus be toppled from his position as chief minister.

He then said, without a trace of a smile on his face, "What I fail to understand is why she does not approach me directly. I know she is offering them [the members of his party in the legislative assembly] one to two lakhs [between ten to twenty thousand dollars]. It would be much cheaper for her to deal with me directly. I would gladly go, for five times that sum, provided some arrangements could be made to take the money out of the country!"

I could not believe that I was hearing this kind of statement from someone who was educated in the West and had a promising political future as a potential national leader in the country. It was not an off-the-cuff remark, nor was it said jocularly in private. In an official interview given to a writer who was due to publish his book in the States, the chief minister was happy to let me record these sentiments on tape!

The Indian masses have taken to democracy and the electoral process with a fierce zest. In the last general elections (December 1984), more than 67 parcent of the electorate went to the polls, there were five thousand candidates for less than five hundred seats in the central legislature, and there were twelve major parties contending in the whole country, in addition to a host of splinter groups and tiny coteries. By and large, the election took place with as much fairness as is possible in a country as vast as India. Western observers noted lapses in individual constituencies, there was *some* violence, but the general verdict was not in doubt. Nor did the

Opposition, utterly vanquished by Rajiv Gandhi's massive majority, rise up in rebellion to complain about the *process* that had produced such an unpleasant result (for them).

Admittedly, religious and communal rivalries (which Mrs. Gandhi did much to stoke and inflame) prevailed. Two states (the Punjab, the source of the recent Sikh troubles, and Assam, in the northeast) did not have elections for fear that there would be carnage. But for a country with an electorate approaching four hundred million, the operation was carried out in comparative efficiency and peace.

If democracy is simply a political apparatus by which a party or leader is elected to power by the expressed wish of the majority of the electorate through the ballot box, then there can be no ambiguity that India has proved over the past thirty-five years that it has vigorously earned the right to call itself the largest democracy in the world. Whether the ethos that dictates the choice of a particular party or its leader is essentially democratic, or whether it is governed by atavistic forces and mythic mechanisms that are precisely antithetical to the democratic ideal, is an altogether different question.

When the successful candidate has had to spend over 15 lakhs of rupees (about $150,000) to be elected to the central Parliament, and the average national wage is $200 a year, it is a little difficult to square the circle and aver that the common man was being fairly and legitimately represented in the highest legislative body of the land. Apart from the obvious and almost indispensable invitation to corruption, gangsterism, incipient violence, and other malpractices, the massive gulf between money spent and official rewards received (the salary of an MP is a miserly pittance of less than $300 a month), will be naturally breached by methods that will not bear close scrutiny.

The forums in which the great issues of state are thrashed out for future legislation bear a facsimile resemblance to the British Parliament. Debates are conducted under identical procedural forms. There is a two-tiered legislature in New Delhi, just as in Westminster. There are speakers in both the Lower and Upper houses, points of order are raised, courteous references to "Honourable Members" are made. But there is a faintly surrealistic air about the whole business, as if it were all happening at one remove from reality.

When the British left, and Harrow- and Cambridge-educated Jawaharlal Nehru became prime minister of independent India, the level of debate in the central parliament was sophisticated and highly instructive. Most members had been educated in the West, their vocabulary was polished, both government and the opposition respected each other.

Since then, much has changed, thanks largely to Mrs. Gandhi's imperious habit of disregarding Parliament, and due to the introduction of a *lumpen bourgeoisie* element through son Sanjay after the 1980 elections.

When Indira Gandhi was sent to prison on a charge of "contempt of Parliament" (even the expression is identically British), I attended the dramatic session in the *Lok Sabha* at which the verdict was delivered. With my naïve faith in the sanctity of the chamber, I was deeply shocked by the screeching and hysterical modalities within which parliamentary business seemed to be conducted.

Innocently, I had hitherto believed newspaper reports that modestly underplayed (though in extreme circumstances the truth had to get out, such as the time when two members indulged in such a rough brawl on the floor of the House that both of them had to be treated at the hospital) the total bedlam that reigned so frequently. I had also blindly accepted the idea that mature, adult men who had been elected by adult franchise to the supreme national body behaved with the solemnity and decorum that their representative status demanded.

For instance, it bemused me no end to observe that not a single report or editorial in the next day's papers drew attention to the fact that the whole of Prime Minister Desai's winding-up speech—on the motion commending Mrs. Gandhi's punishment—which went on for about eighteen minutes, there were only two periods, each lasting less than a minute, during which Mr. Desai was heard in silence by his parliamentary colleagues.

For the rest of the time, there was a continuous din, rising to crescendo in spasms, vocally emanating from the honorable members of the Opposition, some of whom persisted in remaining upright and gesticulating with their hands in a manner that my teachers at school had taught me to consider rude and offensive. All this while, the speaker displayed a benign indifference.

And this was no ordinary occasion. A former prime minister of the country was being charged with having violated the dignity of Parliament and was being put in jail for that offense.

But the other distasteful features of the Indian Parliament went far beyond mere manners. In places where the concept of representative government is held to be firmly established, the procedures through which political affiliation and alignment are displayed took a long time to grow roots. Even with expediency and self-interest motivating individuals in the power game, there were broadly perceptible lines that differentiated contending factions and their human constituents.

In India, the exact converse is almost universally the case. The rule is proven in the unique exceptions of individuals whose stances are dictated solely by ideology or principle. The large mass of parliamentarians are governed by aspirations to retain or gain power and so make money, and nothing else.

It is precisely because fundamental assumptions are so different in the East and West that dynastic succession is accepted with such placid equanimity in the country. But once again we have to go back to the mechanism of the Hindu mind (the vast majority of voters are Hindu), which can contain two diametrically opposed theories within the same mental frame. What the modern mind vehemently repudiates as an absurd and apparent contradiction will be happily accepted by the most refined Hindu, in any kind of sophisticated forum, without the smallest qualms.

This will sometimes perplex, often infuriate the Western visitor. Beyond a certain point, ratiocinative debate will become impossible. A statement will be made, as if it were an axiom that requires no proof.

When I asked Rajiv Gandhi (while his mother was still alive) whether he would like to be prime minister, he did not find the question either absurd or impertinent. To him it was the most natural thing in the world. And I do not believe he was dissimulating.

The ease with which the succession was ensured led one commentator to remark, with a certain literary turn of phrase, on "the loud dissonance" between Rajiv Gandhi "coming into his natural inheritance" and India being projected as "the largest *democracy* in the world." (Emphasis mine.)

The writer had quite missed the ineffable machinations of the Hindu mind. *Dissonance,* after all, is a word drawn from acoustics. There *are* other forms of communication, not least the thermodynamic methods of convection and conduction, and the vastly subtler operations of psychic osmosis.

Rajiv Gandhi became prime minister of India because two divergent processes met and joined hands. The first was a calculated political campaign to install "the heir apparent" on the throne. He had been assiduously built up by his mother, after his younger brother's death in 1980. Power brokers were encouraged to gravitate toward this sprig from the royal tree. When the time came, they duly did what they had been severely programmed to do. That was the first process.

But that extremely efficient political grooming and PR exercise would have been wholly unsuccessful if Mrs. Gandhi had not calculated, quite shrewdly and correctly, that the Indian electorate *would* accept a scion of the family line. Can one ever contemplate that Margaret Thatcher, with all her unassailable present power in Britain, could install her son Mark as the future prime minister of Britain? Or that Reagan could induce his cronies in the Republican party to put one of his offspring in the White House after his time on earth had expired? The people who express reservations about "dynastic" succession are arrogantly telling Indian electors how to cast their votes. Such apparent "progressive" and "liberal" theologizing often conceals a propensity towards a kind of left-wing authoritarianism that I find as equally distasteful as the right-wing variety.

As one writer put it, "It has often seemed that the story of the Nehrus and the Gandhis has provided more engrossing material than anything in the cinemas or on television: a real dynasty better than *Dynasty*, a Delhi to rival *Dallas*." Personally, I am democrat enough to accept a resounding verdict delivered at the polls!

12

Oyster World with Thorns in the Thigh

*I*n the immediate aftermath of independence in 1947, one of the most striking achievements of Jawaharlal Nehru, the new prime minister of India, was preserving and maintaining close links with the departed rulers. He was an intimate friend of the Mountbattens (the last viceroy and vicereine of the Raj), and he had close contacts with the then ruling Labour party in Britain.

Of course there had been bloodshed in 1946, when Hindus and Muslims tore at each other by the thousands. There was much acrimony against the British, who had indirectly brought this about by administering that notorious policy of "divide and rule." But once the fact of partition was accepted, and Pakistan was hived off from the rest of the subcontinent (in effect, a new nation was created, with its two halves strung apart on each side of India—West and East Pakistan), there was surprisingly little bitterness toward the British. Mrs. Gandhi used to tell the story of her last meeting with Winston Churchill, when the old man said he could not understand how the Indians could be so friendly toward Britons, after all the Indians had been made to suffer at their hands. Mrs. Gandhi replied: "We just wanted you out of our country. We didn't *hate*." To which the bulldog barked back, "But I did, madam. I did!"

This cordial connection with Britain yielded considerable political dividends. India remained within the Commonwealth, and using that forum as a stage, Nehru was able to evolve his famous policy of nonalignment—which meant that India would neither belong to the postwar Western camp led by America and Britain, nor become a client state of the Soviet Union. With like-minded spirits such as Nasser of Egypt and Tito of Yugoslavia, Nehru sought to create a third political force in the world, a legacy that still remains with the country today.

After the death of Mahatma Gandhi, Nehru was the only Indian politician known to the world. And he used this unique position to wield a kind of moral authority that was wholly disproportionate to India's military, economic, or industrial might. Nehru's status on the international stage reinforced his power at home and greatly helped to reduce the significance of neighboring countries in the eyes of world statesmen.

Although the policy of nonalignment is still followed by Nehru's successors (albeit with some modification), India's position in the world is no longer solely dependent on rhetoric and moral exhortation.

With its massive population and huge territory, with one of the largest armies in the world, with a rapidly growing and impressive industrial base, with its progress in science and technology, India dominates the region, both because of its international stature and because of its internal political stability. No other country in Asia, except tiny Sri Lanka, is a democracy, and India has amply demonstrated to the West that electoral verdicts do not get set aside by military coups or knives in the night—as has happened in neighboring Pakistan and Bangladesh.

This induces a certain hauteur in India's dealing with the other subcontinental countries, which frequently erupts in malign diplomatic exchanges, minor military skirmishes on the border, and the occasional mudslinging in newspapers on both sides of the divide.

In a sense, it is precisely because India regards the world as its oyster, that its much smaller neighbors can sometimes become thorns in the thigh. After independence, the state of Jammu and Kashmir joined the Indian union. Pakistan disputed this accession, and a war was fought in October 1947 in which India emerged with much the larger share of the cake (including the rich valley of Kashmir). The issue was then taken to the United Nations in New York, where it has lain on the table ever since.

An attempt was made to resolve the problem in 1965, and there was another war with Pakistan, in which India defeated its neighbor once again. Finally, India invaded East Pakistan in 1971, ostensibly because millions of refugees were pouring in as a result of the civil war (West Pakistan had sent in its army, supposedly to quell a rebellion), but in reality to dismember the nation and reduce it to a permanent political and military weakling. In this endeavor Mrs. Gandhi was eminently successful, the invasion was a triumph (from the Indian point of view), and a new nation called Bangladesh was born.

As a result of these bitter military feuds, combined with memories of religious bloodbaths between the two communities (the Hindus and the Muslims), the Indo-Pak relationship is a matter of constant friction. It is also the single cause of a most wasteful expenditure of resources that neither country can afford.

If the superpowers are engaged in an arms race, which includes star wars and ballistic missiles, then India and Pakistan, like two adolescent children emulating their elders, are locked in a similarly futile exercise, which makes no sense to any outsider, but is of vital and corroding concern to the combatants themselves.

Each time the United States sells arms to Pakistan, India goes on a shopping spree to Britain, France, and the Soviet Union in search of even more sophisticated military hardware than the Pakistanis have acquired. And so the game escalates. The press in each country continuously keep the pot on the boil, and mistrust is kept aflame. Frequently, the political leadership in each country uses the bogey of the other's sinister plans to achieve a transient unity within. During the recent Sikh troubles, it was openly asserted in India that Pakistan was harboring and training the separatist guerrillas, feeding them with arms that were smuggled across the border. Similarly, when Zia ul-Haq (Pakistan's military dictator) faces insurgence within and political demands for free elections, he conjures up the Indian dragon, who would be ready to pounce as soon as the country was handed over to weak and squabbling politicians.

Both India and Pakistan use the other as a symbol of an external threat that temporarily unifies the nation. In reality, however, it makes no political or military sense for either country to have aggressive designs on the other. India has enough problems with her own communities to seriously contemplate "swallowing" (a word sometimes used in the Pakistani press) its neighbor. It already has a precarious and hostile border with China in the East, without wishing to extend it to the West. Its eighty million Muslims do not much fancy the rigid Islamization that is currently being imposed across the border. India's interests *were* served in invading Bangladesh, as it helped to dismember the old bifurcated Pakistan. But beyond that, there is no political or economic incentive for it to attempt any kind of military aggression. Kashmir is a slightly different issue, but both countries know that a stalemate has been reached, and from India's point of view, the status quo is quite the most satisfactory situation for which she could hope.

From the Pakistani perspective, it does not make any sense to have two-thirds of its meager army patrolling the Indian border and to go on buying expensive American arms, when more than half the country lives below the poverty line and its economy is in total shambles.

Each country is caught up in a psychological war whose origin lies in distortion and fabrication, but has little to do with current objective conditions. But, as in extreme forms of neuroses, the schizoid disconnection with reality offers no obstacle to a national conviction that the other party is poised to attack. The only people who benefit from this mutually pugnacious posture are the arms dealers from the East and West. While the people of India and Pakistan suffer.

What India does win is the moral and intellectual battle on the issue of democracy. With one small exception (under Zulfikar Ali Bhutto in 1972) Pakistan has been continuously ruled by military dictatorships since 1958.

The other country with which India has been locked in military combat is China. And the Indo-China war in 1962 was a source of immense personal disappointment to Nehru. In 1955, Chou Enlai, the then prime minister of China, came to India, and Nehru signed a friendship treaty with him. There was much rejoicing as flags and buntings went up in the cities proclaiming "Hindi Chini, bhai bhai" ("India and China are brothers").

Then China entered Tibet and "swallowed" it, despite the fact that according to British treaties for over a hundred years, the country technically belonged to India.

Nehru argued that those treaties had been made under Imperial duress, and that he would not stake a claim on a legacy of such dubious origin. He consented to offer refuge to the Dalai Lama, but against strong advice from his cabinet, he refused to contest the Chinese claim or engage in combat. He also dismantled the existing defense positions over the Indo-Chinese border as a gesture of faith in his giant neighbor.

Then, in 1962, the Chinese marched into India and inflicted a humiliating defeat on the Indian army. The ostensible reason was to settle some border disputes that had been simmering for a while. But in reality they ingressed much farther down into the country than the area they claimed. And just as India was preparing itself to repulse this foreign invader, with the country in a fever pitch of chauvinistic frenzy, the Chinese withdrew as suddenly as they had come, having annexed only those areas that they had originally claimed (thousands of square miles in Aksai Chin, where Kashmir and China meet).

In theory, India still lays claim to the land, but in practice she knows that there is no hope of recovering this lost territory. Political pundits have tried to analyze the motive for this inexplicable Chinese action (the land is frozen in snow all year round, and is of no use to anybody), but have not come up with a satisfactory answer.

It was as if the inscrutable giant in the East was out to teach its much smaller sibling in the West a sharp lesson on how to conduct business with an elder brother. It is said that Nehru never quite recovered from the shock, for far more devastating than military defeat and humiliation, his ideals had been shattered. Communist China had violated his trust, and Humpty Dumpty could never be put together again. This state of mutual and wary tension between the two countries persists even today, with occasional torches of amity being lit and minor conferences held. But the old bond has been broken, and only a new generation of leaders, on both sides of the Himalayan divide, without the inhibitions of raw memories, might bring about a rapprochement between the two giants on the Asian continent.

* * *

But China does not exercise the Indian leadership in the mundane transactions of routine diplomacy as some of the other neighbors do. When India invaded East Pakistan in December 1971, it was with the precise objective of repulsing the West Pakistani army, and liberating the Bengali-speaking peoples of the region from the domination of the Urdu-speaking West Pakistanis. Although both halves of Pakistan professed the same religion (Islam), the eastern half of the country had much more in common with India, as both East Pakistanis and West Bengalis (Hindus, mainly) spoke the same language, Bengali.

Pakistan screamed that India was out to *conquer* one half of her land. But Mrs. Gandhi was far shrewder than that. Having vanquished the West Pakistani army, and taken some ninety thousand prisoners of war, the Indian army withdrew into its own territory, leaving the reins of power to the most popular leader of the region, Sheikh Mujibur Rahman. A new nation was created, and Mujibur was elected president of Bangladesh.

But troubles were to follow. The new president was assassinated by a military junta, and an army general was installed as the dictator of the infant state. In turn, he also was ruthlessly butchered, to be replaced by yet another military man. Except at its birth, Bangladesh has had no elections since 1972. It is the most chronic case among Third World countries, where international agencies do not find any reason either to grieve for its deplorable condition or hope for any kind of remedy.

Having been the military midwife, India faces the usual resentment from Bangladesh, which benefactors invariably do from those who receive their gifts. Indian motives are always questioned and there is perpetual friction along the border, as refugees continue to flood into neighboring India in search of food and a marginally better life.

The communal troubles, accompanied by the statutory riots and carnage that have been plaguing the Indian state of Assam (in the northeast), are largely due to Bangladeshi refugees sneaking into the state and competing for jobs and housing with indigenous inhabitants, who demand that these foreigners be expelled from the country.

The Indian government repeatedly approaches Dacca (the capital of Bangladesh) to control its own population, while Bangladesh turns a blind eye to such constant complaints. A country as poor as Bangladesh does not mind if some, or even a sizable number, of its nationals depart for other lands. With a population rising even faster than India's, massive malnutrition and disease are natural corollaries. Yet national pride dictates that the country have its own airline and maintain sumptuous embassies abroad—while India behaves like a weary mother who does not know what to do with a petulant and weakling child, and sometimes wishes that it had never been born.

India's nonviolent international stance was thrice shown up to be the political expedient that it really is, even without the glaring example of Bangladesh. Immediately after partition, there were a large number of "princely" states that had enjoyed a semiautonomous status under the British. Most of these states were offered the choice of acceding to either of the two newly created nations of India and Pakistan, except that the offer was made with the implicit threat of force if the rajahs did not toe the line. Most of these little kingdoms were within the territory of India in any case, so the choice to opt for Pakistan was an exercise in diplomatic euphemism.

The two largest states, however, were Kashmir and Hyderabad, and they were mirror images of each other, with one significant difference. While Kashmir adjoined Pakistan, Hyderabad was entirely within India. In the case of the Himalayan kingdom, it was ruled by a Hindu maharajah, with the majority of the population being Muslim. The Hindu ruler chose to join India; Pakistan disputed his choice, as the original division of the subcontinent was made on religious grounds. Pakistan rightly contended that a maharajah could not and should not decide on behalf of his people, and that the populace should be allowed to choose which nation they would join. India settled the matter by sending in its army, and occupied more than half the state. Pakistan repeatedly asked for a plebiscite, where the people could indicate their choice through a ballot. India has persistently refused, knowing full well that the majority of the Muslim population would opt in favor of Pakistan, if allowed to choose. And there the matter has rested these last thirty-eight years, with might insisting on being right.

In Hyderabad, the exact reverse was the case. Here was the legendary nizam, once reputed to be the richest man in the world, ruling a territory larger than New York State, with a majority of the population of the Hindu faith, while the ruler himself was a Muslim. The nizam refused to accede to India. With a regular army of his own, and a small air force as well (with planes and pilots supplied by Britian), the nizam prepared for battle.

But he had miscalculated the deviousness of the Indian government, and particularly its then home minister, Sardar Vallabhai Patel (who figured quite prominently in the Attenborough film on Gandhi). Patel offered a truce, and suggested negotiations. While preparations for talks were in progress, the Indian army was sent in, and in one of the swiftest operations in military history, the huge territory was annexed in twenty-four hours, with a mere twelve casualties. Nonviolence was all right for world forums and Nehru's speeches, but when it came to the business of vital self-interest, violence won hands down. Hyderabad was a classic example of power dyeing the stainless white sheets of naïve idealism a gory red.

An instance of similar hypocrisy was with an ex–colonial power, and the name used to justify the action was "liberation." After the British left in 1947, there were two French enclaves in India, and three other pockets ruled by Salazar's Portugal.

In 1954, the French withdrew without a fuss. But the Portuguese persisted in staying on. Once again, the Indians offered to negotiate, but the offer was contemptuously turned down by the aging dictator, Salazar. In 1961, the Indian army invaded Goa, Daman, and Diu. The Portuguese threatened to send warships down into the Arabian Sea and shell the Indian garrisons, but in the end, wiser counsel prevailed. Without consulting the people of Goa themselves, the Indian government annexed their tiny island, and over three centuries of foreign domination came to an end At least this was how the war of annexation was presented to the world. But Goans with whom I spoke at the time felt quite differently. One prominent Goan, the poet Dom Moraes, who was living in London at the time, ceremoniously and ostentatiously tore up his Indian passport as a gesture of outrage against the Indian invasion. And incipient resentment still lingers among the island's inhabitants, especially the older folk. But once again, force proved to be a *fait accompli* over which there could be no debate.

Similarly, the tiny mountain kingdom of Sikkim was annexed in 1975, when the Indians unceremoniously seized the territory without so much as a token offer of negotiations with the king. I met the chogyal (the Sikkimese name for king) a few years before his kingdom was snatched from his grasp. The people were happy and smiling, the monarch was a benevolent ruler and totally aware of the currents that were operating against him. His second (or was it his third?) wife was the American woman, Hope Cooke (he had had a child by her), who had been earlier mixed up with the overthrow of Mossadegh in Iran, and various other places around the globe where the CIA was known to have had its finger in the pie. Inevitably, the CIA bogey was raised once again, the issue of Indian security was instanced, the sensitivity of the region with its close proximity to the Chinese border was pointed out, and a military solution was imposed, without the people of Sikkim having any say in the matter at all. The poor king died soon after.

This, then, is the list of Indian nonviolence in action. And the objection is not from the perspective of realpolitik or the protection of vital self-interest, which every nation acknowledges as a fact of life. It is the contrast between what is preached and what is practiced that sticks in the throat. Hypocrisy is the name of the game here, just as it was in 1956, when Nehru swiftly and violently condemned the Anglo-French invasion of Suez, but remained silent for days about the Russian invasion of Hungary.

It is the jargon of moral posturing that Westerners find indigestible in Indian political discourse, and it was the single most offensive streak in Nehru's personality that ruffled the feathers of people like John Foster Dulles. Perhaps, as the nation matures out of its idealistic infancy, we shall hear less preaching and witness more pragmatism in the way it deals with the rest of the world.

The other mountain kingdoms of Nepal and Bhutan do not offer India any specific cause for irritation or worry. Bhutan toes the Indian line in foreign affairs, and due to events that have occured in neighboring Sikkim over the past ten years, it does not make too much noise about anti-Indian feelings that simmer just beneath the surface of an apparently docile and peace-loving people.

Nepal is a different kettle of fish, and has always looked at India with a wary eye. It is the only remaining Hindu kingdom in the world, but the population has never forgotten that its kings have all come from the princely states of India (mainly Rajasthan) and are not *genuine* Nepalese by pedigree.

If India has designs on this toehold in the Himalayas, it keeps its desires securely secret. In any case, Nepal is geographically situated in such an awkward place that invasion and conquest would be a foolhardy exercise. Also, the country occupies a seat in the United Nations, and with the first scream for help, China (with whom it shares a border) would be only too willing to leap in and help, in the hope of administering yet another blow to Indian military pride. But since there is constant traffic between the two countries (India and Nepal) in trade, technical aid, and other matters, once again there is incipient anti-Indian sentiment in the kingdom. The grandfather of the present king sought refuge in India under Nehru when his prime minister attempted to dethrone him. But the monarch returned to his people with Indian help, the prime minister was jailed, and everyone lived happily ever after. The present king, try as he might, cannot unshackle himself from the awareness of this debt, and the populace have not forgotten either. Gratitude here is mixed with a nervous fear. If India could once depose the prime minister of Nepal, why can't she depose the king? But the world is a different place today, and I do not believe that India has territorial designs on this tiny mountain kingdom, which is one of the most colorful places in the region.

Sri Lanka, or Ceylon, used to be called Serendip in ancient times and serendipity is derived from that old Ceylonese word. The people are the most naturally pleasant and hospitable in the whole of Asia. One third of its population derive from Tamil stock from India, and this is where the frictions between the two countries occur.

Hotheads in Sri Lanka have openly accused the Indian government of harboring guerrillas on its soil and encouraging a separatist movement (just as India does about Pakistan and the Sikhs). One Sri Lankan minister even went so far as to declare that Mrs.

Gandhi was planning an invasion. Once again, it is the small fry being intimidated by its vastly larger neighbor and making petulant and unrealistic noises to assert its identity.

I may be wrong, since one can never tell about governmental intentions (although I predicted the invasion of East Pakistan in print in *The Guardian* three months before it occurred), but I cannot see what India would gain by invading Sri Lanka.

At the same time, for its own domestic political reasons, it cannot be seen to ignore the plight of people who are of Indian origin. So it is a case of walking the tightrope between appearing wholly unconcerned about the Tamils in Sri Lanka, and upsetting the government in the island by rabid pronouncements about liberating "our people." Up to now, depite the calamities in 1984, both governments have played their hands with commendable calm.

Geopolitically, then, India commands a magisterial authority on the subcontinent. She has not always shown the greatest tact in exercising that authority, but nor have her neighbors always responded in sympathy to India's own notion that its paramountcy in the region is dictated by geography, sheer bulk and population, an infinitely superior industrial base, and an international status that rises like a giant in comparison to the midgets around. Inequality is written into the geopolitical realities of the region. And it is futile for neighboring nations to expect India to behave like a supplicating child every time a dispute occurs. What she could do, with the prospect of rich rewards, is to display some of the *noblesse oblige* for which Indians are justly famous.

PART FIVE

Currents

Avenues of Ink

The Celluloid Mirage

Ascent to the Apiary

13

Avenues of Ink

*T*he Fifth Estate in India is a polarized amalgam of old dowagers and naughty little children out on a spree in Central Park. There are the broadsheet English-language papers, inheriting their traditions from the dignified reticence of the British, and there are magazines, literally in their hundreds, which pump and squeeze the public imagination with an irreverent abandon.

Each team inspects the "opposition" with wary skepticism, hoping the other will soon vanish from view. But both sides know that this dialectic will persist, as similar confrontations have persisted in India in many other spheres.

The old guard are fully aware that these new young imps (some of them not so young anymore, since the phenomenon sprouted in the early seventies, with juvenile editors in their mid- to late twenties) will not be lectured into nonexistence. Just as the Young Turks acknowledge, with a twinge of detectable envy, that the thundering editorials in papers such as *The Times of India* or *The Statesman,* even today, have a much greater impact on the elite, opinion-forming crust of Indian society than any number of investigative or satirical reports that they may publish in their sprightly little columns.

In a way, this creates a healthy contrast. And in theory, it should keep both sides on their toes. But in practice, it does not. What it does do, in fact, is make each team even more stubbornly insistent about its own virtues, officially ignoring the positive aspects of the other camp. This is typically Indian. Pride is of the essence, and no one is prepared to learn. What may be acknowledged in private will be vehemently and hotly denied and contradicted in public. Pantomime posturing becomes an end in itself, and the visitor, even a former Indian like myself, is left wondering where to look and what to say.

Old myths die hard, and even in the young and rebellious sprigs, ancient loyalties erupt with sudden and unexpected violence. According to the discarded theology, old men had to be obeyed and respected, the mystique of age was sacrosanct (just as the mystique of youth is sacrosanct in the West today). The Young Turks will attack this theology with vehemence, and you might be tempted to think that these young men were modern and agnostic in their outlook. Then you raise the topic of Kashmir or Indian sensitivity about caste, and you will find them reacting in the same hysterical manner as their elders, whom they had just castigated. Once again, you will find yourself in intellectual quicksand, not knowing whether you are on solid ground or rapidly sinking into incomprehension.

For an outsider, there will be certain topics that will be taboo for discussion, among both the old and the new guard. In order of merit, they will be: caste, Kashmir, the proper relevance of "democracy" in India, dowry, bride burning, snake charmers, *sadhus,* the status of Muslims in the country, and finally, the phenomenon of untouchability.

You will be permitted to discuss the economic situation, drought, corruption, everything else under the sun, including sex, especially with the Young Turks, but those forbidden subjects will touch a raw nerve as soon as they are mentioned. The ingenue might persist at considerable risk, the mature and sophisticated observer will acquiescently stay away.

But what will then perplex the foreigner is the fact that the very items that I have listed above will be the subject of lengthy articles in some of the new magazines that have sprung up in the past fifteen years. Those very young men, who will react with a mixture of disdain and contempt bordering on hostility if these things are mentioned by a foreigner, will invite Indians to opine in their pages.

There will be lengthy correspondence following each such article, and the outsider will not know what line to tread.

When I published my first book in Britain, it was reviewed with some fervor by such emiment critics as Cyril Connolly and V. S. Pritchett, and later in the States it received complimentary notices from such noteworthy pens as Edmund Wilson and Lionel Trilling. In India, the same book was savaged by most reviewers, some of them even going on to suggest that such *trash* could not possibly have been published unless I had been funded by the CIA or my wife was a very rich woman who had paid the publishers. I make no claims about the merits or demerits of my book; I merely point out the violent disparity in the Western and Indian responses.

The Statesman was founded in 1818, and is the oldest surviving English-language newspaper in India. Its lineage is even more ancient than that date would indicate, since it is descended from *The Englishman,* whose precise point of birth is somewhat uncertain, but is reckoned to be at least seventy years earlier. If those two figures are added up, it is possible that *The Statesman* is the most ancient directly descended English-language newspaper in the world, older by far than *The Times* (London), which is celebrating its bicentennial this year (1985).

This is to show that the British sowed seeds of their own traditions in the soil of India fairly early on. And the seeds took root. Though it might appear slightly digressive, it is not also unfair to point out here that the Indian National Congress, the party from which Mrs. Gandhi's party (the current ruling party) descended, was founded by an Englishman in 1885, to fight for greater Indian representation on the nominated councils of the land.

To revert to the spoils of Grub Street, the English-language press in India is read by no more than 3 percent of its population, but its prestige and power is wholly disproportionate. The last *Times* (London) reporter reckoned that the English press is read by no more than forty million people in the whole of India, yet what it has to say makes a far greater impact than the vernacular press can ever do (my *OED* defines *vernacular* as *common*).

In the majority, the English papers are a stodgy mess of tired clichés and arch aspirations toward a kind of Britishness that became outmoded in the thirties. But they still cling to these forms. With a few exceptions. the tradition of anonymous reporting is still maintained, the by-line is usually BY OUR OWN CORRESPONDENT or OUR SPECIAL REPRESENTATIVE, and so forth. Individualism is haughtily disdained. Personalized stories do appear, but never under the official imprimatur of the paper itself.

There are five major English-language dailies in India that the Westerner should look at. But just as in America, unlike Britain, there is no *national* newspaper. *The Times of India* is read in the North, most of the center, and a bit of the midsouthern belt. *The Statesman* has a virtual monopoly of readership in the eastern sector, although a new paper, *The Telegraph,* has recently begun to compete. The *Indian Express* is published from ten different cities, and has the largest circulation. But since it aims at a lowbrow, English-educated but lower-income audience, it does not have a commensurate prestige. The *Hindustan Times* is the most widely read newspaper in the capital and its environs. It is abominably written, carries the crudest advertisements, and is certainly a stain on Indian journalism. But it is a powerful organ, because it contrives to support whatever government is currently in power.

There are a few other papers on the fringes, but it would be too tedious to list them all. Besides, they would be of no interest to the Western reader. But all the papers I have mentioned earlier are published from New Delhi, and other stations as well. *The Times of India* headquarters itself in the commercial capital of India, Bombay. The *Indian Express,* forever eclectic, bases itself in Bombay too. *The Statesman,* belonging to the dignified gentry, still resides in Calcutta, the old British capital and currently the cultural nerve center of the country. And the *Hindustan Times,* having nowhere else to go, is securely founded on the earth of *New* Delhi, an invented city if ever there was one.

None of these papers have any evangelical fervor, except when a proprietor is out to get a particular political personality. Most of them kowtow to the ruling party, whichever one it is. There is no such thing as left-wing writing in India, at least in mainstream journalism. Of the five papers I have mentioned, only one is wholly owned by a press baron (not unlike the Canadian Beaverbrook, who made his home in London), with no other commercial connections. Every one of the others is part of a vastly larger industrial conglomerate that carries the paper only to propagate a particular commercial stance.

Although notionally the press is free in India, and far more unshackled than any of its counterparts anywhere in the Third World, it would be wholly incorrect to assert that it was truly unbonded.

As Vinod Mehta, editor of the Bombay-based *Sunday Observer,* told me, "It depends what you mean by *free.* Geographically, if you compare us with others in this area of the world, we are infinitely more free than anyone else. But if you compare us with Britain, then of course we are tied. We are controlled by the quota of newsprint that the government allocates, we are governed by considerations of our advertising revenue, the bulk of which again comes from the government. An editor is constrained by the commercial interests of his employer, which may not always coincide with journalistic impartiality. But other than these factors, of course we are free!"

The style in which these mainstream papers are written is reminiscent of the late Victorian era in Britain, rather than the scurrilous tabloids that were in vogue in the eighteenth century or on-the-spot news coverage with vivid personal interpolation that are popular in the Western press today. As Vinod Mehta confirmed, "No exposé of the dimension of Watergate could ever take place in India. But neither could it have happened in Britain!"

Nevertheless, occasional exposures do take place—every so often a journalist is feted for his part in revealing a scandal, although the public is never aware of the machinations behind the scene. When a proprietor wants to get at someone, it is the easiest thing in the world to feed the correct lines, and out comes the scribe, with his tongue hot in his mouth, spouting on the typewriter, and even honestly believing that he has personally unearthed the greatest dung heap in history. When in reality he has been gently led, like a pig with its snout, and has merely dug up the earth where the truffles were buried.

The new journalism, however, is qualitatively different. It has flair, style, a certain flamboyant self-confidence. The language is not archaic, limits are not set, anything seems to go. The old prurience has been deliberately exorcised. Subjects that were once taboo in print, like wives kissing their husbands in bed, are now openly analyzed. Interior decoration, which is even now regarded as some kind of newfangled philistinism by the oldies, gets an open-hearted hearing. Such unheard-of travesties as opinion polls are beginning to make their appearance.

The young lads who write the editorials in these new magazines and papers have actually gone out there and seen for themselves, in stark contrast to the oldies who are still cocooned in their editorial cubicles, much too highbred and gentlemanly to poke their finger in the earth and *feel* if it is wet and *smell* if it stinks.

It is not simply a matter of the generation gap, either. The difference in attitude stems from an awareness on both sides that one party has got one thing, and the other must grab hold of something else to achieve parity.

Once upon a time this was not necessary. Now is has become vital. When a father like Motilal (Nehru's father) could tell his son not to worry about not being a success as a barrister because "I can earn in a day what you will break your back to earn in a year," and proceed to advise the younger man to go into politics, where he might, just conceivably, make some kind of impact, we begin to see that in India the Victorian age lasted so much longer that it made a devastating impact on every sphere of life, including journalism.

The effects of such late development are only now being felt, and even so, few people realize that they are still paying interest on the legacy they unwittingly inherited from the British. For it is not only in form and manners that the old crusty traditions are perpetuated. They linger in the mind. Deep Puritan inhibitions, intellectual habits, a certain deference to authority, resistance to change, all these characteristics are so deeply ingrained in the Indian psyche that they display themselves all over the place, and nowhere more vividly so than in the press, both old and new.

The startling thing, however, is that what is called "the new journalism" is really as old as the hills, to coin a cliché. There is absolutely nothing *new* about the new tribe of scribes who infest the ink-laden undergrowth. In most cases, they have merely imitated some Westernized version of a format that has long been in vogue elsewhere.

Whether one considers the way a story is reported, or the format of the magazine, or even simply the presentation of facts, there is not one magazine or newspaper in India that can claim any kind of originality. Even this would not be a heinous crime. But the combination of a suppurating conceit with frequent lapses in professional standards leaves the Westerner bemused. At one moment, one tends to be impressed, take the man as an equal. In the very next instant, one discovers that some awful gaffe has been committed, for which a child in its diaper should have been severely smacked on its bottom.

When I last spoke to Rajiv Gandhi, it was on the basis of a commission from the *Colour Magazine* of *The Sunday Times* (London). As it was a magazine story, the pictures were crucial. So, I employed, on the recommendation of the editor at the paper back in London, a photographer who was nationally known in India. I came back with what I thought was a fantastic interview. When the photographs were developed, however, the editor said, "Did this man have a Brownie or what?" He complained that none of the pictures had been "set up." Not being familiar with the terminology, I wanted to know what he meant. He replied, "It looks as if this guy just went on clicking, while you two were talking." I nodded to say that that is exactly what happened. My friend, the editor, screamed at me, "Oh for God's sake, Sasthi, don't you know that we are a *Colour Magazine,* it is the picture that makes the story."

What I had quite forgotten to tell him was the fact that no Indian, whatever his status, would dare tell Rajiv Gandhi where to stand and how to sit, what to do with his hands, and how to smile. A white photographer could have done it, I most certainly did in my verbal interview. But my friend with the camera was an Indian who lived in India, and he would dare no such thing. And like a fool, I had entrusted my project to just such a creature! It wasn't that he was a bad photographer—some of his pictures have appeared in international magazines. But he simply was not up to the job of snapping the son of the prime minister of India for a *Colour Magazine* in Britain!

As Aroon Purie, the editor and proprietor of the most successful fortnightly in India, *India Today,* told me, "We just followed a formula. And we were in at the right time." His magazine is run on an identical format to that of *Newsweek* or *Time,* even the notion of cover stories is identical, as is the "publisher's letter" et al.

At least Mr. Purie did not attempt to conceal the plagiarism. Many others do.

My only query in this sphere is a philosophical one: If a country boasts of a long history and ancient traditions, can it afford merely to replicate external models, and yet insist that it is an independent entity?

I begin to wonder whether there are several types of colonization, the economic and imperial one being the most obvious. Why do bright young men copy a format that their fathers had gone to prison to dislodge? Does India have no authentic internal genius on which to succor its new generation? Or were the British right in assuming that "the natives" will always do what you tell them, provided you do so with a certain authority?

I leave these questions open for the reader. As an Indian myself I have no right to venture into such sacred and volatile territory.

14

The Celluloid Mirage

India's vast dream factory churns out over 1,500 films a year, with an annual turnover that exceeds two billion dollars. No less than the Hollywood of the thirties, the Bombay studios have a rich fauna of stars who bridge the chasm between illusion and reality with a cynicism that can appear monstrous to an outsider. There is no other form of popular entertainment that rivals the attractions of the cinema, in both the towns and in the villages.

The films are very long, between three and four hours each, because the Indian believes in getting his money's worth. In the cities, there is the extra benefit of air-conditioned auditoriums, which, in the middle of an Indian summer (with temperatures swinging merrily around the 100°F mark), is an immense additional attraction. As the prices are comparatively low (about thirty or forty cents a seat), the cinema is the most cost-effective investment for entertainment that exists in India.

There is a rigid formula in each picture that would leave even comic-addicted schoolboys gasping in condescension. Good guy, bad guy; villain, hero; pretty little poor girl weds rich, sensitive handsome boy, and so on. The whole machinery is reminiscent of the great moguls of Hollywood. With this difference. Film stars are not treated with the same kind of skepticism by the populace at large, and they have far greater credibility than most politicians. Since they are seen more often, and are rigorously associated in the public mind with the roles they play, to switch from fiction to reality is hardly an effort at all.

Indian audiences do not have much stomach for "the realist" school of filmmakers. In patronizing the cinema by the millions, they tell the producers that "we have enough *reality* in our daily lives, what we want is fantasy, something that will enable us to *escape*."

The formula is always the same, with a dose of *mirchi masala* (red pepper and spice) thrown in. Boy meets girl is drawn out into a struggle between good and bad, till finally virtue triumphs. There are at least four obligatory songs, two sad, and two happy. In effect, all Bombay movies are musicals. Sometimes the songs from popular films make as much if not more money than the pictures themselves.

The sets are spectacular and wholly unlike anything the viewer is ever likely to see in his own experience. The flashy life portrayed in the character of the hero is also used to encourage the idea that with hard work and good luck, you, too, can achieve such gaudy splendor.

Heroines tend to be buxom and sweet-smiling, with plenty of spare tire round the waist. Heroes, too, are seldom slim, since lack of fat indicates poverty, while affluence is represented by the opposite physical characteristics.

There are other symbols, too. A woman who smokes on the screen is sure to come to a bad end. She is instantly identified by the audience as the vamp who has evil designs on the hero, who undoubtedly will be met with due retribution by the end of the picture—unless, of course, she repents her evil ways, usually when she is dying.

The bad guy will probably smoke a cigar, wear a black curled moustache, drink whiskey, and have a large retinue of evil-looking men as his adjutants. Early on in the film, the characters of the principal protagonists will be set, there will be no final surprises, although the story line will be strong. But frequently the old themes from mythology or religious scriptures with minor variations will be used as the main structure of the plot. The gods will win and the demons will be defeated.

Indian audiences like to idenfity with the righteous; they also like to feel that they know what is coming. Unhappy endings will send an audience into a frenzy of rage, sometimes powerful enough for chairs to be ripped from their bases and thrown at the screen, ticket counters smashed, and total pandemonium to break loose in an auditorium.

I have been in cinema halls where the actions of the villain, especially at points when he appears to have an edge over the hero, have been met with tomatoes and eggs thrown at the screen. In reverse, when the hero wins the heroine, or some particularly virtuous act has been portrayed, great sighs of pleasure and approval rise from the audience, like amens from the congregation in a Catholic church.

Political themes, too, are depicted on film, but once again with the basic elements of fantasy and spice firmly in place. In South India, where the actors currently reign as politicians, film was a very effective medium for these parties to get across their message. It was easy to translate the war between good and evil, between God and the devil, as analogous to the fight between northern domination and southern insurgence. The audience identified, and with unswerving Pavlovian reflexes, cast their votes in favor of the righteous side.

Sex is never directly portrayed on the screen. Several heroines I have met reacted in angry horror when I asked them if they would do a nude scene on film. But nudity is an extreme to which no Indian filmmaker aspires. Even kissing is not allowed, and film censorship is so strict that most producers and directors impose a self-restricting regime that allows a quick flash of bare thigh, maybe, or even a chaste kiss on the forehead. But nothing more.

If belts are being fixed, or the knot on a sari is being tied after a scene that has insinuated lubricious possibilities, the audience knows that naughty nookies have taken place. Women wearing foreign clothes (i.e., anything other than a sari or a *salwar kameez*—tight-fitting pants and long, loose shirt) will be immediately typecast as evil. Men and women will seldom be shown in bed, and if they are, either the one or the other will just be getting up at the beginning of a scene.

Heroines will be doused repeatedly with water (rain scenes are very popular) so that the sari clings to the luscious figure, and suggestive curves hint at explosive possibilities. Similarly, fights between women are common, because they provide the director with an opportunity to show a ripped-off blouse (as perfectly justified in the story line), which enables him to sneak in a quick glance at a bare bosom. This, too, is extremely rare. And if a film that shows such a shot has got past the censor, it will be called "HOT AND SPICY" on the billboards, and the ticket prices will rise to ten times their nominal value.

Any hint of premarital sex is totally taboo. The bad girl might tempt the hero with such evil fare, but if he has any sense, and wishes to keep peace with his fans, he will hover on the edge for a while before finally refusing. Heroines never have sex before marriage. Adultery between married people is permitted provided the participants are a thoroughly bad lot, and have been quite clearly shown to be so. Children do not hear, see, or talk about sex.

The insistence on having happy endings, and on heroes being god-fearing, mother-loving, altruistic souls might appear a little sloppy to a sophisticated Westerner. But it is not as nakedly juvenile as it might appear at first sight. The Indian lives largely by myth. Which is not to say that he cannot make a distinction between reality and illusion. But to him the power of myth and allegory is very strong, because his whole life has been governed by concepts that originated entirely in axiomatic references to legend and past history. The spiritual, moral, and ethical axes of his life are not derived from analysis, they are taken as given. The mind functions on a set of data that is already provided, it does not deduce a code of conduct.

In such circumstances, it is far easier to identify with similar *given* parameters, rather than have to work out paradoxes and solutions to moral dilemmas. Once again, this is not to diminish the enormous intellectual contributions that Indian philosophers have made—after all, those myths had to be invented by somebody—but it is to focus attention on the fact that the majority of Indians live by a mass of symbols and shorthand codes. And these make life a lot simpler than if every time there was a problem a man had to go into his study and devise the correct response to that particular situation.

To make an analogy: The Semitic peoples, whether Jews or Muslims, are exhorted in their religion not to eat pork. To the orthodox, eating meat from the pig is a sin. Of course, every emancipated Jew or Muslim will have to admit that it can be nothing of the kind. (Friends of mine have gone to great contortionary lengths to explain that it wasn't because of *religion,* but that they just didn't like the taste of the stuff and so forth, when all they should have to say is that it is a result of conditioning.) But in the Middle Eastern climate, pork is *the* meat that can carry severe infections in the heat. So, some clever fellow wrapped it up as a religious injunction, and so it has come down over the ages.

Similarly, in India all kinds of very sophisticated points are made in the mythology, but it is simplified enough for the average man to grasp in one sitting. Indian cinema provides a diet for such hunger in capsule form, where right is clearly and totally right, wrong is unambiguously and wholly wrong. The audience is spared the trial of having to work things out for themselves.

This might sound enormously condescending, but in a country where literacy is less than 15 percent, shorthand messages of good and evil, right and wrong, that get across easily are better than none.

In 1982, one of the more spectacular incidents concerning the cinema occurred in India. Amitabh Bachan, the James Dean of the Indian screen and the heartthrob of the masses, was seriously injured while shooting an action scene in a movie. He had severe abdominal injuries and was hospitalized for several weeks, fighting for his life.

The entire nation went berserk over this event. It was front-page headline news in all the papers across the country. Prime Minister Indira Gandhi canceled a foreign trip in order to visit the ailing actor in the hospital (accompanied by her son Rajiv). Prayers were offered across the land, *pujas* were performed in thousands of temples, a day-and-night vigil was installed outside the hospital. Hourly bulletins were issued describing Mr. Bachan's condition, including every medial particular, ranging from the state of the lungs to fecal matter. Most of this medical history was also printed in detail in major publications.

India prayed for a man, barely forty, who was a tough guy on the screen and could fetch the highest price that any actor has ever commanded on the Indian screen. The state of shock and prayerful hope extended far beyond the gullible masses of India. Amitabh

Bachan's condition became the staple fare of cocktail-party conversation in Delhi and Bombay.

Extensive analysis was made of his character, and of the roles he might have played had he lived (it was assumed that even if he did not die, he would never again play on the screen), and all kinds of real-life fantasies were woven round a perfectly ordinary man.

The ingredients in this melodrama were manifold. Mr. Bachan was known to be a "modest" man, he arrived on the sets on time, unlike some of his other colleagues. He was very rich, had earned colossal amounts of money. He was a friend of the then prime minister's son Rajiv. He was a graduate of a university, unlike most other actors who have made their name. Above all, there was a streak of the godly, what the more sophisticated reports called "gentlemanly" streak, in him that endeared the actor to the masses and middle classes alike.

The unique thing about this whole episode was the fact that all his films were shown again in theaters across the country. And in Bombay, the touts were having a field day, selling thirty- and forty-cent tickets for ten times their price. What absolutely no one queried in the country was the sheer singularity of the phenomenon. Is there, or has there ever been, any actor in the Western hemisphere whose travails on the operating table would hold the attention of the entire nation, and for days on end to boot?

When I went to see one of Mr. Bachan's films, it was an entirely novel experience. The audience booed every time his adversary won a point. Each time Mr. Bachan scored a hit there was thunderous clapping and a general crescendo of whistles and screams. It was as if the man were himself present in the hall.

When he recovered, as he was bound to do, because good guys never die in any good film, billboards went up thanking God and various other deities who had been called into action to save this precious life. For days on end, there was jubilation on the streets, and the prime minister made a special reference to this epoch-making medical turnaround in the Indian Parliament. Short of canonization, Mr. Bachan had had the best of both life and death.

I must not leave the reader with the impression that this kind of infantile response is the only one that India can muster in the realm of film. There are serious filmmakers who are highly revered across the world, who have small but highly appreciative audiences in the country. The name of Satyajit Ray immediately comes to mind.

I first met Mr. Ray in London, when he had been awarded an honorary doctorate of literature by Oxford University, the first filmmaker to have been so honored since Charlie Chaplin, sixteen years previously.

There was nothing Indian about Satyajit Ray's looks except the color of his skin. Both his height (over six feet) and his aquiline features set him apart from fellow Bengalis. Sporting a dimple on his chin, the scraggy face reminded me of the early Auden, while the deep resonance of his George Sanders voice suggested an inherited as well as a self-earned confidence. The accent had a slight Indian inflection overlaid by American. The brooding brown eyes were deeply introspective one moment, and full of fun the next.

His handshake was warm and firm. There was an unhurried dignity in every movement he made, the way he lit his cigarette, the manner in which he put his feet up on a bed in his little London hideaway. Even his walk across the room to open the door for the photographer was subtly awesome. Only later did I discover that the man was both pliant and human.

I asked him how it all began. Ray comes from a highly artistic and intellectual Bengali family. His grandfather was a famous painter, musician, and writer, one of whose short stories he has made into a film. His father wrote nonsense poems on the lines of Edward Lear and Lewis Carroll, and founded the Nonsense Club in Calcutta. From his mother's side, his family was very close to the Tagores.

"But," said Ray, "I learned my craft from watching American films. At the age of fifteen, I became terribly interested in Western music." Week after week he collected records of Bach, Mozart, and Brahms. At college he read economics.

"I used to play the Gramophone in those days, and once there was a knock on the door. When I opened it, there was an embarrassed-looking GI standing outside, who said that it was such an unexpected sound coming from a Bengali house ('it was Beethoven's Ninth, I think')."

The GI turned out to be a musician, he played the clarinet. At about the same time, Ray met an RAF (Royal Air Force) officer with whom he shared an interest in chess and Western music. Filmmaking was still nowhere in sight.

But in 1949 he met Jean Renoir, who was out in India hunting for locations to shoot *The River*. Ray had confided his ambitions to make a film someday and talked a little of what he had in mind. Renoir encouraged him. Then the advertising firm for which he was working sent him to England. On his way back by ship, he wrote the first treatment of the film that was to launch his international career.

From this point on the story takes on the character of a fairy tale. "I produced a book of wash drawings, describing the scenario of the film, but none of the producers from top down wanted to know. All the professionals I approached said it couldn't be done. They all said, 'You can't work on location, you can't shoot in the rain, you can't do this, you can't do that.' So I decided I would have nothing to do with the so-called professionals and put together my own crew, including the actors."

Ray did this without any local or foreign encouragement. Five more years were to elapse before the film was actually made. The initial capital came from two life-insurance policies totaling 15,000 rupees in 1950 ($150 in today's money, but allowing for inflation, it would be about $2,000), when Ray was about to cross his thirtieth year. Then he sold his art books, later his records, and finally pawned his wife's wedding jewelry.

The film was cut and edited in record time to meet a deadline set by the Museum of Modern Art in New York. Ray and his editor worked round the clock. "I discovered for the first time that it is possible to work ten days and nights without a wink of sleep, if you are sufficiently committed. I fell asleep with my elbow on the counter as I was handing over the film to the girl at Pan Am."

"I didn't really expect the kind of response that *Pather Panchali* finally got. On the first night in New York, I was there outside the cinema just before the picture ended, and I saw people coming out with tears streaming down their faces. It was an extraordinary sight. There were whites and Negroes, young people, old people and there they were . . . so visibly moved by this Bengali film."

About his first effort, the eminent film critic William Whitebait wrote at the time, "Satyajit Ray has the gift of seeing people as they are, and making them—without violation—beautiful."

At Cannes that year (1956), *Pather Panchali* won a special award, and Satyajit Ray was firmly on the map of internationally acclaimed directors. Since then, many more awards have come his way, from Japan, Venice, Milan, Moscow, and Sweden. But he still lacks a large Western audience. Critical response in India has often been petulant when not downright hostile.

But Satyajit Ray has continued to make films of superlative distinction. The *Apu* trilogy, of which *Pather Panchali* is the first, is widely regarded as being his best, easily ranking him with the giants of the cinema, such as Bergman, Kurosawa, and de Sica. About *The Goddess* (made in 1960), Penelope Gilliatt (former film critic for *The New Yorker*), wrote in *The Observer* (London): "It seems marvellous that he should have been able to register such sweetness of spirit in a film without allowing a trace of softness, and look so harshly at superstition without ever mocking the roots of it. It is the achievement of an artistic integrity as clear as a piece of glass."

Though he has made several other films that make oblique political points, such as *Company Limited* (1971), *The Adversary* (1970) and *The Middleman* (1975), Ray admits he is no good at dogma.

Then there are Mrinal Sen, Shyam Benegal, and an extraordinarily talented lady who has recently taken up directing after having been a child actress herself—her name is Aparna Sen. She directed that wonderful picture *36 Chowringhee Lane,* which was shown in both London and New York.

Admittedly, the audience for such films is small, and producers and directors have a tough time in putting together a shoestring budget.

But film in India is basically a majority vehicle. Its function is to provide fantasy, relief, escape, and some titillation. And this last item on the agenda was well underlined by an editorial in the *Hindustan Times*

> Film festivals in India provide an opportunity for the well-heeled and well-connected to engage in titillation. If there is no nude scene the film is bound to be a flop. If there is the slightest exposure of the female form people will

beg, borrow or steal and consider the effort worth the humiliation. On the surface it is all in the interests of art. But the mass of skin is the message. It could not be anything else for a people so sexually frustrated as the Indians.

At least the masses do not have to "beg, borrow or steal" their thirty cents for a seat. But then they never get to see a nude scene either.

15

Ascent to the Apiary

At the height of imperial power in India, there were just twice as many British as Indian soldiers, who controlled a population of 250 million people. Today, with the colonial influence well out of sight (though not out of mind), there are more than 100,000 Britons who live and work in India. Another 50,000 "foreigners" (non-British) earn their livelihood in the same country that once demanded that all foreign nationals be sent back to where they came from.

The irony here is never underlined, in either the native or the foreign press, for it does not serve the interests of either party to be too particular about issues and feuds that have long been buried.

But it is worth resurrecting this single item, since it figured so prominently on the independence agenda. And it must deserve reflection that something that was once such a bone of contention has now ceased to have any significant relevance. Is it not possible, one reflects, that what we so viciously fight for today might appear marginal, if not totally irrelevant, to our children a year after tomorrow?

The fact that the British left a legacy behind is not disputed either by Indians or by foreign scholars. What is seldom mentioned is the gift that India made to Britain as a result of empire. Apart from the enormous economic windfalls from the colony, the ruling power derived many other benefits, too. The new supplement to the *Oxford English Dictionary* lists more than two thousand words that have come into the language directly through the imperial connection. The American may not be quite familiar with words like *pukka* or *bakshish,* but *punch* will surely ring a bell, a word that was inducted into English some fifty years before Kipling in the officers' messes around the country—originally meaning an alcoholic concoction mixed with five different flavors (*punch* in Hindi means *five*).

It is conceivable that much misconception about the country today is the direct result of decades of misreporting in the past. The Westerner tends to think of the British conquest of India largely through those rose-tinted, apparently liberal glasses that were provided in E. M. Forster's *A Passage to India.* The character of Aziz in *Passage* is fully realized, because an Englishman was meeting a Muslim, and both of them possessed what I call a "modern" mind. And so is Miss Quested fully realized, with her ambiguous responses. But Professor Godbole is a caricature, because Morgan Forster did not comprehend the sinuous complexity of the Hindu mind. Which does not much matter in a work of literature, since the book stands or falls on aesthetic and other criteria. But it *does* matter when a novel is treated as a vehicle of reportage, when descriptions within it are regarded as facts.

Indeed, Occidental knowledge and comprehension about India is based largely on what other Westerners have written about the country. But I am not suggesting that reversing the situation would have produced more desirable results. On the whole, Western writing about India is far more balanced, objective, relevant, and readable than accounts about the country written by Indians themselves. But the fact remains that there is not one single book to which an American or a Britisher can turn that gives an authentic picture of the country as it is and used to be, without turning the scales heavily one way or the other.

The British left indelible marks on the Indian soul. For though the country had been ravaged and conquered many times before, the British were the first (and hopefully the last) invaders who set themselves above the native population and insisted on remaining separate, different, and superior to their subjects. They did not learn any local language. They did not integrate. According to their book of rules, they were not allowed to intermarry (a point nicely illustrated by Forster in his Miss Quested's being invited to India by her husband-to-be, when there were plenty of attractive and educated native women available to him).

The British imposed themselves as a foreign power who ruled by might, not by persuasion.

Professor Kenneth Ballhatchet, an associate Fellow at an Oxford college, has an intriguing theory about the British Raj in India. He claims that he first thought about this idea when he read Kate Millet's book *Sexual Politics.*

Ballhatchet convincingly argues in his book *Race, Sex and Class Under the Raj* that the British kept their distance from the Indians during the latter part of the Raj because domination had to be seen as well as practiced. Sexual connections between natives and members of the ruling (English) class were forbidden because it would break down the rigid barriers that were needed to keep an uncivilized nation under control.

Ballhatchet says:

> Members of the dominant group ascribe to themselves the qualities needed for the tasks they wish to monopolise. They are unable to perceive such qualities in subordinate groups, who are excluded from positions in which they can demonstrate such qualities. Persons of subordinate groups, on the other hand, are perceived as being born with the qualities appropriate to activities involving obedience and subordination, and as they are confined to such activities they duly demonstrate that they do indeed possess these qualities.

Ballhatchet says what many a women's libber has contended before. But he has added a new twist. He describes the hill stations that the British so assiduously built to replicate their cottages in Surrey or Suffolk, and implies that the whole of the Raj was a *tamasha* (pantomime with surrealist inflections).

We get to the kernel of the matter when he asserts:

> Within the dominant group women are perceived as a
> subordinate group but towards all other subordinate groups
> they are expected to display attitudes appropriate to the
> dominant group. In particular they must show distaste for
> any relationship that might bridge the social distance be-
> tween the dominant group and the subordinate group.

Here we have Miss Quested's dilemma in a nutshell.

But much more intriguing is the theory that Kipling went out
to India to booze and wench. And that the empire was essentially
an exercise in releasing the pent-up sexual energies of Victorian
England. If two hundred years ago, the British went out there for
sex and spices, was the British Raj, in extreme psychological terms,
anything other than a gilded exercise in fantasy, which resulted in
the reality of enormous economic riches for the mother country?

You only have to visit hill stations like Simla, Darjeeling, and
Ootacamund, to see how persistently the British influence has remained. Even now, there are liveried butlers, there is still *chota hazri*
(breakfast at seven with a nip of Scotch) in the morning, and there
is polo, snooker, billiards, and a host of other English institutions,
including cricket. Indians are an embarrassingly English race. No
wonder Malcolm Muggeridge remarked, "The only Englishmen
remaining in the world today, are the Indians."

Over a million graduates (between the ages of nineteen and
twenty) are churned out of Indian universities every year. Less than
10 percent of that vast number find jobs in keeping with their educated status. As college education is expensive, and student loans
do not exist, there is enormous pressure on the young man (nowadays, on the woman, too) to find some kind of employment.
Middle-class parents find it hard to carry this extra load as easily
as they were once able to do. Scholarships are available in minus-
cule numbers, but the money does not even pay for the books, let
alone feed, clothe, and house the undergraduate.

Immediately after graduation, there is a huge rush for the small
number of jobs that are advertised in the newspapers. The single
post of a Grade IV clerk in the civil service, carrying a salary of

forty dollars a month, might draw as many as two thousand applicants. The successful candidate will seldom be chosen on the basis of his exam qualifications. Luck will play an inordinate part, and so will influence—an uncle on the examining body or someone higher up the governmental bureaucracy.

In the independent commercial sphere, companies will be far more choosy, and might well demand (and invariably get) candidates with master's degrees, sometimes even doctorates, for posts that require no great talent or education.

In cities, it is common to find university graduates working as bus conductors or waiters in hotels. The physics honors graduate in India who is employed as a menial clerk is not simply earning a bit of extra money with a part-time job. Unless he is phenomenally lucky, that is the job he will have for life, and there will be no light at the end of the tunnel. Changing jobs or careers in midstream are very rare exceptions, not the rule.

The overproduction of educated urban youth is not a problem to which the government appears to be addressing itself with any concern. Potentially, this is as much of a threat to the fabric of society as the population explosion itself. Frustration runs high as the flood of young people from villages and small towns into the great metropolitan centers swells into a torrential avalanche. Opportunities are meager, but expectations have risen exponentially.

The old adhesives are coming unstuck. Youth will no longer quiescently obey its elders. "The mystique of age," automatic reverence for parents and seniors, is no longer as easily accepted or enforced. Violence and rowdyism in colleges and universities are staple items in newspaper reports. The recent troubles in Assam (a northeastern state) were entirely engineered by student bodies strong and militant enough to demand high ransoms from the central government in New Delhi.

Overt political action, such as the Mao-style insurgency movements in the early seventies, are no longer common, but continue to exist in pockets. The more potent force is provided by hopelessness and despair, a feeling that other people are getting a larger share of the cake. Corrupt politicians, with their large retinues of sycophants and gliding cars, incite envy, contempt, and provide the seedbed of violence, a violence that has no specific political complexion but may be exploited by skillful demagogues in the future.

The older generation, the parents and uncles of those who are twenty-five and under, had an identifiable target against which they could direct their anger and their frustrations. The British provided a defined citadel that needed to be stormed. Violence against authority and attempts to demolish existing social institutions were seen as patriotic gestures and were covertly applauded by the nationalist leaders (except Mahatma Gandhi, of course, who believed in nonviolence).

Today, that same violence is beamed against a government that claims direct descent from those same independence fighters, but has failed to deliver the goods. The stock of patience has been all but spent. Indian youth is preparing, however slowly and subconsciously, to claim its rightful inheritance. And when it succeeds in mobilizing itself and unifying its cadres against the ruling elite, the sound of combat fire may well be louder than it was when the British held the fort.

Of course, there is another side to the same coin. Affluent urban youth in cities like Bombay and Calcutta are superficially far more Westernized than the previous generation was or wished to be. They regard the Raj as dear departed phantoms belonging to a remote past about which their sole knowledge is through books and the odd anecdotal story from some old-timer whose memories leaven the nippy winter evenings. There is no personal animosity or any great political urge to right those ancient wrongs.

The British influence is much less overt than the American one. Accents are likely to be much more Americanized than Anglophilic. Pop songs, with transatlantic flavors, are more in vogue. Even slang words owe more to the American influence, as does the faddish cult for grass and coke.

The children of the well heeled may be seen dancing till the early hours in the flashy discotheques of Bombay, Delhi, and Calcutta. These establishments are usually attached to the five-star hotels, where Western visitors invariably stay. So the couples on the floor present a cosmopolitan facade, quite out of keeping with what happens in the rest of the country.

The discos themselves will be decked out with strobes, underfloor flashing lights, and mirrored walls, with dark cavernous spaces on all sides of the room where discreet petting will be in progress. Whatever little "dating" that does occur in India goes on amongst this crust of the nation's urban youth. But the visitor will be mistaken if he thinks that surface similarities of behavior indicate a total congruence.

And though there might be the occasional Indian tune, most of the music will be imports from London and New York. Even crooners in nightclubs (for the slightly older generation) will prefer to sing Frank Sinatra and Elvis Presley numbers, rather than a hit from a Bombay movie.

Women's clothes, even Indian-style, will try to look toward Paris or New York fashion, rather than indigenous couture. The dances will carry the latest names from trendsetting magazines in the Western hemisphere. Leather goods will ape Gucci design, if not carry the original label itself.

Women will smoke (once held to be the lowest form of social depravity) both tobacco and hash, converse with languid familiarity about the latest crazes in Europe and America. At instant glance, there will be no obvious difference between the young Bombay girl of twenty-four, with her sinuous figure and energetic hip movements on the dance floor, and a New York woman at Studio 54. But once again, appearances will prove to be deceptive.

The visitor will be frequently surprised and shocked to discover that beneath that tinsel surface of glittering Westernization, there lurk primeval mental assumptions and values that have nothing to do with the last quarter of the twentieth century.

In sharp contrast, there was Neera. She had actually lived in London and New York. With a ferocious intellect and a sharp tongue, she lashed out at me. "How dare you lump us all together?"

I asked her to clarify. "I know what it is like to live in the West. And I didn't like it a tiny bit. That doesn't mean I like it here, either. I don't *have* to make that kind of choice."

Neera was twenty-seven, single, attractive, with a master's degree in English. She felt she did not belong anywhere. "We have perfected hypocrisy to a fine art. We, the women of India, are not allowed to say anything. There are rules, there are tenets, unwritten assumptions. Sometimes things which are not said are as important as those which are.

"I can behave how I like in New York, but when I come back

to Bangalore I have to perform like a demure litle damsel. And I do!

"But no one understands that there is no subculture in India. That if we wish to revolt, there is no easy or obvious outlet. In London or New York, you can go and dress up, play in a bar, or sell your paintings on the pavements of Soho [New York], but in India, there is no such opportunity. If we want to get out of this rat race, away from all this corruption and philistine materialism, there is nowhere to drop out to. Apart from the very rich, there is a vast unbridgeable chasm that separates the middle classes from those who are down below. I couldn't work as a maid in a hotel or as a waitress in a cheap restaurant. It would drive my parents absolutely crazy. And in any case, the money just wouldn't be enough even to subsist."

Neera's friends from high school and college had got stuck in a groove. At her age she should have been married by now and have produced several children. But she did not wish to enter that universe, and sign that kind of contract.

Did that make her feel happy?

"No Indian woman who is intelligent can ever be happy in this country!" Neera said.

Inevitably, the clash between old precept and new fashion is at its most stark and violent in the realm of sex. And young people in India still suffer from fears and superstitions that even contemporary Western grandmothers discarded long ago.

The vast number of men and women who marry know next to nothing about the sex act. There is very little literature about the subject that exists so openly and in such abundance in the West. A bride-to-be is very often totally ignorant of what is supposed to happen on the wedding night. In rural India, couples are often locked in rooms, so that the new bride does not run out at night, and consummation can take place. One woman told an interviewer that on her wedding night she was ushered into a dark room, only to discover that her husband was already hiding there. She let him do whatever he wanted, gritting the sari between her teeth to prevent herself from screaming with pain.

Ancient shibboleths persist in ways that the Westerner might find comic, if it were not so sad. Young people are constantly warned about the perils of masturbation—"handpractice"—which is supposed to lead to blindness, dizzy spells, headaches, and amnesia.

Even urban youth can fall prey to the quackeries of health clinics and "sex experts" who prescribe herbal cures for enormous fees. Here is an extract from the literature of one such establishment, which speaks of "the horrors of the wastage of semen":

> The human machinery becomes defective; stomach, liver, heart and eyesight go weak. The very imagination of a woman causes waste of semen and young men look old at the age of 25. Many young men have sex many times at night and thus waste this essence of life recklessly. With small production and heavy drainage, supply will exhaust soon and critical consequences will have to be faced.

It may appear incredible that such superstition and medical nonsense can still exercise a firm grip on educated youth even in the cities, who may be expected to know better. But in India paradox and ancient myths weave eternally through the mortal soul. And the gigantic hurdles in the path of enlightenment and emancipation remain stubbornly in place.

Indians will frequently assert with pride that neither divorce nor youthful promiscuity is as rampant in the country as it is in most nations of the West. And, of course, statistically they are perfectly right.

Occidental notions of male-female relationships, within or outside marriage, are totally different from the expectations that a young man or woman might have in India. The very concept of *happiness* is radically different in the two cultures. Obedience to rules and reverence for elders are still highly regarded, especially in rural India. When children of seven and ten are married by parental fiat, there has not been much time for independent ideas of personality to have taken root.

Often such couples will remain with their respective parents till they are old enough to consummate their marriage, which is usually when the boy grows a moustache. Since virginity is so highly prized, an early marriage ensures that the bride can never be contaminated.

Though there is a law that forbids marriage below the age of eighteen, it is observed more in its breach than in its execution. Child marriage is not a unique or secret institution. It is condoned by the authorities, certainly in the villages, and even in towns the phenomenon is not all that uncommon.

The Times (London) correspondent Trevor Fishlock quoted these statistics in his book on India: "The 1971 census figures revealed that 5.4 million children aged 10–14 were married and that more than a third of the people aged 15–19 were married."

The institution does provide a social adhesive, since neither party has begun to develop an autonomous identity at the time they are married. There is no question of *choosing* to accept or reject one's partner, since it has been decreed by elders, and must therefore be considered a *fait accompli*. Imposition of parental dictation becomes far easier, and the bride and groom grow up more like brother and sister than an amorous couple, their habits and personalities developing in tandem. Social harmony is ensured.

The theory is that with the spread of education and economic development, these old-fashioned practices will vanish. That young men and women will begin to think for themselves and assert their independence. But the record over the past thirty-eight years, since the British left, shows that old habits die hard, and neither youth nor age is in too great a hurry to join the twentieth century.

The story of Phoolan Devi, the bandit queen of central India, adds another dimension to the contest between modernity and tradition, youth versus age. In 1981, a young girl in her late teens (there is no way of knowing her age for certain because in the ravines and villages of that part of the country, there are no records of birth) came into the village of Behmai (in Uttar Pradesh State, North India) accompanied by a well-known gang of thugs, and demanded that the villagers produce the two men who had killed her lover.

The peasants told her that the men she was hunting were not in the village at the time, nor had they ever been seen in the region. So, in fury at having been denied her revenge, she ordered thirty men to be lined up beside the riverbank, and squeezed her submachine gun across the whole row, taking care to aim at the genitals first before raising the nozzle to the heart or head. Twenty men fell instantly dead. Her gang looted the village, but by the time the police arrived, there was no trace of Phoolan Devi or any of her followers.

The story was sensationally reported both in the local press and in the rest of India. It was dramatic and thrilling for several reasons. Phoolan Devi was a woman who was reputed to take on men as equal partners, both in sex and in battle. She was said to enjoy making love with other people watching. Newspapers called her beautiful and fiery. That she killed so many men in one incident, and that the men belonged to a higher caste than herself added that extra spice that fitted her superbly for the role of a rebel.

As in that part of the country the *dacoit* (bandit) was already a heroic figure, Phoolan Devi injected a new and sexy element into the myth by being young and naughty. There was also some sympathy because she belonged to a caste that had perennially suffered deprivation at the hands of the higher caste. There was a Robin Hood element in her story that magazines and newspapers played to the hilt.

Two years after that notorious incident, with her activities being recurrently reported, she surrendered her arms at a fabulous ceremony at which the chief minister of the state was the principal speaker—an event that was covered both by All India Radio, and *Doordarshan* (the TV network). Short of deification, Phoolan Devi had achieved a kind of instant immortality in the folktales of the region. She was packed off to Gwalior central jail, where she now lives with the status of a VIP.

When I met her inside the jail compound (April 1984), she was barefoot, a gold ring pinned through her right nostril, and red dye on her toes. Descriptions of her beauty appeared to be wildly exaggerated, although (even with a slight squint) her eyes were sharp and faintly menacing.

She spoke confidently of the time when she would get out of prison, although she had not yet been tried in court for all the charges against her. She told me that she had bought a patch of land that she meant to cultivate after her release, and that she had abandoned her bandit life for good.

When I asked her how it felt to kill people for money, she hotly denied that she had ever done anything wrong. All she wanted to do was take revenge (an honorable sentiment in those parts), and that since she had been unfairly put on the wanted list by the police, the outlaw life had compelled her to raid villages in search of food and clothes (it can get very cold in the ravines). Her gang never took more than what they needed for their bare necessities.

She said she had been raped at the age of twelve, and since then she had been forced to live the life of an outlaw, because her first lover who kidnapped her taught her how to use a gun. Her stories kept conflicting with each other, and I began to wonder whether she knew herself where truth ended and falsehood began.

But she was highly conscious of her unique status, and repeatedly disparaged another (male) *dacoit* who had also surrendered arms, implying that he had never done things on as daring a scale as she had.

The lesson from the Phoolan Devi story can be read in many ways. But the most important one is the impact she has had on the nation's urban youth. Her life has already been made into a movie in Bombay, and I hear rumors that even Western filmmakers are expressing an interest. The romanticized glamour of a rebel and a bandit who is female and openly declares her sexual appetite must provide the raw material for the most vivid fantasies among frustrated young people in India's repressed and moribund society.

And Phoolan Devi must also appeal to that streak of potential rebellion against authority and age that laces the consciousness of India's youth. And if her life story is a source of vicarious dream fulfillment today, who is to say that her example will not be followed in practice in the future, even if in a far less dramatic form?

PART SIX

Epilogue

16

Quo Vadis, India?

*A*midst the cyclic resurrections and recurring burials that Indian civilization has undergone over the past five thousand years, it is perky and defiant to poke a pin on the rim of the turning wheel, and try to divine the message in the crystal ball. But the attempt must be made, because a nation with a sixth of the world's population and the ninth largest industrial base will make a global impact whichever way it turns.

As the most populous "democracy," the result of the Indian experiment will influence the course of other developing countries. The crucial query is whether economic progress and political cohesion can be achieved and maintained within a country as diverse and riddled with centrifugal forces as India, under a system of adult democratic franchise that is essentially foreign to the Oriental temperament.

Its military and international postures currently control the geopolitical realities of the region. In future, with increasing technological sophistication and economic might, this magisterial power is likely to grow into something of an international stature. India's voice, already fairly audible, might begin to be heard with respect in the major councils of the world. Whether the country will be a benign or an inflammatory influence in Asia is a question that is being pondered by the world powers today.

Because of its political system, India's natural affinity is with the Western nations, unlike any other developing country in the world. And the smooth transition of power following Mrs. Gandhi's assassination, despite the subsequent week-long carnage, reinforced the view, in Western eyes at least, that democracy had finally taken root in India. But the event (of Rajiv Gandhi smoothly stepping into his mother's shoes) had a far more profound significance, both for India and the rest of the world. It indicated that political stability in the Orient need not be bought for the price of dictatorship—an assertion that has been made by both Asian apologists of authoritarian rule and some Western political commentators.

When the December 1984 elections were called and the Indian masses endorsed that initial coterie decision, not only was democracy vindicated, the popular verdict showed that the country overwhelmingly wished to remain as one nation rather than be Balkanized into a multitude of fighting factions.

"Unity in diversity" was shown to be no myth, but a living reality. The adhesive powers of Indian culture were tested and found strong enough to withstand the strains of communalism and separatist violence. The result was more than a mere political decision by India's masses. It demonstrated two apparently contradictory propositions. That dynastic succession was not anathema to the country's millions. At the same time, the exercise of his individual franchise was something that the Indian voter took very seriously indeed.

I believe that in the not too distant future the result of the December 1984 elections will be seen to have marked as profound a watershed in the history of the country as the departure of the British in 1947. Rajiv Gandhi is the first prime minister of independent India who does not have any conscious memory or experience of British rule in the country. And he has surrounded himself with like-minded young men who feel neither nostalgia nor hate for the Raj. Age has given way to youth while maintaining a continuity through the family line. This not only provides a sense of stability to the country, it helps to create an atmosphere of optimism and hope, when windows may be opened and new ideas imported, without the constraints of past commitments to worn-out ideological convictions.

322

India's vast potential wealth might at long last begin to be vigorously exploited. It has manganese, copper, coal, oil, the crude
base for nuclear fuel, a mass of cheap labor, a pool of exceedingly
competent technicians, a civil service unparalled in its efficiency in
the developing world, and a highly sophisticated elite that can claim
its rightful status among the bureaucrats of the world.

For the first time, it looks possible that this enormous potential wealth may be translated into real power and that the country
may be plucked from its medieval roots and catapulted into the
twentieth century.

Of course the drawbacks are colossal, too. Inefficiency and corruption are endemic and pervasive, and are unlikely to vanish with
the wave of a wand. Superstitition and caste stubbornly persist, but
education and economic growth might make a substantial impact
on a generation that is both more restless and more expectant than
its elders ever were.

Because of its comparative military strength, India has already
provided a degree of political stability on the subcontinent. While
clouds of nuclear devastation twirl around the horizon, India can
legitimately claim to be a *pacific* nation. In the last four hundred
years of its history, the country has not displayed a specific pen-
chant for aggression. Though Pakistan may deny this in theory (and
it has reasons to do so), belligerence has not been a characteristic
Indian attitude.

Its bloodbaths, of which there have been a few, have all occurred within its boundaries. And though hypocrisy is a national
trait, the theoretical professions of the country are in total conso-
nance with what the Western powers accept as their credentials
of faith.

Even with its professed allegiance to the doctrine of nonalignment, it is possible that the government of Rajiv Gandhi will draw
closer to the West than the country has been since independence.

The psychological and historical distance from British rule will
undoubtedly produce profound changes in the ethos of the nation.
Already there are signs that the servile and obsequious aspect of
Indian personality is giving way to a new self-confidence among
the young, which was not there twenty years ago. Even the peasant, forever downtrodden and accustomed to obeying commands,
is assuming an assertive role in the political process.

* * *

On a trip to Kashmir in 1982, I bought a return airline ticket from Delhi, hoping to be back in the capital within a week. As there was no Telex or phone communication between Srinagar (the capital of Kashmir) and New Delhi, I had to be content with the assurance of the airline official that there should be "no problem" getting a confirmation for my return flight once I arrived in Srinagar.

Instantly as I landed at the airport, I made for the ticket office, and asked for a reservation on the return flight, a week from that day. I was told categorically that there were no seats available for the next six weeks. I explained that I was a journalist, and that I had important appointments with ministers that could not be altered for my convenience. Sorry, the man said, there was nothing he could do. The seats in summer are booked months in advance, and every plane from Srinagar to New Delhi was carrying a full load. In exasperation I queried as to why the man in Delhi had told me that there would be "no problem." If I had known that this was the case, I would not have come in the first place. Sorry, once again, that was not his problem, what the Delhi fellow had told me was Delhi's business, not his here at Srinagar. But did they not both work for Indian Airlines? Yes, but he was doing his job here, while the Delhi officer was doing his job there. There was no connection between the two.

As I was about to leave, he said, "But come back tomorrow morning, and I shall see if I can do something for you."

That seemed to offer a gleam of hope, so I duly reported back the next day. From where I was staying, the journey to the ticket office took over an hour, and by the time I got to see my man, I had spent another hour waiting.

The message was the same, there were no seats available for another six weeks. *But* if I came back in the afternoon, he would see what he could do. So I trudged back again, and there was an identical response. But once more, there was that carrot of hope dangled in front of me. If I came back the next morning . . . This farce went on for two whole days, when far from enjoying a vacation, I had been spending most of my time sitting around in the ticket office, anxiously waiting for my encounter with the airline official. When I was told to come back for the third day running, I asked to see his superior in a fairly acerbic tone of voice. After much shouting and persistence and a ninety-minute wait, I was ushered into the august presence of the superintendent of the outfit, with my original official hovering behind me.

In profusely polite language, and a great deal more of justification—"We have very few planes in India, communications are bad, summer is a very busy time," and so on—I was served up the same story.

By a stroke of luck, however, I was carrying my tape recorder, and it had an interview with Rajiv Gandhi (he was not yet prime minister at the time, but merely his mother's son) on the cassette. So I put the machine down on the table and switched it on. There was a sudden cessation of all conversation in the room (which had sounded like a Baghdad bazaar minutes before), and the eyes of the superintendent flickered with nervous apprehension.

Very softly, I said, "You do know whose voice that is?"

"Yes, of course, sir," he replied. "If you will just wait a moment, I shall expedite." I got my ticket in five minutes.

Next time I met him, I related the episode to Rajiv Gandhi. "Yes," he smiled, "we do have a feudal mentality. It will take a long time to eradicate. When our people no longer feel subjugated, when the memory of the British will have faded into history. But it will take a long time."

With a forty-year-old political novice holding the reins of power, with a new generation in charge of molding the fate of the nation, that time may not be so far away.

Selected Bibliography

Akbar, M. J. *India: The Siege Within.: Challenge to a Nation's Unity.* U.K.: Penguin Books, 1985.

Alexander, Michael, and Shushila Anand. *Queen Victoria's Maharajah: Duleep Singh, 1838–1893.* London: Weidenfeld and Nicholson, 1980.

Ali, Tariq, *The Nehrus and the Gandhis: An Indian Dynasty,* introduction by Salman Rushdie. U.K.: Picador, 1985.

Azad, Maulana Abul Kalam. *India Wins Freedom—An Autobiographical Narrative.* India: Orient Langmans, 1959.

Ballhatchet, Kenneth. *Race, Sex and Class Under the Raj: Imperial Attitudes and Policies and Their Critics, 1793–1905.* U.K.: Weidenfeld and Nicholson, 1980; U.S.: St. Martin's, 1980.

Barnouw, Erik, and S. Krishnaswamy. *Indian Film.* 2nd edition. Oxford University Press, 1980.

Barua, Dipak K. *Buddha Gaya Temple—Its History.* Buddha Gaya: Buddha Gaya Temple Management Committee, 1981.

The Bhagavad Gita. Translated by Juan Mascaro. U.K.: Penguin Books, 1962.

Blechynden, Kathleen. *Calcutta Past and Present.* Calcutta: Printers and Publishers, 1905. New Edition, 1978.

Bose, Aurobindo, trans. *Later Poems of Rabindranath Tagore.* U.K.: Peter Owen, 1974.

Bowers, Faubion. *The Dance in India.* New York: AMS Press, 1967.

Bowes, Pratima, trans. *Some Songs and Poems from Rabindranath Tagore.* India: East-West Publications, 1984.

Calcutta: People and Empire (gleanings from old journals). Selected by P. Chaudhury and A. Hukhopadhyay. Calcutta: India Book Exchange, 1975.

Calcutta 200 Years—A Tollygunge Club Perspective. Text by Samik Banerjee. Calcutta: Tollygunge Club Ltd., 1981.

Cameron, James. *Point of Departure: An Autobiography.* London: Arthur Barker, 1967.

————. *An Indian Summer.* London: Macmillan, 1974; U.S.: McGraw-Hill, 1974.

Chakravorty, P. M. *Systems of Indian Castes and Marriage.* India: Varanasi, 1978.

Chaudhuri, Nirad C. *Clive of India.* London: Barrie and Jenkins, 1975.

————. *Hinduism.* London: Chatto and Windus, 1979.

Colaabavala, Captain F. D. *Sex Slaves of India.* India: Orient Paperbacks, 1981.

Cotton, H.E.A. *Calcutta Old and New.* Calcutta: General Printers and Publishers, 1909. Revised, 1978.

Cowasjee, Saros (selected and introduced by). *Stories from the Raj: From Kipling to Independence.* Preface by Paul Theroux. U.K.: Bodley Head, 1982.

Das, Durga. *India from Curzon to Nehru and After.* London: Collins, 1969; U.S.: John Day, 1970.

Dasgupta, Surendranath. *Indian Idealism.* India: Cambridge University Press, 1933.

Desai, Morarji. *The Story of My Life.* India: Macmillan, 1974.

Desani, G. V. *All About H. Hatterr.* U.S.: Lancer Books; U.K.: Penguin Books, 1972.

Devi, Gayatri, and Santha Rama Rau. *A Princess Remembers—The Memoirs of the Maharani of Jaipur.* U.K.: Weidenfeld and Nicholson; U.S.: J. B. Lippincott Company; India: Tarang Paperbacks, 1976.

Devi, Ragini. *Dances of India.* Calcutta: S. Gupta, 1962; New York: Books for Libraries, 1980.

Digby, Ian. *India.* U.K.: Colour Library International.

Doig, Desmond. *Calcutta—An Artist's Impression.* Calcutta: The Statesman Ltd.

Eck, Diana L. *Banaras, City of Light.* U.S.: Knopf, 1982; U.K.: Routledge and Kegan Paul, 1983.

Edwardes, Michael. *Nehru—A Political Biography.* U.K.: Allen Lane/Penguin Press, 1971; U.S.: Praeger, 1972.

Fishlock, Trevor. *India File*. London: John Murray, 1983; India: Rupa Paperback, 1984.

Forster, E. M. *A Passage to India*. U.K.: Penguin Books, 1924, 1934; U.S.: Harcourt Brace Jovanovich, 1965.

Furbank, P. N. *E. M. Forster: A Life*. London: Secker and Warburg, 1978; U.S.: Harcourt Brace Jovanovich, 1978.

Gardner, Brian. *The East India Company*. London: Rupert Hart-Davis, 1971; U.S.: Saturday Review Press, 1972.

Gopal, Sarvepalli. *Jawaharlal Nehru: A Biography*. London: Jonathan Cape, 1979; U.S.: Harvard University Press, 1979.

Grand Chronicle: A Biography of the Hotel Oberoi Grand. Calcutta, 1980.

Hiro, Dilip. *Inside India Today*. U.K. and U.S.: Routledge and Kegan Paul, 1976. Revised, 1978.

In the Image of Man. The Indian Perception of the Universe Through 2,000 Years of Painting and Sculpture. Catalog of the exhibition at the Hayward Gallery. London, 1982.

Keay, John. *Into India*. U.K.: John Murray, 1973.

Kramrisch, Stella. *The Art of India Through the Ages*. U.K.: Phaidon Press, 1954.

Kripalani, Krishna. *Dwarkanath Tagore. A Forgotten Pioneer: A Life*. New Delhi: National Book Trust, 1980.

Lal, P. (condensed and trans. by) *The Mahabharata of Vyasa*. New Delhi: Vikas, 1980.

Lannoy, Richard. *The Speaking Tree: A Study of Indian Culture and Society*. U.K.: Oxford University Press, 1971.

Majumdar, R. C., and P. N. Chopra. *Main Currents of Indian History*. London and The Hague: East-West Publications, 1979; U.S.: Humanities Press, 1980.

———, H. C. Raychaudhuri and Kalikinkar Datta. *An Advanced History of India*. 4th edition. India: Macmillan International, College Editions, 1978.

Malgonkar, Manohar. *A Bend in the Ganges*. U.K.: Hamish Hamilton, 1964, Pan Books, 1967.

Masani, Minoo. *Is J.P. the Answer?* India: Macmillan, 1975.

Masani, Zareer. *Indira Gandhi—A Biography*. London: Hamish Hamilton, 1975; U.S.: Brown, 1976.

Mason, Philip. *Kipling: The Glass, the Shadow and the Fire*. U.K.: Jonathan Cape, 1975; U.S.: Harper and Row, 1975.

Mehta, Gita. *Karma Cola—Marketing the Mystic East*. U.K.: Jonathan Cape, 1980; U.S.: Simon and Schuster, 1979.

Mehta, Ved. *The New India*. U.K.: Penguin Books; U.S.: Penguin Books and Viking Press, 1978.

Moorhouse, Geoffrey. *Calcutta: The City Revealed*. U.K.: Weidenfeld and Nicholson, Penguin Books, 1974.

———. *India Britannica*. U.K.: Harvill Press/Paladin, 1984.

Moraes, Dom. *Gone Away*. U.K.: Heinemann, 1960; U.S.: Little, Brown, 1960.

———. *My Son's Father: An Autobiography*. U.K.: Secker and Warburg, 1968; U.S.: Macmillan, 1979.

———. *Mrs. Gandhi*. U.K.: Jonathan Cape, 1980; U.S.: Little, Brown, 1980 (title *Indira Gandhi*).

Naipaul, V. S. *A House for Mr. Biswas*. U.K.: Andre Deutsch, 1961, Fontana Books, 1963; U.S.: Penguin, 1976.

———. *An Area of Darkness*. U.K.: Andre Deutsch, 1964; U.S.: Random House, 1981.

———. *India: A Wounded Civilization*. U.K.: Andre Deutsch, 1977; U.S.: Knopf, 1977.

Nehru, Jawaharlal. *The Discovery of India*. London: Meridian Books, 1946; U.S.: edited by Robert I. Crane, Doubleday, 1960.

Pandey, B. N. *Nehru*. London: Macmillan, 1976; U.S.: Stein and Day, 1976.

Pandit, Vijaya Lakshmi. *The Scope of Happiness—A Personal Memoir*. U.K.: Weidenfeld and Nicholson, 1979; U.S.: Crown, 1979.

Pannikkar, K. M. *Asia and Western Dominance*. U.K.: Allen and Unwin, 1959; New York: Collier Books, 1969.

Prabhavananda, Swami, and Christopher Isherwood, trans. *How to Know God: The Yoga Aphorisms of Patanjali*. Madras, India: Sri Ramakrishna Math, 1953; U.S.: New American Library, 1969.

———, and Frederick Manchester, trans. *The Upanishads*. Madras, India: Sri Ramakrishna Math, 1968.

Puri, Rajinder. *India 1969: A Crisis of Conscience*. India, 1971.

———. *India—The Wasted Years, 1969–1975*. New Delhi: Chetana Publications.

Radhakrishnan, S. *An Idealist View of Life*. London: Unwin Books, 1932, 1980.

Rawson, Philip. *Indian Art*. U.K.: Studio Vista/Dutton Pictureback, 1972.

Ray, Satyajit. *Our Films, Their Films*. India: Orient Longman, 1976.

Richardson, Jean, trans. *Indian Art and the Art of Ceylon, Central and South-East Asia*. U.K.: Octopus Books, 1972.

Rushdie, Salman. *Midnight's Children*. U.K.: Jonathan Cape, 1981; U.S.: Avon, 1982.

Sarkar, Sumit. *Modern India 1885–1947*. India: Macmillan, 1983.

Segal, Ronald. *The Crisis of India*. U.K.: Penguin Books, 1965; India: Jaico, 1968.

Seton, Marie. *Portrait of a Director: Satyajit Ray.* London: Denis Dobson, 1971.

Sharma, Dhirendra. *India's Nuclear Estate.* India: Lancer Publishers, 1983.

Sharma, N. K. *Varanasi: The City of Burning and Learning.* India: Varanasi, 1979.

————. *Caste, Custom and Faith in Hinduism.* India: Varanasi, 1979.

Singh, K. *Religions of India.* Delhi: Clarion Books, 1983; U.S.: Humanities, 1983.

Singh, Patwant. *The Struggle for Power in Asia.* London: Hutchinson, 1971.

Singh, Raghubir, photographer, *Ganga, Sacred River of India.* Hong Kong: Perennial Press, 1974.

Spear, Percival. *The Oxford History of Modern India, 1740–1975.* 2nd Edition. U.K.: Oxford University Press, 1979.

Vatsyayana. *The Kama Sutra of Vatsyayana.* trans. Sir Richard Burton and F. F. Arbuthnot. U.K.: George Allen and Unwin, 1951; U.S.: Dutton, 1964.

Wade, Bonnie C. *Music in India: The Classical Traditions.* U.S.: Prentice-Hall, 1979.

Watson, Francis. *A Concise History of India.* London: Thames and Hudson, 1974; U.S.: Scribners, 1975.

Wiles, John. *Delhi Is Far Away—A Journey Through India.* London: Paul Elek, 1974.

Yale, John, ed. *What Religion Is (In the Words of Swami Vivekananda).* London: Phoenix House, 1962.

In addition, I have drawn extensively from newspapers, magazines, and periodicals, too numerous to identify individual issues. The following are the most important publications, which were of immense help: *The Statesman, The Times of India, Sunday Observer, Indian Express, The Illustrated Weekly of India, Sunday, India Today,* and *Seminar.*

Index

aalaap, 161
Abdullah, Farooq, 270–271
Agra, 117, 188, 190, 266
Ahmedabad, 70
Air India, 174, 187, 245
Ajanta caves, 104, 146, 156–159, 163–164
ajanya (untouchables), 29, 223, 224, 225, 229, 230–231, 238, 290
alcohol, 17–18, 34, 46
All India Radio, 24, 317
Amritsar, 21, 43, 214
Anglo-Indians, 226–227
architecture, 73, 161–164, 189–191, 211, 212
ardhangini, 130
aristocracy, 247–250, 252–253
Arjuna, 147, 149
Artha, 210
Aryans, 73, 74, 147–148, 162, 198, 210, 223
Arya Samaj, 108
ashauj, 122–123, 144
Asoka, emperor of Magadha, 161–162, 211
Assam, 272, 281, 311
astrology, 45, 56, 66, 73, 74, 80, 84, 124–125
atman, 168, 211
Aurangzeb, emperor of Hindustan, 22, 192–193, 216
avatar, 199

Bachan, Amitabh, 301–302
Bala Hari, 143
Ballhatchet, Kenneth, 309–310
Banaras (Eck), 193, 207
bandar lok, 113
Banerjee, Surendranath, 107
Bangladesh, 44, 154, 277, 278, 279, 281–282
Basu, Jyoti, 113, 117
BBC, 34, 36
Benares (Varanasi), 80, 145, 163, 169, 193, 201, 204, 206–207
Bengal, 16, 17, 24, 51, 53, 92, 93, 100, 102, 107, 113, 114, 116, 117, 119, 120, 153, 202, 227, 241, 248, 252, 303
Bentinck, Lord William, 29, 104, 132
Bevan, Aneurin, 218
bhadralok, 98
Bhagavad Gita, 44–45, 146–147, 149–150, 198, 199, 207, 241
bhang, 45
Bharat Natyam, 159
Bhutan, 284
Birla family, 115, 262, 265
birth control, 125–127, 251
"Black Hole" of Calcutta, 100, 101–102
Bodh Gaya, 211, 212
Bombay, 46, 51, 109, 116, 120, 136, 139, 163, 189, 262, 264, 292, 293, 297, 302, 312, 318

Brahma, 74, 209
Brahmacharya, 210
Brahman, 80, 142, 209
Brahmins, 30, 34, 55, 81, 123, 124, 202, 204, 219–232
Brahmo Samaj, 198
British:
  in India, 19–20, 22–24, 73, 92–96, 100–104, 109–112, 162, 226, 237, 259, 276, 307–310
  India viewed by, 25–27, 110, 111
Buddhism, 145, 146, 157, 161, 162, 163, 164, 197, 198, 199, 211–212, 223
bustees, 92
Butler, David, 41

Calcutta, 15–18, 46, 51, 60, 70, 83, 91–119, 136, 137, 139, 143, 169, 190, 216, 225, 260–261, 262, 292, 312
  culture in, 106–107, 114, 117–118
  history of, 95, 100–104, 117
  population of, 91, 105, 260
  traffic in, 16, 92, 97, 115
castes, 29, 30, 32, 47, 86–87, 142, 199, 204, 210, 213–214, 216, 217, 218–232, 238, 290, 323
censorship, 34, 127, 136, 299–300
Chakravarti, Sasthibrata, 219
Chakravorty, P. M., 224
chalita bhasha, 118
Chand, Prem, 154
chandals, 143–144, 145
chapatis, 18
chaprasis, 17
Charnock, Job, 95, 100, 132
Charulata, 153
Chatterjee, Bankimchandra, 154
Chatterjee, Sarat Chandra, 154
Chaudhuri, Nirad C., 118, 203–204
childbirth, 121–124
China, People's Republic of:
  India compared to, 39, 86, 87, 142, 197, 258
  India's conflicts with, 279–280
choola, 18
chota hazri, 310
Christianity, 131, 142, 145, 197, 198, 209, 216–217, 230–231
Churchill, Sir Winston, 99, 104, 218, 250, 276
Clive, Robert, 73, 92–93, 102–103
clothing, 17, 43, 46, 48, 61, 62, 72, 74, 137, 144, 268, 269, 299, 313
Cochin, 158, 197, 215
Colaabavala, F. D., 140

communism, 94, 98, 99, 104, 113, 116, 240, 241
Congress (I) party, 42, 241
corruption, 39, 94, 126, 236, 269, 270, 271, 272, 311, 323
Cotton, H.E.A., 106
Curzon, Lord George Nathaniel, 104–106, 265

dacoit, 317, 318
dal, 18
darshan, 77, 79
Darshana, 208
Das, C. R., 107
death rituals, 142–145, 193, 204, 214
Delhi, 18–19, 22, 25, 30, 38, 46, 51, 70, 95–96, 117, 136, 139, 162, 190, 312
Delhi durbar, 95, 109–110
Desai, Morarji, 25, 34, 37, 231, 244, 268, 273
desam, 269
devadasis, 159
Devasthanam, 76
Devi, Gayatri, 189, 247–250
Devi, Phoolan, 316–318
dharma, 168, 210
dhotis, 43, 62
Discovery of India, The (Nehru), 157, 228
divorce, 47, 58, 65, 136, 246, 315
Drake, Roger, 101
Dravidians, 74
dunda, 26, 259

East India Company, 19, 73, 92–94, 100, 101, 103, 109
Eck, Diana L., 193, 207
Einstein, Albert, 151, 152
elderly, veneration of, 124, 126, 290, 311, 315
electricity, 91, 260
Eliot, T. S., 120
Elizabeth I, queen of England, 19, 93
Elizabeth II, queen of Great Britain, 16, 236, 250
Ellora caves, 163, 164
Emergency regime, 25, 27, 34, 37, 38, 126–127, 239, 240, 249, 251
Epstein, Jacob, 163

famine, 262
film, 55, 64, 118, 136, 153, 270, 297–306, 318
food, 18, 34, 45, 48, 63, 65, 82, 86, 116, 138, 140, 188, 222, 225, 254, 255, 259, 261, 269, 300–301, 310

Forster, E. M., 96–97, 308–309
Furbank, P. N., 96

Galbraith, John Kenneth, 86, 235
Gandhi, Indira Priyadarshani Nehru, 35–44,
    66–67, 84, 87, 112, 155, 204, 214,
    221, 225, 236–245, 269, 271, 272,
    273–275, 276, 278, 281, 291, 301
  assassination of, 21, 24, 39, 40, 41, 213,
    236, 237, 242, 322
  political defeat of, 28, 33, 38, 41, 127,
    231, 240, 251
  tyranny of, 25–28, 34, 44, 67, 113, 126–
    127, 237–238, 240, 249, 273
Gandhi, Mohandas Karamchand (Ma-
    hatma), 23–24, 29, 37, 38, 40, 41,
    50, 99, 110–111, 112, 143, 191,
    229, 237, 256, 277, 312
Gandhi, Rajiv, 24, 37, 38–41, 42, 44, 112,
    204, 227, 238, 241, 245, 272, 274–
    275, 295, 301, 302, 322, 323, 325
Gandhi, Sanjay, 37, 38, 39, 126, 127, 273,
    275
Gandhi, Sonia, 39
Ganges River, 46, 81, 83–84, 91, 95, 143,
    201, 204–207, 222
Garibi hatao, 43
Gautama Buddha, Siddhartha, 211
George III, king of Great Britain, 93, 104
George V, king of Great Britain, 95, 109–
    110, 189
ghat, 81, 144
ghazals, 139
ghee, 143
Gilliatt, Penelope, 305
Gitanjali (Tagore), 152
Gladstone, William Ewart, 109
Goa, 283–284
Godrej, Mr., 264–265
Golden Temple, 21, 43, 214, 242, 243
Gopal, Ram, 160
gopis, 167
Grihastha, 210
Guardian, 25, 27, 286
gurdwaras, 197, 214
gurus, 84, 85, 109, 199–203, 208, 213

"half-caste," 47, 226–227
Harappa, Pakistan, 147, 161
Hare Krishna movement, 199
Hari, 143, 229
Harijans, 229, 231
Hastings, Warren, 93, 104
health, 98, 125, 261, 301
  childbirth, 121–123
  disease, 91, 92, 96, 108, 138, 259

folk medicine, 34, 141, 269, 315
  unsanitary conditions, 91, 92, 106, 115,
    121, 202, 205–206, 228, 259–260
Hinduism, 19, 29, 34, 44–45, 74–83, 108–
    109, 120–124, 129–131, 145, 148–
    150, 162, 164, 193, 197–211, 213,
    225, 227–228, 242, 274–275, 278,
    281, 282–283, 284
  gods of, 74, 98, 108, 111, 112, 130–131,
    142–145, 159, 163, 206
  wedding ceremony of, 60–66, 224
Hinduism (Chaudhuri), 203–204
Hindu-Muslim riots, 23, 97–98, 276
Hindustan Times, 135–136, 292, 305–306
Hitler, Adolf, 26, 148
Hogben, Lancelot, 151
Hooghly River, 95, 100, 101, 143
hookahs, 43, 251, 255
hotels, 83, 104, 116, 138, 187–191, 235,
    250, 260, 311, 312
Hussain, M. F., 155–156
Hyderabad, 117, 282, 283

illiteracy, 24, 91, 127, 243, 256, 301
India:
  culture in, 106–107, 114, 117–118, 146–
    168, 312–314
  history of, 19–20, 22–24, 73, 92–96,
    100–104, 109–112, 147, 162, 165–
    166, 237
  languages of, 22, 24, 45, 55, 62, 73, 153–
    154, 173, 216, 244, 248, 254, 269,
    281, 308
  names in, 52, 219–220, 231
  Nobel Prize in, 108
  political system of, 24–29, 37–41, 225,
    230–231, 236–245, 249–252, 262–
    263, 268–275, 322
  population of, 86, 125, 126, 307, 321
  races of, 73–74, 226–227
  traveling in, 169–193, 235, 262, 324–325
Indian Airlines, 174, 324–325
Indian Express, 38, 292
Indian National Congress party, 41, 108,
    291
India Today, 295
Iqbal, Mahomed, 154
Islam, *see* Muslims
ITN (Independent Television News), 34, 36,
    244

Jack, Ian, 114
jagrata, 74
Jainism, 145, 162, 164, 197, 212–213, 223
Jaipur, 189, 247–250
Janata party, 37, 231, 251, 269

jauhar, 132–133
jewelry, 48, 61, 62, 72, 317
Johnson, Lyndon, 37, 40
Judaism, 197, 209, 215, 221, 300–301
Jumna River, 87, 205

Kailasa temple, 164
Kaldor, Nicholas, 250
Kali, 98, 225
Kalidasa, 150
Kaliyuga, 209–210
Kama Sutra (Vatsyayana), 128–129, 137, 210
Karma, 80, 81, 142, 166, 211
Kashmir, 21, 169, 171, 227, 253–256, 266, 271, 277–278, 279, 280, 282, 290, 324
Kathakali, 159
Kennedy, John F., 40, 99, 189, 221, 247
Kerala, 113
Khajuraho temple, 129–130, 169, 170
khalsa, 213
Kipling, Rudyard, 87, 104, 113, 226, 310
Konarak temple, 129, 130, 159
Krishna, 131, 147, 149, 159, 167, 199, 207, 229
Kshatriyas, 223, 224, 232

Laplace, Pierre de, 150–151
Lenin, Nikolai, 99
Let There Be Sculpture (Epstein), 163
lingams, 130, 167
Lingaraj, 19
Listener, 96
literature, 47, 85, 118, 147–155, 224, 243
Lok Sabha, 239, 240, 273
Lutyens, Sir Edwin, 38, 162

Macaulay, Thomas Babington, 107, 216
Madras, 73–74, 100, 163, 227, 270, 292
Mahabharata, 22, 124, 131, 149, 207
Maharishi Mahesh Yogi, 199
Mahavira, Vardhamana Jñatiputra, 212
makeup, 48, 61, 143, 269, 317
Manas, 168
Manipuri, 159
mantras, 65, 77, 123, 144
marriage, 30–33, 46, 47–51, 53–54, 56–72, 86, 122, 131, 133–136, 139, 210, 225–226, 231, 290, 309, 314, 315–316
   Hindu ceremony for, 60–66, 224
   intercaste, 226
   intercommunal, 227
   polygamous, 131, 136, 249
Marx, Karl, 104

mathematics, 150–152
Mathematics for the Millions (Hogben), 151
maya, 152, 168, 209
media, 24, 33, 34, 36, 39, 127, 136, 243, 244, 268, 273, 278, 289–306, 317–318
Mehta, Vinod, 293
melas, 207
Midnight's Children (Rushdie), 155
Millet, Kate, 47, 309
mirchi masala, 298
Mir Jafar, nawab of Bengal, 102
Mogul civilization, 19, 20, 22, 158, 162, 216
Mohammed, 199
mokhsha, 130, 145, 210, 211
mon, 153
monsoons, 91, 101, 260
Moorhouse, Geoffrey, 92, 103–104
Moraes, Dom, 154–155, 283
Muggeridge, Malcolm, 155, 310
mukti, 77
Murdoch, Iris, 27, 42
Murshidabad, 100–101, 266
music and dance, 17, 107, 146, 150–160, 163, 224, 298, 312–313
Music in India (Wade), 160
Muslims, 23, 97, 131, 133, 142, 145, 155, 162, 197, 199, 209, 213–216, 217, 230–231, 278, 279, 281, 282–283, 286, 290, 300–301

Nanak, Guru, 213, 214
Narayan, R. K., 154
nashbandi, 126–127
Nehru, Jawaharlal, 24, 25, 29–30, 37, 38, 39, 40, 41–42, 43, 53, 55, 99, 111, 112, 157, 190, 205, 220–221, 225, 227–229, 237–238, 240, 245, 251–252, 259, 269, 273, 276, 277, 279–280, 283, 284, 294
Nepal, 111, 284–285
New Delhi, 26, 34, 37, 51, 162, 190, 230, 236, 241, 244, 251, 269, 271, 292, 311
Newley, Eric, 205–206
newspapers, 24, 33–34, 38, 95, 99, 127, 135–136, 273, 289–295, 317
New Yorker, 114, 247, 305
New York Herald Tribune, 104
New York Times, 27, 115, 155, 243
Nirvana, 211

Observer (London), 105, 155, 251, 305
Odissi, 159
Oh! Calcutta!, 114
OHM, 209

Oppenheimer, Robert, 146–147
Orwell, George (Eric Blair), 218
Ovid, 16

painting and sculpture, 155–159, 161–164
Pakistan, 21, 23, 44, 148, 154, 276, 277–279, 281–282, 286, 323
pandas, 206
Pandit, Vijaya Lakshmi, 29–30
parent-child relationships, 30–33, 46, 52–53, 55, 58–59, 106–107, 111, 122, 125–126, 140–141, 244, 315–316
Parliament, British, 93, 272
Parliament, Indian, 24, 25, 27, 30, 239–241, 247, 272–274, 302
Parsis, 145, 197, 214
Parvati, 130–131
Passage to India (Forster), 96, 308–309
Patel, Sardar Vallabhai, 283
Pather Panchali, 304–305
Patna (Pataliputra), 162
Paul, Swraj, 263, 264
Philip, prince consort of England, 16, 189, 250, 265
Plassey, battle of, 102, 103
poverty, 15–16, 21, 39, 43, 81, 92, 98, 106–107, 116, 126, 171–172, 259–262, 279, 298
prajahs, 252
Pralaya, 209
predestination, 80–82, 125, 150
prostitution, 138–140
pujas, 21, 65, 74, 79, 81, 124, 142, 144, 167, 207, 222, 301
pukka, 47, 227, 308
Punjab, 21, 24, 272
punkah, 111
purdah, 55
Purie, Aroon, 295

Race, Sex and Class Under the Raj (Ballhatchet), 309–310
Radha, 131, 159
radio, 24, 39, 243, 244, 317
ragas, 160–161
Rajasthan, 117, 133, 158, 169, 247, 266, 285
Rajya Sabha, 240
Ram, Jagjivan, 231, 239–240
Rama, 150, 270
Ramachandran, M. G., 270
Raman, C. V., 108
Ramanujan, Srinivasa, 151–152
Ramarao, N. T., 269–270
Ramayana, 150, 207, 270
Rammohun Roy, Raja, 108

Rao, U. S., 265–266
"Rape of the Lok" (Brata), 25
Rau, Santha Rama, 247
Ray, Satyajit, 118, 153, 303–305
Reagan, Ronald, 41, 44, 270, 275
Red Fort, 158, 192–193
reincarnation, 80, 81, 142, 150, 166
religion, 19, 21, 34, 44–45, 52, 60, 73, 80, 87, 98, 108–109, 111, 120–124, 128–131, 142–145, 146, 148–150, 159, 160, 164, 167, 197–217, 225, 229, 230–231, 241, 242, 270, 272, 278, 282–283, 300–301
see also individual religions
Renoir, Jean, 304
Rig Veda, 148, 208–209
rishis, 128, 149, 150, 200
Ross, Ronald, 108
roti, 140
Roy, Jamini, 155
Rushdie, Salman, 155

sadhus, 80, 83, 170, 199, 201, 203–204, 206, 208, 290
salwar kameez, 299
Sanskrit, 62, 73, 111, 147
Sanyasa, 210
Sardarji, 242
saris, 17, 48, 62, 72
Sen, Aparna, 305
servants, 17, 49, 51–52, 63, 71–72, 81, 138, 222, 247
Setna, A. M., 190
Sex Slaves of India (Colaabavala), 140
sexual relations, 18–19, 32, 46, 47, 51, 58–59, 60, 63, 64, 65, 86, 127, 128–132, 136–142, 167, 200, 210, 268, 269, 299–300, 305–306, 309, 310, 314–318
Shah Jehan, emperor of Hindustan, 192–193
Shakuntala (Kalidasa), 150
Shankar, Uday, 160
Shastri, Lal Bahadur, 42
Shergil, Amrita, 155
shikara, 171
Shiva, 74, 130–131, 146, 163, 206
Shiva Linga, 164
Shiva Nataraga, 163
shiv puja, 19, 167
shunya, 151
shuva drishti, 63
Sikhism, 21, 43, 44, 80, 197, 213–214, 236, 242–243, 272, 278
Sikkim, 284
Singh, Charan, 231, 239, 268, 269

Singh, Guru Gobind, 213
Singh, Khushwant, 137, 243
Siraj-ud-daula, nawab of Bengal, 101–102
skin coloring, 46–47, 53, 73–74, 133, 223
Sona Marg, 253
Spear, Sir Percival, 101
Spectator, 244
Spivak, Gayatri, 118
sraddha, 144
Sri Lanka (Ceylon), 277, 285–286
Statesman, 17, 33, 95, 289, 291, 292
Stewart, Charles, 92
stupas, 161
Sudras, 223, 224
Sunday Observer (Bombay), 293
sutra, 128
suttee, 29, 132
swastika, 147–148, 213

tabla, 160
Tagore, Rabindranath, 47, 108, 112, 114, 118, 152–154
Taj Mahal, 87, 116, 146, 158, 162, 169, 171, 191–193, 266
tamasha, 309
tantric Hinduism, 130
Tata family, 262, 264, 265
taxes, 46, 76
Telegraph, 292
telephone service, 83, 91, 174, 188, 244, 260, 324
television, 34, 36, 243, 244, 317
Thatcher, Margaret, 41, 44, 238, 275
Third World, 41, 85, 87, 92, 103, 258, 293
Tibet, 94, 280
Tilak, Lok Manya, 113
Time, 84, 295
Times (London), 27, 41, 110, 135, 164, 291, 295, 316
Times of India, 17, 289, 292
Tirumala, 74, 76
Tirupathi, 74–79
Twain, Mark, 100, 207

unarya, 147
unclean *(ashauj),* 122–123, 144
Untouchability (Offences) Act, 229

untouchables, 29, 223, 224, 225, 229, 230–231, 238, 290
Upanishads, 148–149, 198, 207, 208, 209, 220

Vaisyas, 223, 224
Vanaprastha, 210
Vanar Sena, 42
Varanasi (Benares), 80, 145, 163, 169, 193, 201, 204, 206–207
vasectomy, 126–127
Vedanta, 209, 220
Vedas, 147–148, 198, 207, 208–209
vegetarianism, 34, 48, 63, 73, 82, 138, 212, 225, 255, 261
Victoria, queen of Great Britain, 93, 94, 109, 110
Vidyasagar, Iswar Chandra, 108
violence, 97–100, 134–136, 272, 299, 311–312
Vishnu, 74, 111, 131, 143, 153, 199
Vivekananda, 108–109
Vogue, 247

Wade, Bonnie, 160
wages, 76, 92, 104, 138, 243, 261, 262, 272, 310–311
Washington, George, 103, 104
wealth, 17, 92, 104, 114–117, 190, 247–250, 260, 262–265, 323
Whitebait, William, 304–305
women:
  murder of, 134–136, 290
  religious practices of, 19, 122, 130–133, 167
  status of, 28–33, 45–51, 53–72, 81, 120, 122, 134, 173, 244, 249, 255, 310, 313–314
  widowed, 29, 48, 63, 108, 132, 143

Yoga, 82, 200, 210
yonis, 130, 167
Yugas, 209–210

Zoroaster (Zarathustra), 145, 197, 214